Books by Valentino Zubiri

Dollman the Musical
A Memoir of an Artist as a Dollmaker

Hocus Pocus Lately
A Paranormal Memoir of a Soon-To-Be Famous Anonymous Artist as a Reluctant Healer or Real Healing Lessons From a Psychic Surgeon & How You & I Can Do It Now

Wonder
A Memoir of Relative Importance of a
Soon-To-Be Famous Anonymous Artist

1-Hour Mentors
Leadership Rubs: A Memoir of an Artist as a Masseur

Valentino F. Zubiri:
Nude Drawings & Paintings from 1995 to 1996

Books by Valentino Zubiri & Silverio Perez

Valzubiriagenda
The Viral Groundbreaking Way to Achieve
Your Profits through Global Art Investment

Coming Soon:

more about #valzubiriagenda

VALZUBIRIAGENDA
The Viral Groundbreaking Way to Achieve Your Profits through Global Art Investment

by
VALENTINO ZUBIRI
Author of Dollman the Musical, Wonder
Hocus Pocus Lately & 1-Hour Mentors

& SILVERIO PEREZ

Copyright © February 2018 by Valentino Zubiri and Silverio Perez

All rights reserved. No part of this publication may be reproduced, distributed, or transmitted in any form or by any means, including photocopying, recording, or other electronic or mechanical methods, without the prior written permission of the publisher, except in the case of brief quotations embodied in critical reviews and certain other noncommercial uses permitted by copyright law. For permission requests, write to the publisher, addressed "Attention: Permissions Coordinator," at the email address below.

Valentino Zubiri
P.O. Box 409312
Chicago, IL 60640
email: valzubiri@gmail.com

Printed in the United States of America

Publisher's Cataloging-in-Publication data
Zubiri, Valentino & Perez, Silverio
Valzubiriagenda, The viral groundbreaking way to achieve your profits through global art investment
p. cm. 296 pages. 6 x 9 inches. 15.24 x 22.86 centimeters
Library of Congress Control Number: 2017919797
ISBN-13: 978-1982082659
ISBN-10: 1982082658
1. Marketing. 2. Art business

First Edition

Editing, cover design, book design: Valentino Zubiri
Contact valzubiri@gmail.com for your book projects

All Font Software used is licensed under the SIL Open Font License, Version 1.1.
Alfa Slab One - JM Sole, info@jmsole.cl
Autoradiographic - Ray Larabie, typodermicfonts.com
Blenda Script - Seniors Studio, behance.net, Facebook@seniorsstudio, Twitter@seniorsstudio
Bubble Gum Sans - Angel Koziupa, Alejandro Paul, sudtipos@sudtipos.com
Catharsis Expresso & Catharsis Macchiato - Christian Thalmann, cinga@gmx.net, www.cinga.ch
Caveat font family - Pablo Impallari, impallari.com, Twitter@pabloimpallari
Clicker Script Regular - Brian J. Bonislawsky and Jim Lyles, Astigmatic AOETI, astigma@astigmatic.com
Creampuff Regular - Nick Curtis, nicksfonts.com
Fira Sans Condensed - The Mozilla Foundation and Telefonica S.A.
GoodDog Plain - fonthead.com
Lakmus - Emil Bertell, fenotype.com
Lemon Cookie - Shara Weber, sharasfonts.com
Smudge Stick - Shara Weber, sharasfonts.com
Vollkorn - Friedrich Althausen, www.friedrichalthausen.de

Stop calling me names, dummy!

For All Countries · For All Budgets
From Janitors' Closets to Cafés to High–End Galleries
From the Poorest Street Artist to the Most Famous

hashtag #valzubiriagenda

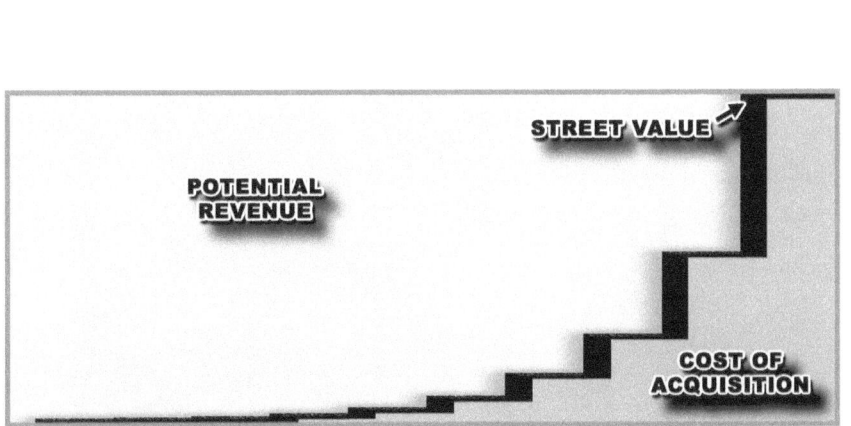

Table of Contents

Books by Zubiri & Perez ii
Copyright iv
Preface xiii
Introduction xv

PART 1: ART, PRICING, SCARCITY & BOOK PUBLISHING ... 3
Special Section #1 4
1. The #valzubiriagenda The Basics 5
2. Here's a Simple Business 15
3. Let's Crunch Big Numbers First
    The Yet Unusual Big Challenge 19
4. How All This Started Years of Evolution
    So You can Use This Now! 33
5. Really Stupid, Really Easy Technical Knowledge
    Just So You Know 37
6. Why Books 41
7. Scarcity & Pricing The Next Pair 47
8. Reselling to Friends & Colleagues 51
9. We will All Become Marketers & Collaborators 61

10	Use Hashtag #valzubiriagenda to Find Each Other	65
11	Ideas for Banks & All the Other Financial Companies	71
12	Cafés, Restaurants, Offices & Other Locations	73
13	YouTubers, Other Videographers & Their Followers.........	79
14	Galleries Some Considerations	81
15	Homeless Street Artists, UFO Abductees, & Others	85
16	Tips for Publishers, Writers, Ghostwriters, Editors, Book Designers, Proofreaders, Lawyers, Photographers, etc.	89
17	Business Authors, Business Writers & Economists	93

	PART 2: PREPARING YOURSELF	**97**
	Special Section #2	**98**
18	Preparing to Become a Writer	99
19	Permissions & Apologies	103
20	Who the F#%k Told You to Get Yourself Published?	109
21	Becoming Artists & Writers	115
22	Become an Artist Now & Join #valzubiriagenda It's Never Too Late!	117
23	The World's Easiest Way to Produce Books!	127
24	Easy Technical Knowledge To Help Make You Stop Flinching	133
25	Book Production Preliminary Basic Knowledge	147
26	My Encounters with a Very Famous Author	149
27	Internal Conflict Preparing Your Mind to Write	153

i: Table of Contents

28	Try this: Publish First	
	What Your First Book Will Do for You	163
29	External Conflict How Others can Affect You	165

PART 3: WRITING & EDITING 177
Special Section #3 178

30	You can Use Other Writers or	
	Write Your Own Book!	179
31	How to Come Up with 2 Books from 1 Draft	181
32	Do Warm Ups	
	Pretend You're Already Writing	185
33	Beginning to Write	
	Some Nice Simple Pointers	189
34	Secrets Before You Begin Writing	195
35	Actual Writing Bigger & Better Tips!	201
36	My Writing Secrets	
	Get Started with These Techniques	207
37	Editing & Proofreading	
	Read Your Work 8 Times	213

PART 4: PUBLISHING BOOKS, E-BOOKS & OUR FUTURE ... 221
Special Section #4 222

38	A Quick Lesson in Publishing	223
39	Which Print on Demand Company to Use	229
40	Publishing Your Book	
	What You Should Watch Out For	233
41	Producing Your Art Books Before You Proceed	255
42	The Basics of Producing E-Books	
	Just an Overview	261

xii   **#VALZUBIRIAGENDA   ZUBIRI • PEREZ**

     Special Section #5 264
43 Beginning #valzubiriagenda
         Let's Organize & Make Progress! 265

ABOUT THE AUTHORS 269

INDEX 271

IMAGES
T-Shirts (mentioned in Chapter 41 page 260) 18
Valentino Zubiri's 4 memoirs (pages 49, 159, 265, 269) ... 36
Artist Richard Lau's 3 art books
     (Chapter 41 pages 256-259) 70
One Porcelain Doll in Fur Coat & Boots
     (pages xxviii, 4, 120 & 269, *see index for more*) 80
A Selection of Mixed Media Porcelain Dolls
     (pages xxviii, 4, 120 & 269) 84
Silverio Perez, Untitled, porcelain & permanent
     marker, 2018 (pages xxviii, 4, 120 & 269) 116
Jerry Miller's & James Miller's books
     (Chapter 33 pages 191 & Chapter 37 page 218) 146
Bob Couttie's book (Chapter 40 page 246) 152
Silverio Perez' art, commentary
     (pages xxviii, 4, 120 & 269) 162
Porcelain Doll Heads
     (pages xxviii, 4, 120 & 269) 164
Porcelain Doll Shoes
     (pages xxviii, 4, 120 & 269) 188

Preface

Hello Everyone!

We just want to let you know that this book is written as if Valentino Zubiri wrote it. It was easier to do this than to go back and forth between co-authors Valentino Zubiri and Silverio Perez.

Our challenge is to help you, non-writers and non-publishers, to write *and* publish your books and e-books—memoirs, biographies, autobiographies, articles, essays, manifestos, full-color art books, etc.

We don't just hope that you will learn from the book. We hope you get yourself to the point where you will see your books and e-books available to investors, art collectors and everyone else.

Your books will end up in various locations—more than the number of bookstores in your town.

This book proceeds not so much as a how-to, but as a series of stories, knowledge and examples.

We will have more related books. A second related book is already in the works.

Relax and enjoy the book!

By the way, if you are busy and you have subordinates, get them to read the book. Simply order a few copies, and hold a meeting.

Introduction

Christmas Eve, December 24, 2017

Silverio and I had been wondering what to tell you for the introduction. It is December 2017, right now, between Christmas and New Year.

We planned months in advance that we were going to Midnight Mass, or Christmas Eve Mass. Silverio lives in another state with his girlfriend. He had no plans to spend Christmas with his girlfriend's family, so he drove here to Chicago to spend it with me two days before Christmas, on December 23.

I was taking for granted this Christmas "Eve" mass. I was thinking we will just go to an afternoon mass. To cut the story short, it was only on that day, December 24, that I even bothered to find out if the church two miles away had Midnight Mass. They did, and it was to start at 11 p.m.

Because it was nighttime, and finding new parking was going to be difficult if Silverio moved his car, not to mention it snowed earlier that day, he and I walked those two miles, at 10:30 p.m. We were a little late. After the mass, we walked back. It was cold and windy. The temperature was below freezing. This was our sacrifice.

Silverio is also an eccentric guy. Even though he knew it was cold outside, with snow on the sidewalks, he went out with his constant trademark look: a thick, plain, white t-shirt, a hoodie, a pair of jeans and white gym shoes.

I was just my usual. I had pajamas under my jeans, four layers of shirts, and an insulated black leather jacket with pocket zippers that no longer worked.

I saw a friend, Dan, at church, and he also walked a few blocks from home. After mass, the three of us walked in the same direction. We paused at Dan's gate for a moment, I gave him a hug, Silverio touched knuckles with him, and then Silverio and I continued to walk home for another mile.

So I'm writing now, between Christmas Day and New Year's Day. Going to mass to worship was not in my mind to tell you. This means that we already had an introduction prepared. We decided to change it. Here now is why.

The Christmas Eve party

That afternoon, Silverio and I went to a small party. I was invited by a friend whom I had once in a while mentioned in my earlier books. She was staying at her friend's home downtown. Her friend was a locally famous classy lady whom I had not yet met.

At noontime, I called my friend to cancel because it was still snowing. By 5 p.m., Silverio said it seemed okay to go to the party, so I called my friend back to reinvite ourselves again.

My friend is certainly another eccentric, a really nice one. She would remind you of Olympia Dukakis from the TV show **Tales of the City,** except that my friend is a real female. Dukakis' character later revealed that she used to be a man—we're not tackling that in this book. I'm just saying my friend loves everyone and smokes pot—for health reasons.

For the few years that I had known her, she told me that her friend, the host that night, was also a writer. The host supposedly had book-length manuscripts who must have published some works somewhere. I had gone online and could not find any book title of hers. No blog entries, nothing.

This was why, on that afternoon, Christmas Eve, I thought that I should bring my book samples to show her, and see if she would want to self-publish. If she did, I would help her. Because my backpack still had space, I also planned to bring a few of my porcelain doll art to show her.

Because it snowed, there was a total of six people at the gathering. They said people started to call to cancel, just like myself, so it was good that Silverio and I changed our minds.

There was the host whom I would not describe for now (she's locally

Introduction xvii

famous), my friend who invited me, myself, Silverio whom I invited, and two ladies. There was a total of six people. Let me focus on the last two ladies.

The two ladies and I talked about art

One was probably in her eighties and the other one was younger, probably in her fifties. So Silverio and I were the last to arrive.

After introductions and a little conversation, the older lady continued to ask the other lady for tips on how she can represent an artist whom she believed in.

Before I joined the conversation, I overheard the younger lady say that she could not help her, because she only bought art in London for her clients. This was when I joined in. The younger lady explained that she was an interior designer and she used to buy art in New York, but now London is the place to buy art and she has stopped going to New York in favor of London.

I can be smart and stupid at the same time. Having been seriously into writing books, I flip-flop between reading between the lines during conversations, blanking out and not listening at all, being careful of what I say, and, in this case, saying too much.

I opened my big mouth and said, facing the older lady, "Oh you should know that art can be political. If you've never been in the art business, you should prepare yourself. Art can be political."

The host's residence was on a high floor. Across the street was a museum. It was so easy to point to it and exclaim, "The owner of an expensive gallery once told me that the executive director of that museum has never set foot in her gallery. The gallery represents some artists that the museum also has, except that the art pieces were obviously not bought from her."

I added, "The gallery owner said that she and the other galleries had figured out, why would anyone from the museum come to them, for the price of a taxicab fare, when they can have a vacation, with first class plane and hotel accommodations, expensive meals paid for, etc., if they go to New York to buy the art?"

Then I joked, "Seriously, if I had that ability to get myself to another city, all expenses paid, and we're talking art, everything would be first class... I would do that same thing. My conversation with the gallery owner happened more than 10 years ago, and she was referring to whoever was current then. But if that practice continues, I don't blame them. Then again, it's a matter of how we perceive things and which side we're on."

As I will tell you later, writing is 99% editing. When we speak, we don't have time to edit. This is why we can psychoanalyze conversations. I began to realize that the interior designer, a respectable guest of the party where I was only a surprise guest at, may have been hurt by my disappointment of the museum's practice, because she herself did the same thing: fly elsewhere, this time to London, and forget New York(!), to buy art for her clients. Whatever was offered in Chicago must *never* be what she can offer her clients.

Then I placed myself back on the ground, saying, "But I should feel some degree of responsibility and every once in a while spend on cab fare to visit and get to know at least some of the galleries in the city. We're talking about the museum.

"It's a nonprofit, so the galleries feel that the museum should have a connection with the local galleries. Are they representing the city's art community or are they bringing art from the outside to show and educate the city?

"But private citizens are different, we can do whatever we want. We don't need to have a mission to do what we do.

"Except me," I added, as a joke.

As I have said, I did bring my art and my books to the host. Later on, the interior designer made up an excuse not to even look at my art and my books. I wasn't offended, but this is a real world reaction which has a solution—we just need to convince her clients to look for us, and that is what this book is about.

The host and the older lady listened to me. I explained to them what I call the #valzubiriagenda. I made the older lady realize that in order to get people interested in her protégé's art, art is still a business, there are trends, there are politics involved, and people who buy art might follow trends.

All of us learn about trends. We don't necessarily follow them. We all still need to make money right where we are located. Let's set a worldwide trend so we don't have to follow the interior designer to London.

Introduction

I don't blame the interior designer for leaving too early. Between the six of us at the dinner party, she was the most normal. She did not fit in. We might still end up being friends in the future.

Her real world reaction was good. Consider this: If you want someone like her to buy your art, you will have to make her clients insist on buying your art. You will have to set a trend.

I'm in Chicago. I cannot convince *her* to buy my art. I have to convince *her clients* to get her to take a taxi to come and visit me—as soon as now, or yesterday, or tomorrow! Only a trend, a movement, can do that.

For now, I might have some understanding of her. Not counting Silverio and I, why would she be with old, widowed and single ladies on Christmas Eve? It was an "almost business" call. She was an interior designer and our host was a real estate agent who got in the news for a huge, historic real estate sale.

If I told you what the host was able to accomplish at about age 80, just a few years ago, you would laugh, because it's familiar and part of American pop culture that's so well-known to the whole world.

My "unofficial designation"

There is something I should mention here. I also explained to the ladies that I had become known in 2007 to some high-end galleries in the city. I had met with the with the director of their association, so the unofficial title given to me was "Friend of the Galleries."

That night at the party, I probably sounded like I was the enemy of those who don't care about the local galleries. I probably became perceived as such by the interior designer.

Once again, we are talking money here. The way to make money and earn commission is to represent a client and go to another city or country to acquire art. With all expenses paid.

She successfully separates artists and galleries from her clients. That's good. I know an interior designer who was not able to keep clients and had to stop practicing. He lost his condo and he now lives with his relatives.

I will wake you up a little bit more later, but December 24 was a special, surreal time for me and Silverio.

Silverio and I went to a party with a few people. It was like a movie scene. Silverio only drank water, but I had wine, so it made me look at the situation in a life-changing way. I seldom drink.

Then Silverio and I went to church at midnight, sacrificing our health to get to church by walking at night, just after the snow. I worried that we might not make it if we got lazy, because I got tipsy and Silverio might just simply decide not to go.

Our going to the party and the conversations we had there, going to church, writing this book, and now, you reading this book, and, later on, wondering how you can get involved, even write a memoir—these all reflect our constant, active search for meaning.

We should not have to go to hell for art

Here is a reminder that I always tell myself:

"We should not have to go to hell for our art."

Why would we create something just so we will end up in hell, after living and creating art here one earth? Please remember this. We will now ask you to at least be drawn toward the #valzubiriagenda. How to hopefully make money through art in the real world. We should be responsible. We should deliver. We should be thankful for being creative. We should find creative, thoughtful ways to help other fellow artists, fellow investors, fellow art collectors, fellow writers, fellow book designers, fellow editors and everyone else who want to join in. Some of us artists might be mentally deficient—we should help them get ahead as well.

If and when we succeed or at least move ahead using the #valzubiriagenda, I'm sure we will still end up in this hierarchy of snobbery. That's probably okay. At least, along the way, we have connected more and helped some people advance together with us.

During that conversation with the interior designer, she asked, "If the galleries know you, then why aren't you represented by them?"

It was obvious by that time, having mentioned a good number of things, that we were becoming polar opposites. The more she knew about me, the more she can tell others. I wanted to get back on her good side.

I answered her with this remark. "Well, I obviously know about what is going on in Chicago. I'm working to get represented in New York!"

She exclaimed, "Hah! See? I knew it."

Introduction
The business of galleries

There was something I did not care to explain to her. Galleries can take 50% to 60% of the retail price. The artist receives 50% to 40%. They also might require exclusivity for their city. I hesitated to ask any gallery in 2007 to represent me.

In 2006, I gained a little more "real world," not imagined, confidence in myself, because I had just written my first full-length tangible book. It was my first attempt to write a memoir from an artist's perspective. Even though I took it out of circulation because I had written too much and I needed to reorganize what I wrote, it leveled up my confidence by a billion points. It made me feel like I was headed in the right direction.

Although I had been painting, I was not really set on my art yet.

I had been painting and drawing from the late '80s to the '90s. I had also joined a theatre group, joined group art shows, done street fairs selling rubber stamps, and painted and drew—nudes for the most part.

I also had a monthly column which featured the arts in a free monthly paper. I eventually became the paper's #2 guy, helping the owner/publisher/chief editor as an assistant editor/layout artist, besides maintaining a column. I left the paper in 1996. I learned a lot, and now I can confidently write and make books.

It was in 2009 when I started getting into porcelain doll-making

I'm almost positive that you will agree with me about this, if you haven't already done so. Maybe you will feel this in the future as soon as you finish your first book-length draft.

I put a huge amount of effort coming up with each and every single one of my memoirs and other books. No gallery asked me to write a memoir so they can represent me. After the effort of writing a book, it did not make sense to accept 40%-50% out of an asking price of 100%. It also did not make sense to be exclusive to a gallery.

The only way this would make sense, in my opinion, was if there were no exclusivity within any city.

It did not make sense to put in a lot of effort to get myself to a higher level, only to allow a single gallery to profit from a demand that I myself may have generated.

The galleries whom I call friends do not represent me. I have this joke that I am ambitioning to become the first-ever artist in Chicago whom all the galleries and agents represent. The vision is still alive in my head and still unachieved. Not yet real world. If I get myself famous and in demand enough, it will happen.

We all make rules to include and reject

I am not really familiar with the conditions of becoming a member of the association of galleries, but someone told me that to become a member, the gallery must only sell art, not gifts. This means that the counters should not have handmade necklaces, even if the walls have original art. Giclées are probably out of the question as well. Very strict.

If you opened what you would consider a gallery, and applied to the association only to get rejected because you did not realize they were so strict, you would be disappointed and have nothing good to say about them.

You made smart decisions regarding your gallery, and selling lower-priced items could be one of them. It's not about adhering to the rules, but some gallery owners did envision themselves opening a gallery that only sold original art.

Some galleries I know stuck to that premise until when they had to close for good. I'm talking about my time when I hung out at the galleries just before the 2008 real estate crash.

In my mind, too, I envision the reopening of some galleries that had closed. What happened in 2008 was harsh. Even some members of the gallery association had to close.

This book contains stories with lessons that I can share because they happened to me. I hope they become as valid to you as they have been to me. Sometimes, we just need to hear someone else say the same thing that we have been thinking of and considering to do.

Those struggling galleries, some of them have closed. I did become friends with a few. Besides the complaint that the museum people and interior designers don't bother with them, here are a few more things that I can tell you.

The galleries reject a lot of artists

The galleries will not tell the public that they are struggling. Part of the illusion is success and money, to beget success and money.

They reject artists even without viewing the works. Here is why. We

Introduction

are talking about Chicago here, which is a big city.

In the United States, there is a hierarchy of cities in the minds of most people. People in Chicago like going to New York. People in the cities of Indiana and elsewhere, like the city of St. Louis in Missouri, like going to Chicago. Silverio likes to come to Chicago, because he thinks his smaller city is boring, although he calls his city Shitville #1 and Chicago, Shitville #2. His more favorite city is in California. He also has been to New York City. He envisions himself moving to New York City someday.

Returning to the rejection of artists even without viewing their works, top galleries in Chicago, and this is according to a friend who owned a gallery, and who had to close because of lack of business—they can receive as many as 50 inquiries a day from artists from the rest of the United States, and all over the world, asking for representation. Before the internet and current computer technology, the inquiries were in the form of snail mail and phone calls. Now they get phone calls, email messages, email with attachments, inquiries on their websites, mailed CDs, DVDs, USB flash drives and visits to their galleries. Still, they don't get a lot of queries from New York.

As I said, I was actively hanging out at the galleries in 2007. I have met many artists who have told me, "How dare these galleries reject me without even looking at my art!"

There is also a gallery here who only represents 10 artists. The only way a new artist will get represented by the gallery is if an artist they represent dies.

A gallery would call the group of artists that they represent their "stable of artists." Stable, like a horse's stable. It's just a word. I don't find it derogatory. However, imagine if the gallery keeps growing its stable, just to accommodate all the artists who inquired to get represented. The stable would get unmanageable.

Imagine a visitor with money, thinking of buying works that should become higher-priced in the future. A gallery with a lot of artists would feel watered down compared to a competing gallery with only a few "select" artists.

"Oh Val, we're all doing the same thing!"

Here's another instance to wake you up. There was a panel discussion that happened every once in a while. I don't know if they still do it now. The panel consisted of one or two art experts, a gallery, an art collector and a bank CEO. You might want to attend to watch their discussion.

So I went online to research about the panel members. To my astonishment, I discovered that the art collector was looking for a job, and he posted his resume publicly for potential employers and strangers like myself to see. It was too easy to find, so don't blame me for spotting it. Nowadays, you would have online job sites, but this was more than a decade ago, he had one of those free pages provided for by sites like Geocities.

There's more to this story—a gallery told me that they did the panel every year. They were friends who were into the art field. The experts would mention artists. The artists were represented by that gallery in the panel. The art collector would attest to collecting art as investments and being happy and satisfied with his collection. And yes, he buys from the gallery in the panel. The bank would have available money to lend to the potential art collectors and investors in the audience. All of them were always available for later consultation.

I was in a gallery when I initially saw the panel's postcard. It was the gallery who explained the above system to me. The gallery assistant said it's a modern day snake oil approach to selling art.

I said, "Then that's a bad thing they are doing."

The gallery assistant laughed out loud. She said, "Oh Val! That's pretty much what every gallery is doing!"

How galleries define these two groups of people

A gallery owner defined something to me. There are people with art collections and there are people who are art collectors. Some visitors come in to tell galleries that they are art collectors, just because they bought collectible art decades ago.

If they stopped actively buying or collecting art, then they are no longer art collectors. They become people with art collections.

She said this is not snobbery, but more for the galleries to define, because the galleries have monthly bills to pay. They cannot actively sell to people with an art collection so their focus should be on art collectors. Art collectors are the ones who get invited to art openings.

Introduction

Wondering about expertise

I joined a gallery tour one time. When the tour got to this one gallery, the curator talked to us.

She introduced the gallery to the group, and in the course of her presentation, she said she had been working at the gallery, for decades, as the manager, that even though she had no degree in art *nor* a college education, she considered herself an expert in art.

Then she pointed out things about brushwork on two paintings which someone in the group later commented were stupid.

If you're an artist, and you went to art school to become profound, and you applied for representation at that gallery, you can guess who rejected you.

There was a practice that she did which I never saw other galleries do. Every time I was at a scheduled gallery tour that included her gallery, checks paid out to the gallery were laid out on her desk. As visitors came in, she looked like she just happened to be busy for the day, behind the desk, looking as if she was busy with the checks. I would not tell you this if I had only seen this once. Gimmick!

My mild stroke theory

If you used to look at art magazines in the '70s and '80s, and saw names of galleries which are still open now, in the 21st century, you might want to save up some money to visit these galleries. It will feel like visiting a sacred place.

I have this phrase I keep in my head: "mild stroke."

I know some people who had mild strokes. Some of them had changes in their demeanors—they got meaner and uncaring. Maybe I had a mild stroke. For now, let me focus on the art world.

I just want to point out that there have been a few galleries in Chicago, over the last 30 years, who were caught reproducing much too many "limited editions" of lithographs and whatever else. They only got caught later. They probably stopped being careful.

There was a gallery who sold works by a street artist who died about 13 years prior to this. I saw the gallery owner thumb tack four works on paper by this long-dead artist on his gallery's wall. The four works were pristine, with no creases, no violations, up until four thumb tacks penetrated each corner of each art piece.

Why did he do that if they were selling for at least $11,000 each? I would think he would have glass-covered frames in storage for displaying pieces. By the way, those works can be easy to fake.

This is exactly why I am encouraging everyone to archive their works in art books and catalogs. I'm really just using "catalog" to appease those who use that word.

You will discover that as you make your own "catalog" of works, you will put in so much effort in and appreciation for the activity that you will refuse to use the word "catalog." You made an art book.

If you systematically stack 5 to 20 images of your art pieces in one page, that's probably a catalog. If you dedicate one art piece to a page, I would call that an art book. If you add some text, that's an art book. Whatever works.

What I'm saying here is that we should chronicle and archive our works to prevent fakery. We human beings become old. We forget, we get mild strokes, our brains get rewired, we stop caring and we die. Our books and art can outlast us 300 to 3,000 years.

My encounter with a very classy rich lady

Here is why I am encouraging all of us to write memoirs and biographies... all in book form.

I was at a gallery I frequented. There was a classy lady in her sixties or seventies, nicely dressed in something that looked very expensive. She also wore large, classy chunks of noticeable jewelry. She was looking around. I had noticed earlier that she had just paid for an art piece. I approached her and we talked.

She was just waiting for her driver to come pick her and the art piece up. She said she buys art for her husband's office and for their home.

I said, "I hang out at this and some other galleries. I noticed you bought an art piece that I had gotten visually familiar with. I just have one question to ask. Do you know who the artist is?"

She answered, "No I don't."

"Let's say you have a party, and people walk around to check out your collection, wouldn't it be a good thing to tell your guests something about the art and the artist?" I asked.

Introduction

What she said was simple, but relevant to me then, and this may be relevant to all of us now.

She answered, "My husband is a jealous man. I cannot know the artist because he might think I'm seeing him."

Here is where our memoirs and biographies, in book form, come into the picture.

Imagine her at her party. She points to our original art pieces. Next to them are our books. Some of the books are memoirs and art books by the artists, investors and fellow art collectors. One of the solo art books includes the original art piece she owns.

I'm a lazy person myself. If I were busy making art, I would certainly not want to be hobnobbing with people too much. The presence of our books would suffice. People will get to know us without having to see us.

So I hope you find a way to come up with your books. If you are illiterate, have someone else do your books for you. If you are lazy, do the same. Let a writer or even a ghostwriter write a book for you.

The way I visualize my doll art is this: A straight man has a party, and in the middle of a room is my art, encased in glass. The art has the porcelain dolls, gemstones and precious metals. People look at the work. They also see the books about me on a nearby shelf.

I visualize that everyone has heard that my art is currently in the 8 figures. They also talk about my musical that won an award, that was based on my book, **Dollman the Musical, A Memoir of an Artist as a Dollmaker.**

The man says he has this one art piece and four more in other rooms. He lets his guests know that he's selling two and keeping three. This is why I call my art "chick magnets."

The art itself becomes irrelevant to the investor. It's just an investment. As he entices the next investor to acquire his acquisition for a profit, he simply gives away copies of my books, including an art book that has the art he is selling.

I'm the one responsible for my art and my books so he would not have to. In fact, I added the gemstones and precious metals in my art, to justify the higher prices in case I did not get known.

He's responsible for the business. This is okay. This is a good relationship.

I'm still just visualizing. I'm as poor as a church mouse.

(Note: You can see my doll art on pages 80, 84, 162, 164 & 188, & Silverio Perez' art on pages 116, 162 & 164)

The galleries have seen this before

Let me tell you another incident. One time, I had just come out of a gallery, and a couple approached me. They were both middle aged. They said they were from out of town, checking out the galleries because the lady, the wife, was an artist. They came out of the gallery with an art piece, so they obviously bought the piece.

They initially went in to see if the gallery can represent her. They bought the art piece, made by someone else, because they also collected art.

I said their purchase was a good one, because I always regularly visited that gallery to check out what they have out on display. I said I wouldn't be there if I didn't like the place.

Obviously, I'm not one to shatter illusions, not unless you buy a book called **Valzubiriagenda.**

They bought a piece. They should be happy with it. I cannot have them see my face telling them that bribing a gallery would not make the gallery agree to represent her. I could be wrong. I can be bribed, duh. Kidding. I just hope that, by now, she has representation.

This artist from Manhattan publishes his books

Here is a story I included in my memoir, **1-Hour Mentors, A Memoir of an Artist as a Masseur.** I was a masseur then, I got a call from someone young. He came to Chicago to be away from New York City.

He told me that he was an artist who was going to have an art show in less than two months. He had paper strewn about on the hotel room floor. I asked him what they were.

He said they were his writings, and he needed to finish his book so that even those who cannot afford his art can go home with a book. The gallery will get the book printed and will make the book available at the show's opening reception.

This would be the precursor to what we are doing right now. I believe his was a book of poetry and a few essays. The weak part of his

Introduction

book was that it was only going to be made available at the gallery. This was around 2003. Like what I will be explaining in this book, self-publishing trended in 2006.

The artist was in his twenties. He said he was lucky enough to have inquired at and gotten accepted by a Manhattan gallery just before he graduated from art school in Indiana. He told me that some of his classmates are still working as waiters and baristas.

He also told me that he had seen galleries drop artists who don't sell. He said that during show openings, the gallery allows his friends, fellow artists, art collectors and investors to mix. He even gave me details to his show, in case I want to come.

He said his gallery has its own warehouse-sized space, where its artists can make art. He also said there is a bar across the street which can take care of the overflow of guests on opening night.

The proud artist I know

I want to tell you about this artist I know who volunteered at the same church I used to volunteer at. One time, I showed him my memoirs. He shrugged. The next year, I showed him Richard Lau's art books—I will mention Richard some more later. I made three books of Richard's art for him.

This fellow artist and parishioner made a decision to avoid Richard and I. I thought it was funny. When you get published yourself, you will take other people who dislike or even insult you in stride.

I remember the moment he probably decided to start avoiding me.

One time, we were picking up about 300 pots of Easter lilies to decorate the church. While we were in the church's van at Home Depot, waiting for the deacon to give us the go signal to get the plants, he told me he used to work for a gallery.

The gallery he mentioned was a commercial gallery. They carried original art and giclées. He begrudgingly told me that they let him work there, but never let him display his art. So he finally quit.

I said I had become familiar with some galleries, and they can get political. That was all I said. I think he thought I was defending his enemies.

People who will experiment with what I call the #valzubiriagenda definitely will feel varying degrees of positivity. We will slowly see the glass being half full. We will reject the bad and store good things in our minds.

This introduction is mostly tidbits about high-end galleries, because a lot of us still think that being accepted in a gallery is the be-all and end-all of success. I have pointed out that some galleries can't even keep themselves open. You're the one who is still here, who continues to survive.

In my memoir, **Wonder,** I had a chapter on being an artist versus being a brain surgeon.

Art versus brain surgery

From the time when any (would-be) brain surgeon goes to school, there already are amenities so that the brain surgeon comfortably continues to study, finally graduates and works as a brain surgeon.

There are parking lots, elevators and air-conditioned rooms where things about brain surgery happens. There are well-manicured people smiling at the hallways. There are books on anatomy and whatever else. There are instructors teaching exact ways. Finally, when the brain surgeon shouts, "Give me the saw for the skull!" someone hands him one, in a very nice, careful way.

We artists have to keep figuring things out for ourselves. What I call the #valzubiriagenda is the best that I had come up with. I still cannot call this book a textbook. Art doesn't follow an exact science.

The artist who died in the '90s

In the early '90s, I read an article in a local magazine that featured this artist who had just passed away.

The article said he died bitterly, according to his widow. She said that his dedication to the city he loved was not fully returned. The phrase the article used was that the artist in his older days felt that "the city owed him."

Owed him what? The city as a living breathing organism is a concept. The article indirectly said that the city should have made him more in demand, more famous, and more commercial. It boils down to this—the city should have made him money.

After reading the article, I went to the lobby of the nearby building where the article said had some of his works. It felt to me like I was paying tribute.

Introduction

I happened to be working at an office back then. On the following Monday, I was in the elevator with a coworker who asked me how my weekend was. I told her I went to the lobby of a building to check out the works of this artist, after reading the article in the local magazine.

What a coincidence. She said he was a friend of hers. She then mentioned that the city should have done more for him. She said the same idea: "The city owed him."

What has this artist been promoting? He died with a grudge.

In retrospect, thinking about him now, I get the feeling that he too may have had a mild stroke, that he never met his interior designer neighbor who always went out of town, that he should have known how many graduate from art schools a year, that he never understood the politics of art and that he never heard about the hierarchy of cities in the world.

Here is a way to move forward

Despite knowing some galleries here, some of which had shuttered their doors, I chose to look more into the #valzubiriagenda.

There *is* a method to the madness. One day, I still hope I will be represented by all of my beloved galleries. Those who have closed, I will encourage to at least represent a few of my works.

I owe them all so much for all the insights I have garnered to the point where I bravely and strongly believe I should not yet be represented by them. When the magic happens for me and them, I hope they will all profit.

So there's our introduction. It's a lot, but it is for those who still feel that galleries will represent 1,000 artists out of 1,000 who inquire.

Maybe, one will get accepted. Maybe there are places which will accept the 999 others. In this book, I will mention the owner of two coffee shops whom I talked to.

He said that he cares enough for the community that he welcomes local artists to display on his walls. He has also envisioned himself seeing one of his artists becoming famous, highly collectible and super expensive.

He was also hoping that the famous artist would also make him rich.

If he followed the status quo of the high-end galleries in our beloved city of Chicago, he would open a full-fledged gallery, with the strict conviction that nothing else would be sold, not even coffee. If he followed the interior designer I mentioned earlier, whom I am using now to change our lives and decisions, he would move to London to open a gallery—that still did not sell coffee.

As you can see, it's all about perception. We have a hierarchy of perception. His café is good enough. Cafés! He has two.

Our challenge is not to convince those museums and interior designers to change their ways.

Our mission is to become so irresistible that collectors and investors will insist on giving their interior designers and buyers taxi fare to the nearby venue, even a café or a janitor's closet, to buy art.

We have to give investors and collectors no choice but to notice and demand for our works. We have to make people unable to say no to our art or at least close to that.

The #valzubiriagenda is also about perception, *and* at the same time, it's also about our tangible books and predictable pricing and scarcity.

My challenge is to get all of us to set goals and programs for ourselves that will help investors and art collectors make money, chase art and collect local and international art within their budgets.

Another challenge is to get non-writers to write and get everyone into publishing and self-publishing.

Let us meet and help each other. Let's barter our skills to keep costs down if we are not yet financially okay.

Giving commissions is important. I always joke that I can be bribed. Be generous with commissions. People know people and sometimes, they know people you don't. Someone somebody else knows can change your life forever. You also just might have something that can change other people's lives forever.

Everyone needs money to eat. I'm already looking forward to treating you. If you succeed, maybe you can take me to eat somewhere.

Let's do our best to help one another. Let's do our best to leave no one behind.

There might be an unknown force who knows what we're up to. And once again, people go to hell for killing people. We should not have to go to hell for something as stupid as art.

For All Countries · For All Budgets
From Janitors' Closets to Cafés to High-End Galleries
From the Poorest Street Artist to the Most Famous

hashtag #valzubiriagenda

VALZUBIRIAGENDA
The Viral Groundbreaking Way to Achieve Your Profits through Global Art Investment

by
VALENTINO ZUBIRI
Author of Dollman the Musical, Wonder
Hocus Pocus Lately & 1-Hour Mentors

& SILVERIO PEREZ

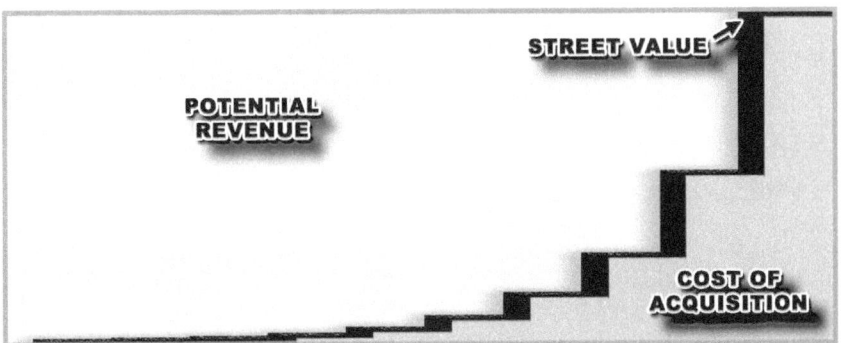

hashtag #valzubiriagenda

Part 1

Art, Pricing, Scarcity & Book Publishing

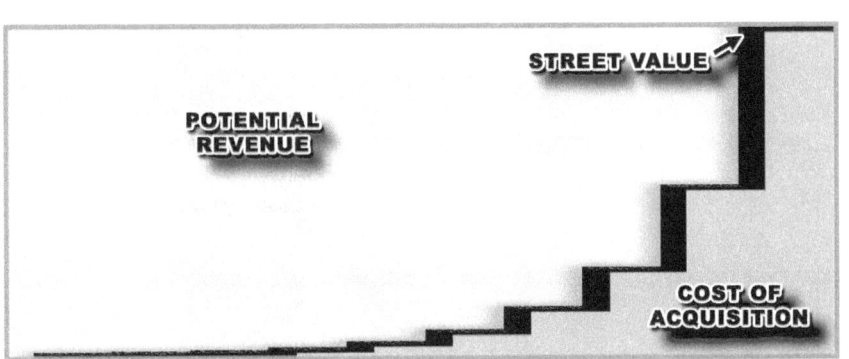

SPECIAL SECTION #1

www.ValentinoZubiri.com
valzubiriagenda@gmail.com

ATTENTION EVERYONE! GET ON MY LIST NOW!

If you want to be on the cue for earning commissions, direct reservation for my art, Silverio Perez' art or Richard Lau's art, please email me at **valzubiriagenda@gmail.com**.

Use the subject line in English:

"*Interested in Representing Val Zubiri, Silverio Perez or Richard Lau*"

"*Interested in Selling Art by Val Zubiri, Silverio Perez or Richard Lau*"

"*Interested in Reserving Art by Val Zubiri, Silverio Perez or Richard Lau*"

"*[Something else...]*"

You can opt to immediately reserve or do a wait and see and pay only when the next price point is soon to be reached.

ALSO FROM CHAPTER 9 PAGE 62

I was suggesting that we can publish group collaborations.

My suggestion is that you immediately form your own group by informing your friends and colleagues. Then go online and use the hashtag #valzubiriagenda and grow your group some more. Immediately place your stake as soon as you decide to do all this even if you still don't have any books nor enough art.

As soon as you decide to use #valzubiriagenda, email me at valzubiriagenda@gmail.com so you can also be in my cue.

As soon as I can finance books, I will help publish others like yourself. It might take a while, so if you can publish others now and form groups now, do so. I'm still currently busy contacting my own investors and art collectors.

You still have the option to choose which projects you want to join in, but it would be good to be in the know.

Some of these collaborations would be for the first 50 to 500 in a category such as:

1. First group in your city, town, province, state or country
2. First group in deciding to join the #valzubiriagenda
3. First group investors and art collectors
4. First group in your medium of art (watercolor, oil, dolls, pastel, cards, paper, outsider art, nudes, fine art, acrylic, metal, mixed media, jewelry, birds, flowers, etc.—be creative)
5. First group in your social category (veteran, enlisted army, homebound, new age, activist, LGBTQ, celebrity, nurse, pilot, drag queen, teacher, age range, cancer victim, student, homeless, etc.—be creative)
6. Suggest other ideas

Use this on the subject line *"List me as first in my city for ..."* or something else.

I will not be judgmental, and everything you send me will be confidential.

I will also send you and everyone else a regular newsletter without sharing your email addresses.

- Val Z.

valzubiriagenda@gmail.com

Next special section is on page 98

Chapter 1

The #valzubiriagenda
The Basics

I will give you the basics now, just in case you are impatient to know this.

Chapter 2 will give you a simple idea to implement this. For people with available selling locations, which is pretty much all of us. We can sell online and from our homes.

Chapter 3 will then be for higher-end individuals and companies. In case you need a huge amount of money *and* you're busy.

There are a few conditions. You don't have to follow everything. Pick and choose what you are comfortable with. As you get more savvy, then you might adopt a few more into your mix.

The purpose of the #valzubiriagenda is to make money sooner than later through art.

The #valzubiriagenda is for the following people or companies:

1. If your non-art company needs money
2. If you're an artist, you will become the source of art
3. If you want to earn commissions by matching art pieces from the artists, investors and art collectors with later investors and art collectors
4. If you want to help as a writer, ghostwriter, lawyer, editor, proofreader, photographer, book designer, desktop designer, etc.
5. If you have a following, you can make art and sell to

your followers

6. If you need money for something, you can also make art

The #valzubiriagenda

The first two conditions

$Zero-cost self-publishing and "print on demand" are now possible online. The first two conditions are related to this.

1. **Publish written books that are about yourself and art. These can be the following: memoirs, biographies, autobiographies, artistic essays, manifestos, storybooks and others**
2. **Publish art books of your works. In order to prevent fakes, include as many works as you can. Publish *all* of your art pieces**

Everyone—artists, cafés, offices, homes, investors, art collectors, etc., can publish written-through books and art books.

Publish solo and collaborative group books.

This book will explain self-publishing and print on demand.

The second two conditions

Art is unregulated, portable and global. Stock brokers cannot sell stocks valued at $10 USD for $1,000,000. Realtors cannot sell houses valued at $100,000 for $1,000,000. They will get in trouble.

If you sell an art piece that you got for $1 later, or yesterday, or a year from now, or even today, right now, for $1,000,000, you will get praised. The idea is to buy art early from artists who will:

3. **Entertain scarcity by announcing a fixed quantity of art pieces that they will produce in their lifetime**
4. **Announce a schedule of increasing prices per number of pieces. Because art is unregulated, the price increase can even be exponential**

Examples:

For people with lower budgets, a $10 piece of art can reach $5,120 in

1: The #valzubiriagenda The Basics

ten steps, if the artist follows exponential pricing by a factor (or exponent) of 2:

$10 each for 300 pieces ⇒ $20 (300 pcs.) ⇒ $40 (300 pcs.) ⇒ $80 (300 pcs.) ⇒ $160 (300 pcs.) ⇒ $320 (300 pcs.) ⇒ $640 (300 pcs.) ⇒ $1,280 (300 pcs.) ⇒ $2,560 (300 pcs.) ⇒ $5,120 (300 pcs.)

For companies and individuals with higher budgets, here are the numbers if a still-unknown artist starts with $100,000. $100,000 can reach $51,200,000 in ten steps:

$100,000 (300 pcs.) ⇒ $200,000 (300 pcs.) ⇒ $400,000 (300 pcs.) ⇒ $800,000 (300 pcs.) ⇒ $1,600,000 (300 pcs.) ⇒ $3,200,000 (300 pcs.) ⇒ $6,400,000 (300 pcs.) ⇒ $12,800,000 (300 pcs.) ⇒ $25,600,000 (300 pcs.) ⇒ $51,200,000 (300 pcs.)

The investors can resell to other investors and art collectors at a discount. Even later investors just need to wait for the next price point to claim that their investments doubled.

We can call this the price and scarcity schedule or chart, which may change in time. It would also be good to be able to list the 3,000 works, together with their provenance (past and present owners of the art pieces).

Find one another

5. **Use the hashtag #valzubiriagenda online and in venues to be found**

Add the hashtag to be seen. Search online for people using the hashtag. Use the hashtag if you want to collaborate with people. You can call for meetings. You can call for submissions for book projects.

The following should discover and meet each other:

Artists, investors, art collectors

People and companies with commercial locations and venues, resellers

People who want to earn commissions

Writers, ghostwriters, collaborators, editors, book designers, graphic artists, photographers, proofreaders and others can find nearby and online projects

Lawyers and law firms for contracts are needed

Financial companies can help transfer funds

Computer professionals can come up with apps and software we can all use

Snowball the demand and trade contracts

6. To increase the street values of the artists at a fast rate, come up with ways to snowball the demand

7. If the works are slow to produce, trade the paperwork, which is actually the artist commission. The art pieces get delivered to the current owner of the paperwork

The most important factor for your financial success

8. Give commissions to middlemen

People know people. You can become an agent. Find artists and resellers you can help. Even agents can publish books.

Everyone can give commissions or rewards of some kind to instrumental people. Make sure to show your appreciation and gratitude. Give importance to people.

That's it! Begin now, attend local and online meetings and find a group or groups you can work with.

By the way, don't just trust anyone to take your finished art without any written receipt or agreement.

Your numbers if you start at $100,000

- ☐ $51,200,000 each x 300 pieces
- ☐ $25,600,000 each x 300 pieces
- ☐ $12,800,000 each x 300 pieces
- ☐ $6,400,000 each x 300 pieces
- ☐ $3,200,000 each x 300 pieces
- ☐ $1,600,000 each x 300 pieces
- ☐ $800,000 each x 300 pieces
- ☐ $400,000 each x 300 pieces
- ☐ $200,000 each x 300 pieces
- ☑ $100,000 each x 300 pieces

Total pieces: 3,000

The top last 300 pieces do not have to sell. Please refer to Chapter 3 for the explanation of the values below.

Cost of Acquisition for 2,700 pieces:
= $15,330,000,000

Street Value for 2,700 pieces based on the 2701st artist's asking price of $51,200,000:
2,700 pieces x $51,200,000 = $138,240,000,000

Potential Revenue from 2,700 pieces:
$138,240,000,000
- $15,330,000,000 = $122,910,000,000

Total Contribution to Society:
$51,200,000 x 3,000 pieces = $153,600,000,000

Your numbers if you start at $10,000

- ☐ $5,120,000 each   x 300 pieces
- ☐ $2,560,000 each   x 300 pieces
- ☐ $1,280,000 each   x 300 pieces
- ☐ $640,000 each   x 300 pieces
- ☐ $320,000 each   x 300 pieces
- ☐ $160,000 each   x 300 pieces
- ☐ $80,000 each   x 300 pieces
- ☐ $40,000 each   x 300 pieces
- ☐ $20,000 each   x 300 pieces
- ☑ $10,000 each   x 300 pieces

Total pieces: 3,000

The top last 300 pieces do not have to sell. Please refer to Chapter 3 for the explanation of the values below.

Cost of Acquisition for 2,700 pieces:
= $1,533,000,000

Street Value for 2,700 pieces based on the 2701st artist's asking price of $5,120,000:
2,700 pieces x $5,120,000 = $13,824,000,000

Potential Revenue from 2,700 pieces:
$13,824,000,000
- $1,533,000,000 = $12,291,000,000

Total Contribution to Society:
$5,120,000 x 3,000 pieces = $15,360,000,000

Your numbers if you start at $1,000

- ☐ $512,000 each   x 300 pieces
- ☐ $256,000 each   x 300 pieces
- ☐ $128,000 each   x 300 pieces
- ☐ $64,000 each   x 300 pieces
- ☐ $32,000 each   x 300 pieces
- ☐ $16,000 each   x 300 pieces
- ☐ $8,000 each   x 300 pieces
- ☐ $4,000 each   x 300 pieces
- ☐ $2,000 each   x 300 pieces
- ☑ $1,000 each   x 300 pieces

Total pieces: 3,000

The top last 300 pieces do not have to sell. Please refer to Chapter 3 for the explanation of the values below.

Cost of Acquisition for 2,700 pieces:
= $153,300,000

Street Value for 2,700 pieces based on the 2701st artist's asking price of $512,000:
2,700 pieces x $51,200 = $1,382,400,000

Potential Revenue from 2,700 pieces:
$1,382,400,000
- $153,300,000 = $1,229,100,000

Total Contribution to Society:
$512,000 x 3,000 pieces = $1,536,000,000

Your numbers if you start at $100

- ☐ $51,200 each   x 300 pieces
- ☐ $25,600 each   x 300 pieces
- ☐ $12,800 each   x 300 pieces
- ☐ $6,400 each   x 300 pieces
- ☐ $3,200 each   x 300 pieces
- ☐ $1,600 each   x 300 pieces
- ☐ $800 each   x 300 pieces
- ☐ $400 each   x 300 pieces
- ☐ $200 each   x 300 pieces
- ☑ $100 each   x 300 pieces

Total pieces: 3,000

The top last 300 pieces do not have to sell. Please refer to Chapter 3 for the explanation of the values below.

Cost of Acquisition for 2,700 pieces:
= $15,330,00

Street Value for 2,700 pieces based on the 2701st artist's asking price of $51,200:
2,700 pieces x $51,200 = $138,240,000

Potential Revenue from 2,700 pieces:
$138,240,000
- $15,330,000 = $122,910,000

Total Contribution to Society:
$51,200 x 3,000 pieces = $153,600,000

Your numbers if you start at $10

- ☐ $5,120 each   x 300 pieces
- ☐ $2,560 each   x 300 pieces
- ☐ $1,280 each   x 300 pieces
- ☐ $640 each   x 300 pieces
- ☐ $320 each   x 300 pieces
- ☐ $160 each   x 300 pieces
- ☐ $80 each   x 300 pieces
- ☐ $40 each   x 300 pieces
- ☐ $20 each   x 300 pieces
- ☑ $10 each   x 300 pieces

Total pieces: 3,000

The top last 300 pieces do not have to sell. Please refer to Chapter 3 for the explanation of the values below.

Cost of Acquisition for 2,700 pieces:
= $1,533,000

Street Value for 2,700 pieces based on the 2701st artist's asking price of $5,120:
2,700 pieces x $51,20 = $13,824,000

Potential Revenue from 2,700 pieces:
$13,824,000
- $1,533,000 = $12,291,000

Total Contribution to Society:
$5,120 x 3,000 pieces = $15,360,000

Chapter 2

Here's a Simple Business

Here is the traditional situation with galleries

The gallery wants exclusive representation of your art for a territory. They take 50%-60% of the sale.

Here is the traditional situation with cafés

You get into an agreement with a café. They display your work for a month or two, then you take back your unsold art.

Here is the new #valzubiriagenda approach

For the artists, you will need:

1. Your art
2. Your books
3. Your price and scarcity chart or schedule
4. Your venues and other locations

Publish all your works in book form. Your locations, sellers, collaborators, investors and art collectors can also publish their own art books. This increases the number of books you will be included in.

Go to a participating location such as a café and leave one or two art pieces, one or two books and your price and scarcity chart.

Go to another participating café and leave one or two works, one or two books and your price and scarcity chart.

Go to as many locations as you want and leave one or two works, one or two books and your price and scarcity chart.

You will probably have a lot more works at home or in storage.

Everyone sells your works using the art books. All sellers can accumulate as many art books and artists as they can handle.

You (artists and resellers) don't have to supply everyone with an art piece. This way, even million-dollar art can be sold by any approved location or representative, even those without physical locations.

Email your contacts regularly

Email everyone regularly to update them on which art pieces are no longer available.

As soon as you reach the number of works for the current price point, notify everyone so that everyone's asking price is changed to the next scheduled amount. Everyone's commission is changed to the next, higher price point.

The locations can give discounts or raise prices if they decide to do so.

Potential buyers can always look at your online blog or website to learn of your "official" current price and official locations. Anyone can get directly in touch with you. Set up a system to rightfully continue to give commissions.

Have a website that lists all of your art pieces together with the following:

1. Updated provenance
2. Updated books per art piece, as investors and art collectors include the art pieces
3. The current asking price

Additionally, provide the following:

1. Locations where your art is sold
2. Individuals selling your art
3. Your contact information
4. Conditions and disclaimers

The buyers, current owners, investors and art collectors of your work can also resell your works or their contracts at the same location.

2: Here's a Simple Business

Even art commissions can be sold.

You might no longer be a part of any agreements between the locations and the resellers if you have been paid and your finished art has been delivered. However, you might still need to maintain updates for still-unfinished, undelivered art and the provenance of all your works, to show your progress from when you started this to the present, to help investors and art collectors decide to acquire your art.

Everyone's asking prices will also be based on your current asking price. Everyone can discount or increase the works and contracts as all of you please. Everyone needs to watch out for fraud, so it is up to everyone's discretion as to how you all will deal with everyone else.

Your art can be sold in another city or country if you want as long as there is mutual trust between you and the other locations. Have written agreements. You will be in charge of shipping your art from where it is located once it is finished.

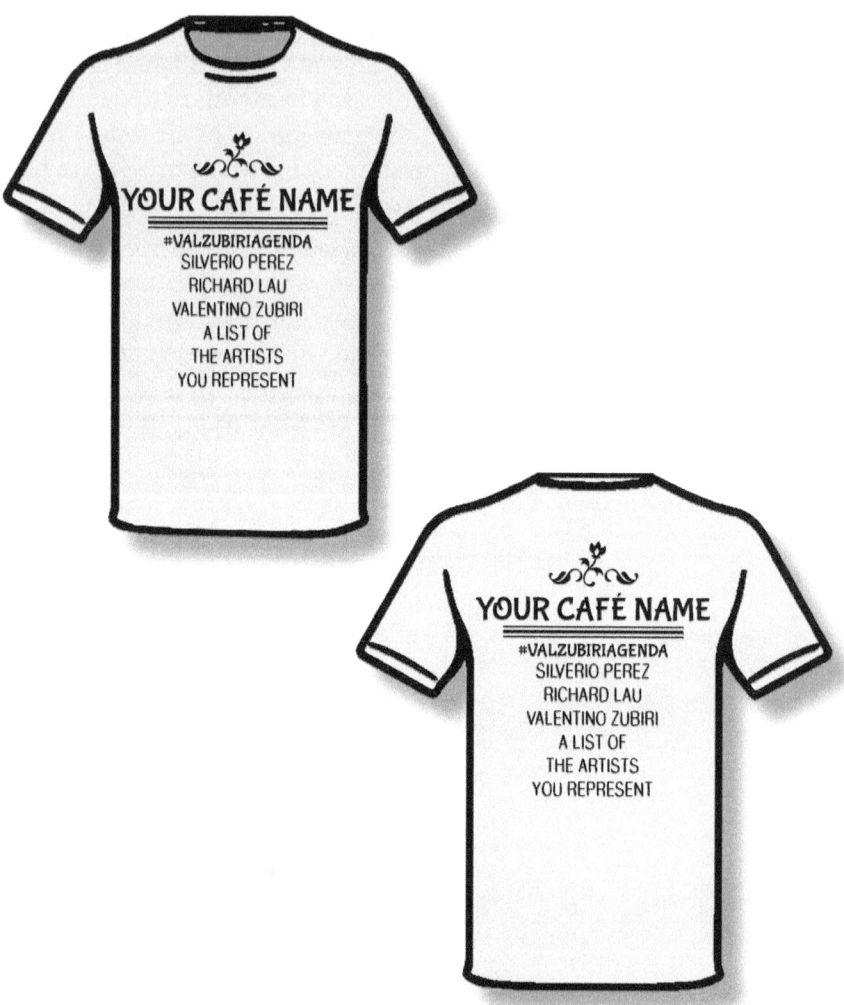

Refer to page 260, for the discussion on t-shirts

Come up with ideas to promote your place of business and your artists. Design t-shirts and mugs. Make them look like rock concert merchandise, etc. Do this as soon as your artists start paying off.

Your artists can also come up with their individual artist versions—the mugs can have their full-color designs.

This can be done because now, your artists will be at your locations on a more permanent basis.

Next image is on page 36

Chapter 3

Let's Crunch Big Numbers First
The Yet Unusual Big Challenge

First of all, thanks for acquiring this book. After focusing on artists in the Introduction, let us entertain our higher-end investors and art collectors, and the individuals, companies, government agencies and even entire countries that need help. I will talk about how all this came about in the next chapter.

Some popular mentions of large-scale finance

1. During World Wars 1 & 2, the banks that thrived held "confiscated" art
2. There was a Germany-based bank that was recently in the news because they needed €8 billion euros or $8.5 billion dollars to keep operating. They eventually raised the needed amount. They went public with their need, probably because they could not figure out how to make the money from their normal channels
3. There was another bank that got in trouble because employees got financially "creative" by opening unauthorized additional accounts for their clients
4. There are government pension funds that are claiming to be losing money. Government agencies do use private investment companies and returns have not been enough
5. Cook County in Illinois, in 2017, imposed a soda tax

by charging a penny per ounce of sugary drinks for a few months. They had to repeal it after a backlash. The county had hoped to make money for other purposes by taking pennies from the general public
6. In the news, even countries like Greece and Cyprus cannot pay debts
7. Bernie Madoff went to jail after his Ponzi scheme got discovered in 2008. The size of the fraud amassed by just one single individual was $64.8 billion dollars. If you do the math, one single artist could have helped him get out of his situation
8. There must be other felonious individuals and companies like Madoff who have yet to be found. They still have a chance to save themselves
9. There must be even more legitimate and honest individuals and companies that nevertheless need to be saved

What is your status quo?

I want to show you how a friend stopped #valzubiriagenda in its tracks before I show you how it could work for you.

I have a friend who happened to be a vice president of a bank. This was in 2007 before the real estate bubble. They, or his department, specialized in lending money related to real estate.

I wanted some feedback, so I told him about my idea of escalating prices and asked him if financial institutions would be interested in something like this.

He said something important. He said yes. And then he said something else, even more striking and relevant to us.

He reminded me of his status quo. He said he cannot introduce this idea to his bank for one simple reason.

He was on his way to retirement. He had put in decades of work with his company to get to where he was. He said if he introduced this idea to his bank, and that bank in the long run loses money, he might get shamed or become a scapegoat, be asked to quit, and lose his retirement.

3: Let's Crunch Big Numbers First The Yet Unusual Big Challenge

He then said that he did not like his company enough to care about their future income. He also said he has superiors who will make more money than him.

There was, therefore, no need to stir the waters.

I think when the real estate bubble happened in 2008, a year later, his company continued in their business. They probably repossessed homes. Maybe it was business as usual for them.

Those who lost their homes, some of us included, should probably have been the ones looking into this #valzubiriagenda.

The difference between my friend then and you now

You might have the same sentiment now as my old friend had in the past. Still, there is a marked difference:

You're reading a publicly available book. You can pass this book along in your office. Everyone now has access to the information here. Everyone can brainstorm and see if the idea can be enhanced.

If other companies and individuals will do this, you might as well do it too before it becomes too late. You're safely joining others.

My friend in 2007 only heard an idea. Even if I made a presentation, I would not have had this book, my memoirs, my art books, and my original art to support me.

Your first move

We're still assuming that you're busy.

Purchase a good number of copies of this book and ask your subordinates and other people to read it. You can start with individual meetings with them, get their individual inputs and then decide if you should have a meeting.

Have this book to pass around. I priced it to sell, at $13.95, so people all over the world can hopefully afford it. I don't intend to profit from this book. My focus is my own art, investors, art collectors and collaborators, and you, if you want to work with me.

Public meetings

Be ready to have a designated presenter.

Your company might have a meeting room that you can regularly use. This can be a way to have better control of your interests. You can call for the more public meetings.

Meet people, choose artists and choose whom you would want to collaborate with for your book projects. Find out if it's beneficial to form your core group.

You can conduct separate meetings for separate groups and art budgets. Find ways to manage people with different interests, especially if huge crowds show up.

What will motivate you and your company to do this?

How much influx of capital can you use for yourself or your business? As your company continues to profit from your regular industry, you can get into all this on the side.

Maybe your company is currently making less than you had hoped. There are some companies and government agencies that are desperate to make money. This is a new idea that might be worth the risk. If everyone is doing it, and it's at an early stage, then consider doing this for the meantime.

Get a pen, paper and a calculator and play with numbers. What will be your affordable price range? Only purchase art that you can easily afford.

You're supposed to spend only what you can afford

This is not like investing in real estate, which has a fixed price range. You can start with $1, $1,000, $100, $200, $50 art. You look at each artist's chart for scarcity and pricing and study the acceleration of demand to predict if the investment is smart.

If your goal is to make a lot more money, then you can look into artists who will have a scarcity and pricing chart that will meet your criteria.

Your circle of friends and colleagues

Would it not be safe to assume that someone who can afford $100,000 for art might have a circle of friends who can afford $200,000 or $400,000?

Would it not be safe to assume that someone who can afford $12,800,000 will know someone who can afford $25,600,000 or $51,200,000?

3: Let's Crunch Big Numbers First The Yet Unusual Big Challenge

I am suggesting that everyone spend within their means. Collect $5-dollar art if that is all you can afford, as long as the artist has announced the top goal of $50,000, more or less.

The #valzubiriagenda is not like real estate, where everyone has to afford the same budget range.

As you progress with all this, you can begin gathering contacts and contacts of contacts who can afford higher ranges.

Not all 3,000 will circulate

We're still playing with the 3,000 quantity for art pieces, just as an example here.

Investors and art collectors might want to, for example, purchase 8 works, and resell only 4. If you have 4 children, leave them with 1 art piece each. So, if I made 3,000 works, chances are only 1,500 will keep circulating, while others want to save what they got. Art collectors also tend to keep art.

Selling lower

Discounts can be added incentives. Investor #1 can resell to Investor #2 at a discount. For example, if the current asking price by the artist is $400,000, and Investor #1 acquired the art for $200,000, Investor #1 can resell for $325,000. Investor #2 then waits for the next price point. If the next price is $800,000, Investor #2 can resell to Investor #3 at a discount as well.

The artists can do this as well, because the artists' goal is to get to the next official price point for everyone's benefit.

The way to attract investors, to your own specific art pieces, can be through the books you will be able to produce for yourself, which will include your art acquisitions. Publish your own memoirs and art books if you want.

You can also get into an agreement with your artists, to be an agent as well. You can pass along discounts from your commission to your own contacts, so they can buy through you. Now you can choose between selling your own works and selling what your artist has available. You can still make it appear as if you bought the art pieces or contracts, even for just a moment. You can still include the art in your books.

How to get your money back fast

If you, for example, bought 10 works from the same artist at $100,000 each, and the next scheduled price is $200,000, sell 5 at that price. Now you have 5 left. You can resell these at a profit.

Trade the paperwork

An artist who becomes in demand might agree to sell the contracts before the art even gets started. The contracts are the art commissions, so whoever owns the contract will receive the art piece.

The contracts can include the scarcity and price chart and permission to publish the art piece. It can also include upcoming book projects, including the assurance that the art piece will be included in an upcoming art book by the artist.

All this information will help the sale and all future sales as the contracts pass from one investor to the next.

Everyone decides to trade based on the specific stipulations in the contracts—on a per artist, per contract basis.

What if the artist died?

Some art pieces can be fast to produce. Andy Warhol's silkscreen work was relatively fast.

Some forms of art are finalized by foundries and other companies. The artist simply emails the 3D computer file to the foundries. Foundries can also scan the artist's original, small prototype, and reproduce them to the specified, much larger size, in the correct final medium, like bronze or concrete.

There are also some art forms which need assistants in the studios. The art will still get delivered in case something happens to the artist.

I personally plan to employ assistants. It makes sense to be paid up front if the paperwork will be traded as soon as the investors get their hands on it. It all depends on the artists and the buyers seeing eye to eye. It also makes sense to have a nonrefundable amount because bills have to be paid.

Is $100,000 to $51,200,000 realistic?

Some artists already charge $100,000 dollars for their art pieces. I have been to galleries that sell relatively unknown artists at that price.

3: Let's Crunch Big Numbers First The Yet Unusual Big Challenge

These artists might sell faster if they declare a higher price point.

My idea for myself was 3,000 works and no more.

$100,000 for the first 300 pieces

$200,000 for the next 300 pieces

$400,000 for the next 300 pieces

$800,000 for the next 300 pieces

$1,600,000 for the next 300 pieces

$3,200,000 for the next 300 pieces

$6,400,000 for the next 300 pieces

$12,800,000 for the next 300 pieces

$25,600,000 for the next 300 pieces and finally,

$51,200,000 for the last 300 pieces.

As you can see, in ten steps, $100,000 can become $51,200,000. An early investor can net $51,100,000 from one art piece.

The earlier you get in, the better. However, the later investors and art collectors all continue to be okay. Everyone at any price point would only need to wait for the next price point to be able to claim that their investments just doubled.

I love Picasso's works, so I stop at $51,200,000 for this series of prices. 3,000 works are also less than Picasso's 4,600 paintings, not counting his other media.

I believe that there would be artists who will succeed in doing the #valzubiriagenda at this quantity and price range. This can be adopted to help big business and big investors and art collectors. Even big business can start with $10 art pieces.

I'm sticking to these numbers as my maximum. If I give a smaller quantity now, and I increase the quantity later, investors would get mad. If I don't sell much, I can always quit or slow down, and this will lessen the circulating quantity, which investors would appreciate.

How to save yourself from going to jail

Mr. Madoff's scam was discovered in 2008. He was just one single individual with such an influence that he "promised" returns of $64.5 billion.

He almost did not have to go to jail had he successfully started raising money through this idea. Here's some math, with 1,600 works and a starting price of $100,000. He could have used an artist with an announced total of 1,600 works. Get a pen, paper and calculator.

Starting from $100,000 for the first 160, all the way to asking for $51,200,000 for the last 160, Madoff could have bought the first 1,440 art pieces from that individual. The 1,441st would then have a street value of $51,200,000.

This would bring Madoff's 1,440 works to that price.

The total market value or street value for 1,440 works, will have been about $80 billion. The cost of acquisition: $15 billion. The net potential revenue: $65 billion. All he would have needed was one artist, publicity and marketing, 10 salespeople who will work on commission basis, his own database of contacts, and the empty, unused office space down the hall.

It's just too bad that this idea was not around in 2008, but now you have this idea floating around, safe, and in a publicly available book.

See how much you need to make for yourself in your currency, either as an investor or artist.

If you're an investor, imagine promoting one or two artists at the high prices. If you're an artist, start with your current comfortable price and look into increasing your price realistically.

Your quarterly and annual financial statements

I'm not a financial expert, but this is how I see all this in your financial statements.

In the simplest way I can propose, there are three numbers for your financial statements:

The Potential Revenue is the difference between the Current Street Value and the Cost of Acquisition. I also call the Current Street Value, Current Market Value or Current Asking Price by the artist.

Current Market Value = Current Street Value
= Current Asking Price

Potential Revenue =
Current Market Value - Cost of Acquisition

3: Let's Crunch Big Numbers First The Yet Unusual Big Challenge 27

Art is unregulated

If you look at the schedule of prices, you will notice they are increasing by a factor of 2 from the recent. They keep doubling. If you're an artist with lower starting prices, you have the option to increase your prices by more than 2.

This is because art is unregulated. You cannot do this with real estate nor stocks.

You cannot sell real estate for a million dollars if the current general value in the area is only $200,000. You cannot sell a stock for $1 million dollars if the current value is $50. Those people who overprice stocks and real estate can get into trouble.

You can do this with art. If you bought an art piece for $1 and sold it sometime later for $1,000,000, you will get praised. If you bought art for $1 and sold it on the same day for $1,000,000, you will get phenomenal praise.

You can even sell your art piece for $10 million dollars even if the current asking price by the artist is $2 million dollars. Each art piece is unique. You might be holding something that someone else just has to have.

Maybe there is a long waiting list, and someone wants something in time for a birthday. Maybe you have something in a very unique color.

How the high prices might be reached soon

For every artist, for the first art piece to become valuated like the last art piece, all art pieces must have a degree of similarity with each other, such as the time spent on each art piece, the range of sizes, the cost range for gemstones and precious metal used, etc.

If the current price of the artist is $12,800,000, and a collector pays an investor $25,000,000, all the other investors can use $25,000,000 in their financial statements as the current market value.

There was an artist who secretly bought back his own art at an auction. I read this one online. That was a sneaky, legal move.

The snowball effect might happen

If a huge company orders or commissions 300 works from one artist, other investors would follow suit. The company just assisted in making the price of the artist go to the next level or levels.

It will be safe to say that the large company intends to profit from the deal. The artist and the company have something up their sleeves. They have the means to promote that artist, and make that artist famous. Fame cannot be reversed.

Some people might see this as the "bandwagon effect" or "herd behavior," but remember the limit of 3,000. If you understood the Madoff discussion, only 2,700 really needs to be sold and circulate.

"Connect ten"

Once you make a purchase, let ten contacts know.

If everyone keeps doing this, the demand for the artist might snowball.

Anyone can go on Twitter, for example, and make the announcement. The frequency of announcement for an artist can induce others to invest in the same artist sooner.

If you're maintaining a newsletter, encourage your recipients to invest in the same artists you have.

Email: A way to entertain a cue for reservations

Anyone can use email as the cue for reservations and whatever else. All you need to reserve with an artist is email.

"Wait and See Program"

What if everyone reserves and only pays the artist when the quantity for that price point has been reserved?

I would not mind doing that for myself. So only as soon as 300 art pieces at the same price point get reserved will everyone get charged.

Venues will matter less

Where you bought the art piece will matter less with the #valzubiriagenda. Each art piece will have a life of its own and a unique provenance. Each art piece will get included with other art pieces in a unique set of books and lineage of investors and art collectors. Book collaborations that will include many artists will also add to the prestige of each work.

The books may mix the famous ones with the more obscure ones. The expensive ones may mix with the cheapest ones.

The prestige of a gallery may help the art piece become collectible at the beginning, but in the long run, it would matter less. Cafés and other venues may start with lower-priced art, and the artist will still end up expensive.

If I priced my art at $100,000 to start, I would not mind being represented by cafés, gift shops and laundromats. We're all the same, after all, here to make money for our families. All of our businesses opened because we all had, and still do have, brilliant ideas.

I will just require my sellers and resellers to have my memoirs and this book available to their own contacts. My art takes time, so my art books will also take time. I will be happy to participate in group collaborations with people who have book projects. I would not mind being published with the poorest artist.

I can't be a snob. I'm hoping to set an example for everyone else. I came up with this idea.

The best way to show the spread of an artist is online. For now, while no app or software is available yet, each artist can maintain a list that has each art piece produced or promised accounted for. Underneath each piece can be a growing list of publications and provenance, or owners. Some entries can link to other sites. All the books can link to where they can be bought.

Nothing can really cheapen art

Airlines, for example, already have catalogs with items for sale. They can add a page or two to sell art pieces at any price. It does not cheapen the art pieces, because everyone is doing the same thing—maximizing publicity.

Artist's charts that show the schedule of prices and quantity can even be included.

As we all know, department stores have started to close because they cannot sell enough smaller-priced items.

We have all seen some stores and lobbies displaying high-priced art in high-traffic areas. It would not hurt for them to place price tags and price schedule charts next to the art.

When I was young, I had an uncle who let me use his condo for about two years. I went to the nearby mom and pop furniture store to see what they had. They showed me catalogs where I can also choose whatever I wanted that was not in their store. I got furniture from their catalogs and I can still, right now continue to feel the excitement of my purchase.

Just imagine this. Art can have the prices of cars, without the needed car showroom space.

Once again, the internet and our books will show the spread and collectability of the artists.

You can form groups and focus on the same artists

Just like when a single financial institution is able to afford a large quantity of art pieces from the same artist, a group of art collectors and investors can do the same.

A collective group can purchase larger quantities from the same artists and advertise what they did on national papers, so other investors can join your group or purchase the same artists.

The artists themselves with a higher price range can form their own groups or collaborate with their collectors and investors and afford to collectively promote themselves.

A full-page newspaper advertisement for a national daily in the United States may cost $50,000-75,000. If the goal is to get the artists to reach 7 figures, then this advertisement could be minimal.

Here is an idea that came from the galleries

We can all go online and maintain a list of our own art pieces. The best an artist can do is help maintain the list of all the works he or she has, and maintain a growing list of ownerships and publications produced per art piece.

This idea came from the galleries. We have all been to art shows where the folder with the price list also includes a list of famous people and corporations who already have works by the artist. The galleries who do this obviously want their visitors and collectors to know who else already owns works, but they stop at that single page. The list also hints at the prestige of the gallery.

The three regions of sales

I think that every artist's exponentially increasing bar graph, like the one on this book's cover, in the long run, will have the following:

1. An early bird region
2. An acceleration region, and
3. A plateau region, where sales slow down

The artist can decide on the top price

If an artist's demand slows down, and the price plateaus, the artist can still raise the price to much more than double and stick to that price.

An artist who has been successful charging 7 figures would be comfortable enough to raise the price many times the last price and stick to that price, helping all the earlier investors to claim that as the current artist's price, or current street value.

The artist is the gatekeeper

Here is another workaround. For the 3,000 pieces, let's assume that the artist stuck to the price schedule. The last piece sold for $25,600,000 will be the 2,700th piece. As promised, the asking price for the 2,701st piece will be $51,200,000. This will become the street value, even though none has been sold yet.

If someone finally pays $51,200,000 for the 2,701st piece, then that's really just another good claim.

The artist really does not need to sell anything anymore. It's just that the artist gives himself that highest price point for the benefit of the investors and collectors.

The artists are the gatekeepers. I don't think the earlier sellers, buyers, investors and art collectors will like the artists lowering their prices just to make an additional sale.

The artist also announces right from the start, the maximum quantity of art pieces, then the artist retires. I personally would not make more. Probably less. This will be up to all artists to decide.

The artist commission for upcoming art is a contract. If it includes the condition of producing no more than a certain quantity of art pieces and sticking to prices, then the artist will have to stick to that agreement or risk lawsuits.

Art book copyrights

Throughout this book I'm only suggesting that artists allow their art to be included in art books.

Everyone makes their own specific rules.

What is also important is that the artists know where their images will appear, so that they can tell their groups, investors and collectors where to get more and more books to add to their book collections.

I cannot suggest to yet unknown artists to give up all the rights they have for their art. I think all this is a matter of individual agreements.

You might realize that the art is almost inconsequential

Investors might start going for artists with the most profit potential. I've been thinking about this for years—the art is almost negligible.

I would not mind allowing my investors and collectors to trade the art commission and being okay for people to earn commissions, because I fully believe I can deliver.

We artists can still be mysterious in our art, ourselves and our books, but we are taking the mystery out of quantity and pricing to help businesses and individuals make money from art.

It is the artist's responsibility to make art and deliver. I'm not even saying that it is our responsibility to make good art, you can make bad art, this is relative. The two most important conditions are that you:

1. Follow your contracts, and
2. Deliver your art

This is how we match the needs of investors to our needs. We as artists are responsible for our art as much as investors and art collectors are responsible for their business transactions..

I propose complicated art because I want my resellers, investors and art collectors to succeed in reselling my works.

I also propose to use gemstones and precious metals, because I want my resellers to justify the prices even if I did not become famous.

In the next few chapters, I want to tell you how all this evolved and then introduce the #valzubiriagenda to the lower priced sellers and artists. In 1998, I wanted all this to only be for myself, so I feel you should now know how the idea started.

Chapter 4

How All This Started
Years of Evolution
So You can Use This Now!

Self-publishing trended in 2006. I started attending publishers and booksellers conventions in 1996.

Since 1996, I saw what looked like long copy machines sold by different companies. Each time an operator pressed a few times on the LED pad on one end, out came one book, sometimes more, on the other end. The book produced had a 4-color cover, a glued spine and trimmed edges—exactly what a book should be.

There is one major convention for publishers and booksellers in North America. It is now called BookExpo America or BEA. When I started attending, it was called the ABA, or the American Booksellers Association Convention and Trade Show.

In 2006, the convention's daily supplemental newspaper reported that Lulu, or Lulu.com, the online self-publishing company, reported $10 million dollars in sales, up from $1 million dollars the previous year. Print on demand for self-publishers had finally trended.

Print on demand publishing is when the printer prints one copy of a book as one gets ordered. The companies were, in the past, proposing that the machines be in the back rooms of bookstores.

As I said, I started attending the convention in 1996. I saw trends every year, which I felt was useful to someone like me, who wanted to become an author. I will talk more about the trends later.

By 1998, I became a masseur to see if I can write a memoir related to being a masseur, with an artist's perspective.

I had visions of being on the bestseller lists with an artist's memoir, while a high-end New York gallery sells my expensive paintings. This was my exclusive, secret idea. I started getting into doll art later in 2009.

I finally wrote in 2005, finishing in 2006 just in time for attending the 2006 BookExpo. I went to that year's convention, only to find out that anyone can now get self-published. Any artist can write a memoir, just like me!

I decided to look into promoting this idea for everyone.

When I returned home from the convention, I designed my first book cover and interior—2 separate pdf files. I then uploaded my book files on Lulu.com to get a few copies, then I took it out. A few days later, my books arrived.

I saw my name on the cover of a book! It was very encouraging! The book still needed editing, but to flip through a thick book, that I had written, was an ego booster when I needed it. Just don't read the contents. I had yet to edit the book!

It made me feel accomplished. It gave me a higher level of confidence.

In 2007, with the confidence that I can write, I started hanging out at the galleries. I got to know the business and politics of art.

Just because an artist made art, does not mean they get recognized.

I started to figure out how an artist can get known, even without the galleries.

It was in 2007 when I learned that a well-known science fiction author was also a graduate of a local art school. Her fame as an author did not equate to getting known as an artist.

The best her exclusive Chicago gallery can do was talk about her whenever someone walked in their door.

I realized that the galleries are not the gatekeepers of the art business. Everything is about perception. The imaginary line can be moved. All of us can do better.

The gallery the artist was in had since closed. Even after decades of being open, the gallery owners retired.

4: How All This Started Years of Evolution So You can Use This Now!

Publishing memoirs and art books by the artists, investors and art collectors themselves *can* move the imaginary line from the front of our faces to behind our backs.

I'm sticking to my belief, that our books will continue to be here, 300 to 3,000 years from now. This is better than gallery owners who still had to retire.

Now, imagine being an owner of a café. You allow art to be posted on your café's walls. If you produced collaborative books yourself with profiles of the artists that you have, and also carried the books produced by your individual artists, you would have surpassed pretty much all the art galleries who have not produced a single book.

Imagine if the artists you have in your café are also sold elsewhere, and everyone else has their own books. Then you would all have surpassed the active promotion a single gallery would have of their exclusive artists.

All you need to do is to keep the art books of the artists you represent on a shelf and display a sign by the window that says "#valzubiriagenda."

In time, we might set a trend. All this is an easy trend to do, because everyone gets involved. As you can see, just like me, realize that it's not about getting into a gallery. The 1,000 you got rejected by galleries could be the 1,000 times you got accepted by other locations who could use the money you can potentially produce for them. Just set the terms so no one gets defrauded.

Let me introduce you to just a tiny bit of super basic technical knowledge to make you more confident in moving ahead with the rest of us.

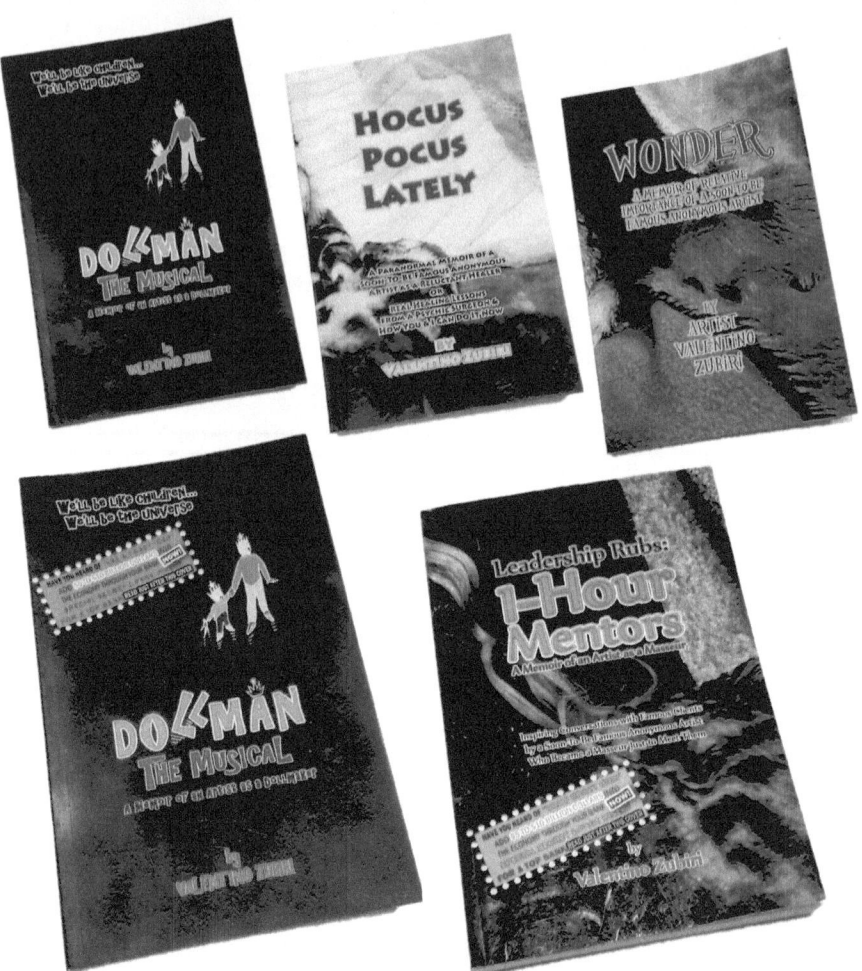

Refer to page 45, the discussion on "Triangulation"

My current 4 memoirs, **Dollman the Musical, Hocus Pocus Lately, Wonder,** and **1-Hour Mentors.**

I made 2 print and 2 e-book versions of each of my 4 memoirs, so you will see 8 books & 8 Kindle versions on Amazon.

The 4 books became 16 versions because I added a "Bankers' Secret Insert" to the 4 book and 4 e-book regular versions. The regular versions have a lower price; the bankers' versions have a higher price.

The secret insert explains the main ideas of the #valzubiriagenda. The bankers' versions have an added sign on the cover and title pages.

Next image is on page 70

Chapter 5

Really Stupid, Really Easy Technical Knowledge Just So You Know

This early chapter will encourage you to keep at this. I will extrapolate on this later, so for now, here are a few technical tidbits related to publishing.

Let's begin with a non-technical tip

You might notice that your country does not have access to an online print on demand company for self-publishers—keep on reading like all the rest of us.

Only do this after you have produced your book files. Get in touch with a relative who lives in another country where self-publishing is possible with Amazon.com, CreateSpace, Barnes & Noble, Lulu.com or another outfit. Ask your relative to help you. CreateSpace is Amazon.com's self-publishing arm.

The online company might need a bank account and a mailing address, so that income from book sales will get deposited directly to your relative's bank or get mailed. Ask for help from someone you can trust.

Come up with a username and password, so you can upload your book files from your country.

Only ask for help after you have written and designed your book. If you ask your relative for assistance before you even write a book, you are asking for trouble. You're giving your relative enough time to think of an excuse not to get involved.

Prove that you have put in a lot of time, real talent and effort. Produce your pdf files first. More information about pdf files later.

An accepted publishing practice

Other writers can write your book! Ghostwriters are writers who will agree to not being named as collaborators. Co-authors are those who get recognized together with you.

Our new practice for #valzubiriagenda

You can actually simultaneously ask several writers to write several separate books about you! Simply dictate to them various "eras" of your life. In just a few months, you can have several books about yourself.

I claim to be the living, contemporary artist with the most memoirs, and I don't really bother confirming that, because anyone can one up me on this.

Of course, I can still claim to be the living contemporary artist who *has* written the most memoirs, written from an artist's perspective, to date. I still would not bother to prove this.

The biggest misconception people have

People think that just because e-books are cheaper than printed books, they are easier to produce!

E-books are more difficult to produce!

This is because different private brands of e-readers use different proprietary formats of e-books to be opened and read. E-books need different file formats for different e-readers.

Only two pdf files are needed for printed books. One is for the cover and the other one is for the interior.

The file for the printed cover should be a single page or spread that includes the back cover, the spine and the front cover. The spine is the middle of the book. Its width depends on the number of interior pages.

Colored images only need to be 300 dots per inch

Unlike HD television screens and the new digital cameras, the general size and required resolution of books hasn't changed. The colored images for printed books only need to be 300 dpi, or 300 dots per inch.

You can use your digital cameras at the highest resolution. Use those images to produce the books. The software for producing the pdfs will be the one to take charge of shrinking the images to acceptable book size.

Self-publishing is now cheap

You can now see your books listed on Amazon.com, Barnes & Noble (online and in the databases of their stores), Lulu.com and elsewhere for $0 zero cost, if you know what to do.

Choose the company that will only make money when someone orders your book. Avoid the other companies for now.

This is called "print on demand." One single copy of your book gets printed when one single book is ordered.

Self-publishing vs. vanity presses

The vanity presses still exist, but they require money. They might also require additional fees at different steps in book production and distribution.

Look for talented individuals in the #valzubiriagenda community first to collaborate with you on your books. Barter with them.

Prefer to meet local talent. As you work together, learn from each other.

Here's the minimum number of words for a book

An acceptable enough book can have about 55,000 words. It can be less if you add pictures—maintain the thickness of the book.

If you want to know now, how thick 55,000 words is, for this book, including the Introduction, feel this book up to page 174. Page 193 also explains that I used 11.3 points (the font size).

Selling price varies for color and black and white books

If you decide to include pictures in your memoir or biography, you can use black and white pictures to maintain a lower price compared to a colored book. Produce a more expensive colored book for your art book.

The two most important lessons from a publisher

The two most important lessons I learned from my former boss, a publisher of her own monthly paper:

1. The book is not a term paper, and
2. Producing the book is like giving birth

This means that the book does not have to be perfect. No teacher nor professor will grade your efforts. You do have to watch out for the public because they can still rate your book.

People also tend to stop themselves from writing because they think they are supposed to come up with the "Greatest American Novel" right from the first attempt at writing. Just write!

The second is probably more important than the first. It means you will experience a high, but you also will experience some sort of post-partum depression.

Producing a book is a project-oriented activity. Once you see the final product, a published book, you will feel a great sense of accomplishment. Because it's over, you can also get depressed.

You need to become aware that even the most famous and accomplished bestselling authors get depressed. This is why publishers and literary agents tell stories about being counselors, friends, shoulders to cry on, psychiatrists and psychologists to their writers.

As self-publishers, we need to learn how to cope with bad feelings. We may have less support from others. The good thing is that we don't experience rejection letters and emails.

Because this book encourages non-writers to write and publish, I will provide you with stories so you will know what to expect and have better and healthier ways of coping emotionally and mentally.

Chapter 6
Why Books

Your art vs. someone else's

Imagine an art collector or an investor, facing two artists: yourself as an artist and a second one. The investor or art collector can only purchase one art piece.

You have a book about yourself and the art you are selling is in another art book. The other artist does not have any book at all. Who do you think has a better chance at getting purchased?

Imagine yourself with a book about yourself and the other artist still has no book but is being represented by a top gallery. Who do you think has a better chance at getting purchased?

It should still be you, but you have to tell the investors and art collectors where you are.

You can do this online, directing them to two places: your web presence with your contact email, and your physical location, where the art can be found. Even with all the sales pitch from the gallery, it would still seem that the investors and art collectors have a better investment with you in the long run.

I always say that books last 300 to 3,000 years. You cannot beat that.

Self-publishing and POD or print on demand

As I explained earlier, self-publishing and print on demand trended more than 10 years ago. I kept my idea a secret to be able to say that if I can do this—become an artist and a writer and publish books, so can you.

Traditional fiction and nonfiction authors have taken it upon themselves to self-publish and not wait for literary agents and traditional publishers. We're now doing the same thing.

Triangulation

There is this business concept called *triangulation*.

Imagine two points. If you connect the two points, you only produce a straight line.

Imagine three points. If you connect the three points, you produce a triangle.

Triangles, in the mind, feel more stable than lines.

The path between the artist and the investor or collector, even with a gallery, feels like a straight line. If there are books written by or about the artist, the added element of published books makes up the more stable triangle.

Books vs. postcards

I have hung out in the galleries, and they even now have been very generous giving away postcards of upcoming shows.

The thing is, after having worked for a local monthly free paper that uses a printing press, seeing even high-end galleries use inkjet and laser printers which everybody can now use, to announce art shows with expensive art, doesn't feel right.

Imagine having your own memoir and art book, or even just one of these, and comparing them with a stack of postcards, brochures and a curriculum vitae. Which one do you think has a better chance at promoting yourself?

The old art collector might be used to postcards, brochures and a CV, but don't you think the new investors and art collectors just might prefer your books?

Now, imagine having a stack of your books, postcards, brochures and business cards, all next to your art piece. Then imagine a place 300 years from now where your art piece still survives. Which printed material stays intact with the art?

I always say books last 300 to 3,000 years. These are better than anything else. Spend time producing your books, or spend years convincing people that postcards work just as well.

6: Why Books

Being online only maintains our availability for the moment. Anyone can be online. Not everyone has an excuse to have a book—we do.

Self-publishing

Because self-publishing is now available to everyone, anyone can now write memoirs and biographies and produce art books. Investors and art collectors can do it. Even cafés and offices can do it.

The images of the art can repeat in multiple books, if investors and art collectors also produce their own books. In case the heirs of an artist decide to discontinue the artist's books 300 years from now, the images are still assured to be in another book if the investors and art collectors continue to publish them in more and more future books.

I compare this to multiple triangulations which keep increasing like the facets of a dynamic, growing crystal.

This will also hopefully discourage fakes of your work in the future, including 300 to 3,000 years from now.

Right now, we are using the word "self-publishing" to describe what we are doing. Later on, you might realize that us as publishers just might surpass traditional publishers.

The bestselling sci-fi author and visual artist

I already mentioned this sci-fi author. One of the galleries I used to frequent represented her as a visual artist. I saw her art. The gallery also showed off a few boxes of her science fiction book.

A famous Hollywood movie company was in production, making the movie version of her book when I walked in the gallery that represented her with a gallery tour group. Unfortunately, the gallery owners themselves said she was still not established as a visual artist despite being an author and getting the movie made.

The gallery owners had retired. Their gallery is now closed. The artist/author is still not known as a visual artist.

This is why I'm telling everyone to get into the #valzubiriagenda by first writing memoirs, biographies, artistic essays, artistic manifestos, and whatever else that would be related to the visual art we are selling. We're putting the same hours to writing our books, let's write something that introduces both ourselves and our art. Write a novel later.

I believe that getting our artistic essay or article included in a collaborative book of artistic essays will advance us more than writing a full-length unrelated novel.

The author/public speaker/television interviewer

In my book, **1-Hour Mentors,** I mentioned meeting a man who was the following:

1. An author of bestselling business and leadership books
2. A public speaker who commanded more than $80,000 to speak before an audience for a few minutes to three hours, who flew all over the world for speaking engagements
3. A news channel reporter, interviewer and profiler of business leaders

You might think that he did many things, but everything he did was his successful version of triangulation.

By being a news channel reporter and profiler of business leaders, he gets to meet the business leaders. He gets the chance to get to know them better for possible future mentions in his upcoming books.

These CEOs and other business leaders also tend to invite him to speak at their conventions. After he speaks, he sits by a table with his books, so that the attendees have the chance to have him autograph and dedicate his books to them. This is part of the celebrity experience which reinforces the lessons from the business talk.

His books are sold in bookstores. The books are like permanent business cards. When I was with him, he told me he had a contract with his publisher to deliver a new book every 2 years, for 5 books total. I believe he received an advance of $10 million dollars.

Here is a good example of triangulating oneself. I'm encouraging you to write and publish your art-related memoirs, biographies, essays, manifestos and your own art books because I've seen triangulation done by people like this man.

If only we meet people like this person regularly. What I share with you are my own real encounters. These are not rehashed ideas from other books. I have read about these things, and the events in my life confirmed them to be real.

The triangulation continues with the CEOs he befriends and features on TV. If you're a CEO, and he interviewed you as a great business leader on a news channel, that prestige can be reinforced further. You can invite this person as a speaker in your next convention. Your image as a leader gets reinforced.

My triangulation
(Note: You can see my memoirs on page 36)

My own attempt at triangulation includes not just writing and publishing memoirs per se. Each of my memoirs has a different topic.

Hocus Pocus Lately is about the paranormal and psychic healing. I was interviewed about it in October 2015 by Richard Syrett on his radio show, **The Conspiracy Show with Richard Syrett.** His show is based in Canada, but syndicated internationally. Look for my interview on YouTube. Search for "Richard Syrett Hocus Pocus October 2015." It's my first interview in a long time, so I'm sure it could have been better, but I'm still proud of it. I wish we had more time.

I feel I successfully added a paranormal angle to myself as an artist and memoirist.

I also wrote **Dollman the Musical, A Memoir of an Artist as a Dollmaker.** My initial idea was to sell doll art, while the show gets staged. The show obviously has not happened yet. This is triangulation with another envisioned future triangulation.

I have had years of theatre experience, so I wrote a musical for the stage. This is not my only musical. I have written another one.

A famous film company that specialized in animation in Hollywood noticed **Dollman the Musical** and wanted to see if an animated movie can be made, but my book's underlying topic is adult-oriented. I wrote it for the stage, after all.

I *was* given priority when the woman from the animation company called me at exactly 9 a.m. Hollywood/California time on a Monday. I was first on her list and that's a good sign.

Wonder is about my childhood which includes more tips on being creative, including what I call "creative procrastination"—I used to delay my goals by getting into something related but time-consuming.

I mentioned bartending and having been a waiter in this book. I have plans to write a related memoir in the future, which is a further triangulation.

1-Hour Mentors is about my time as a masseur, when I met celebrities, actors, singers, authors, business leaders and many others who gave me life-changing lessons on keeping my artistic ambitions alive.

I met well-known people as a masseur. I'm sure that will pay off further in the future. I also mentioned something about scents and a few other topics that I can further triangulate on in the future.

Here now is my fifth book, **Valzubiriagenda,** and you're holding it, which also has lessons to learn, based on my stories. The triangulation continues.

Chapter 7

Scarcity & Pricing
The Next Pair

Scarcity and pricing

I started hanging out at the galleries in 2007. I saw this happen twice on separate occasions as I had mentioned in the Introduction. They were memorable because they happened twice.

Let me just recreate the scenes here.

Both days were Saturdays, after lunchtime. On both occasions, a group of men walked in. They were not the same group of men, but both groups were dressed in suits and ties, as if they just had their corporate meetings. Chicago *has* world-class corporations.

They were gregarious and probably had something to drink during their lunch. They were confident to a high degree, like they were a new corporation with new money and things were looking up.

They asked the same question:

"Do you have art that we can invest in, that you can guarantee will go up in value?"

The two different gallery owners, on each of those two instances, told them the same thing:

"We cannot guarantee our art as investments, you must only purchase what you like."

The men immediately left and did not bother to look around. They obviously felt like they would be wasting their time by staying longer. They exhibited the same groupthink and behavior.

If one of them even paused to look at an art piece, just to be polite, the rest in the group would have frowned on him.

Both galleries had art that were priced between $8,000 to $15,000.

I analyzed the answers of these two galleries. They were right and honest to answer the visitors that way. They smiled at the visitors and continued to smile as the visitors headed for the door.

The gallery owners both shrugged at me and said people like these come in once in a while.

The response by the gallery owners were not what the visitors wanted to hear.

Groups like these men are exactly the people we want to meet.

The gallery status quo

The galleries have their own status quo. These two galleries I was in had been open for decades. They planned to keep themselves open for years. They cannot tell people that prices will go up, because... what if the prices stayed the same?

The artist decides for himself

What if the gallery artists themselves decide to follow our ideas on scarcity and pricing and simply relay their decisions to the gallery owners?

It would become easy and honest for the gallery owners to convey this message to the groups of men on those Saturdays.

A great lesson from the comic book industry

If you live in the United States, you will have noticed the closure of bookstores. People have not been buying books at the bookstores.

Even if you are not into comic books, you know that there are more comic book stores than there are bookstores to begin with. You know that one or two comic book stores may have closed from out of 5 to 8 that you can remember. People still read and collect comic books.

If you know nothing about comic books, here is one bit of information. The comic book companies themselves admit to manipulating the demand for their products.

For example, they have proven to themselves that if they renumber their series back to #1, there will be a surge in sales.

7: Scarcity & Pricing The Next Pair

They also come up with cover variants of the same issue. Sometimes, an issue would have the normal cover and an additional four different foil or hologram covers.

Comic book collectors get prompted to buy. This behavior is predictable. It has sustained the publishers, the artists and their stores.

The publishers also discovered that after publishing separate comic book issues, they can republish the complete story arc as book-length graphic novels.

Read more about the comic book industry online. They even killed Superman at one time.

A suggestion if you cannot decide on pricing and scarcity

There are those artists who are not yet becoming comfortable with pricing themselves and becoming scarce.

Imagine a brain surgeon who is not sure how much to charge their patients. We artists have chosen art to be our careers. If anything, we should look into outsmarting brain surgeons.

Try this: write your first book. It takes time to write a book. As you dedicate your time writing your book, entertain pricing your art. You most probably *will* eventually come to a decision.

My confidence in presenting numbers keeps getting stronger as I publish more and more books through the years. I wrote my first draft in 2006. In 2008, I produced a book with nude drawings and paintings.

I remember it was around winter 2008 when I came up with the pricing and scarcity idea and then months later, Madoff was in the news. I once again took out my calculator, wondering if my idea could have helped him.

In 2012, I finished my first acceptable memoir.

In 2013, I simultaneously started writing four memoirs. By 2014, I came up with three full books and a fourth that had chapters and stories, but no closure.

Once in a while, I look at my idea of scarcity, prices, memoirs and art books. It keeps feeling more and more right and stable.

So if you're not comfortable with pricing and scarcity right now, look into producing your books first.

Then write the numbers you want to work with. Here are two exam-

(Note: You can see my 4 memoirs on page 36)

ples with escalating prices:

$10 ⇉ $20 ⇉ $40 ⇉ $80 ⇉ $160 ⇉ $320 ⇉ $640 ⇉ $1,280 ⇉ $2,560 ⇉ $5,120 ⇉ $10,240 ⇉ $20,480 ⇉ $40,960

$100,000 ⇉ $200,000 ⇉ $400,000 ⇉ $800,000 ⇉ $1,600,000 ⇉ $3,200,000 ⇉ $6,400,000 ⇉ $12,800,000 ⇉ $25,600,000 ⇉ $51,200,000

See if you have become more comfortable with them.

Back to the gallery with the investors

Imagine the gallery situation again. If the investors confidently come in and ask who might be worthy of investing into, the gallery might be able to match their confidence and say,

"We have one artist who is following the #valzubiriagenda. Here are some already published books, and the schedule of pricing and scarcity.

"All of this artist's works in the gallery will be included in an upcoming art book, and the artist will send you a couple of autographed copies of the book once it's published.

"Now, remember, we are just the gallery. The decision to get into the #valzubiriagenda was purely the artist's, so whatever happens in the future is not the gallery's responsibility.

"Would you like to see the art we have available?"

Chapter 8

Reselling to Friends & Colleagues

Looking at ourselves as kids again

If you ever got into trading cards either with sports, sci-fi and fantasy art or comic book characters, look at trading art this way.

Trading cards, for those who don't know, are those sealed packs of cards. There are several cards in each pack, but a full set of that pack's edition can consist of 90 to 120 cards, or even more. If you like the edition, you'll have to buy more sealed packs. When the cards start repeating, you trade with friends who are also trading the same cards and completing their sets.

Past the set of 90 cards would be the rarer special or "bonus" cards. We used to call them "chase" cards, because if you really got into this, you would chase after them from store to store. There are usually 5 to 8 chase cards. The set of 90 would be the usually full-color printed cards. The chase cards have a special finish, like 3-D hologram, chromium, prismatic or metallic. They stood out.

If you got into trading cards, remember how you used to actively trade cards with friends to complete your collections? Actually, a friend of mine and I did this in our twenties around after the death of Superman. Superman died in 1992, so my friend and I got into sci-fi and fantasy art trading cards in 1993! We also collected the art books by the artists whose cards we collected. You may have done this when you were younger, or older, like me and my friend.

My friend got so much into fantasy art trading cards, that he got to the point where he started buying unopened, factory-sealed, display boxes of the cards. He discovered that each box can complete four sets, with a few chase cards added in. The box must be bought factory-sealed.

Obviously, the factory had a way to shuffle the cards so that the card shops and comic book stores can give us customers the chance to complete a set from the same box in the same store.

I learned to "feel" for the rare cards in the sealed packs. They felt heavier or thicker than the packs with no chase cards. I went from store to store and felt for them. Some stores didn't allow people to feel for the cards, unfortunately. I avoided those stores. Part of the fun was feeling for them. I felt a rush in my system. Highly addictive.

While this was happening with me, I also went to a sport card shop which held auctions for their cards. They specialized in decades older sport cards. The cards would be in protective material and secured on their walls in a row so collectors can examine them. Each item had a pad where bidders placed their names and their higher bids. This was downtown, so the bidders were mostly the 9 to 5 people. The bidding usually ended on Fridays. I wasn't able to afford those cards.

This #valzubiriagenda comes from matching higher-end collecting from galleries with what I have learned from trading cards. This is why I'm encouraging artists to declare their quantities. This time we are entertaining original art.

The sets of 90 sci-fi and fantasy art trading cards had 90 art works. The first card was as artistic as the 90th and produced by one artist or a collaborative pair. There was enough to be traded with other collectors. Imagine if only twenty cards were circulating—what's the use?

There has to be enough art to generate enough followers and enough talk. 3,000 works, all comparably similar from #1 to #3,000 sounds enough for the moment. 2,000 sounds even better.

I'm only saying I want to produce 3,000 art pieces just to be on the safe side. I can opt to make less, not more.

Here is one way to get prices to the next level fast

If you are supporting an artist, get the quantity that will get the price to the next level.

Then you can begin reselling the art or the commission at the next price level.

You can also form a group of investors and art collectors to make

8: Reselling to Friends & Colleagues 53

this happen if you or your company cannot do this alone.

If you got a few from a certain artist, let your friends and colleagues know the artist you just bought. Let them know the next price point. They might follow suit.

The moment you spend money on an artist, will be the moment you will actively keep promoting the artist, so that demand and sales go up. Everyone else who bought the artist will be doing the same thing. The idea is to get the artist's price and demand to go up.

This is so much more active and different from just visiting a gallery, interacting with a few people, and getting the art passively situated in your home or office.

Instead of waiting for years for the perception of the artists in the traditional galleries to get better, the rise in prices will be faster and observable.

Follow the leader

If you can only afford one or two pieces from within a price range, invest in the same artist that a huge institution bought a lot from.

You can be sure that plenty more will take notice and collect.

You can safely assume that the large-scale investor will have a budget to promote the artist further. You're piggybacking on the potential, active promotional effort of the larger companies.

Entertain agents and commissions

Allow people to work for you on commission.

You can also work on commission.

You can also work to get a commission and an art piece. This will get you collecting art as well, and eventually, you can also have enough art pieces to publish in book form.

You can end up with art that will be substantially higher in value in the future than the 10-20% commission per art piece you might earn for the meantime.

Different price ranges for everyone's various budgets

Human beings tend to socialize within their economic range.

As I have said before, if you were an investor who was able to afford $50 US dollars for an art piece, then it might be safe to assume that you would have a circle of friends who can afford $100 for an art piece. You may not know someone who can afford $100,000 for an art piece at the moment.

If you were able to afford $10,000,000, then it might be safe to assume that you can resell to a contact, friend or colleague who can afford $20,000,000.

People and companies who can afford higher prices would also have a list of contacts who can afford to pay the next one or two higher prices.

Investment companies will have a database of clients who can afford higher prices.

We should all support everyone who will have different capacities.

Do not succumb to pressure to spend on art that is not within your budget.

Spend on art that you can afford and then proceed to nurture and expand your network.

Magic the Gathering for adults

There is a nearby gaming store which continues to be open from 6 p.m. to 10 or 11 p.m. every night, so kids of all ages sit down to play different card and board games.

What they are doing is obviously addictive and habit-forming.

The owners of gaming shops might have ideas on how to hold meetings so people can trade original art.

The separation between artists and collectors

Artists communicating only with artists isn't enough anymore.

Everyone has the notion that galleries deliberately separate artists from investors and collectors. I don't think that's the case. I've seen artists at their art openings give away their business cards to anyone who asks.

The issue is availability. Galleries are more available to the public because they have store hours, unlike their artists.

We're slightly varying our business approach. We need to become more predictable and more in contact with each other. Just being online can make a difference, coupled with the 24/7 availability of our books online, in bookstore databases and all the stores, offices and other venues that will be reselling for us.

This time, the best person per artist who can maintain contact with everyone else and who can promote further sales between investors and art collectors would be the artist himself or herself.

Looking at ourselves as traders

Traditionally, galleries see investors and art collectors as the ultimate consumers.

If everyone participating, including those who trade their book publishing talents for art, looks at himself or herself as a trader, then everyone becomes open to reselling their collections upward.

This is no longer about the artists and galleries profiting from everyone else. This is about the artists providing a way for everyone else to profit.

Taking over the work of the galleries

We are not really taking over the function of the galleries. We are doing more.

You as an investor or art collector will only be responsible in reselling what you have, just like everyone else. However, everyone who also owns or is reselling the artist's works helps in creating buzz around the artist.

Galleries also usually take 40%-60% of the retail price.

This time, you are taking ownership of works so you can make even more money.

What if you got an art piece for $100,000, and it now retails for $51,200,000. That's a 51,200% increase in your investment.

From janitor's closets to cafés to galleries

I always say that even janitor's closets can hold and sell art. The venue doesn't matter. There are even empty store fronts that can be used temporarily. What matters is getting seen online, knowing where the related books can be bought and the current physical locations of art by the artist.

Galleries can get involved anytime. Anyone can decide to open a gallery and collaborate with others in the community. Old galleries can join in anytime. The trend just has to happen.

Your area of business

You can open your own #valzubiriagenda gallery. People can leave their art and books with you. Come up with a good, profitable system.

I saw an eBay drop-off business operate for years before they closed. People dropped off their used items so they can resell on consignment.

I had the feeling they closed because the profit margin for used clothing was too small.

This time, if you open a #valzubiriagenda gallery, you can require art for yourself from artists, and a percentage of sales from artists and resellers. Come up with your own requirements.

You can also help match writers, book designers and other publishing professionals with people. You can maintain contacts and databases, a website and broadcast live once in a while.

You can be the go-to gallery who also knows which cafés, offices and other venues in the area carry the same artists that you have or just ran out of.

Enticing investors and collectors with books

In my mind, I was thinking that a simple declaration of this increasing pricing plan, matched with set quantities per price point, can be enough to be noticed by investors and art collectors. The declaration can be an artistic statement itself. The problem is, even scammers can do it and be noticed.

The declaration of pricing and quantity also might only work with people who have connections. It does not even out the playing field.

What continues to be fair and yet brings everyone to a higher level is the presence of the books. Whose art seems more collectible? A homeless person with cheap art who was able to produce books or an established, expensive artist with no books?

Getting the next investors and art collectors to produce books

Look into our own creativity in writing and publishing. Encourage your contacts to do the same thing.

Writing a book is a liberating experience.

8: Reselling to Friends & Colleagues

Publishing and seeing our names on book covers after all the time and energy invested is very rewarding.

We are not traditional publishers

I don't want to name names, but according to a traditional publishing company's CEO, in an online report:

1. Between 2010 and 2015, in a 2016 report, there has been a steady "explosion" of self-publishers in the United States alone
2. Combined with the introduction of new titles from the traditional publishers, the new titles can reach 1 million each year
3. An observation by the CEO was that despite the explosion of new titles, they consider total book sales as stagnant
4. Another observation of his is that a book now has far less than 1% chance of being stocked in an average bookstore

You may have noticed that there are some traditional publishers who have also finally given in. They have also offered self-publishing services online.

Here is where we begin to differ from traditional publishers

We publish books to sell art.

We care more about selling our art, because this is where the money is at. We will only make a few dollars from the books themselves.

Our books are about ourselves, so that our art investors and art collectors can know more about us. We can all display our books next to the art.

As publishers of our own books, we can get one or more copies at the printer's wholesale price. We might include our books with the sale of our original art. *Don't forget that we can get our books at wholesale prices.*

As investors and art collectors pass our art along to others, they can order our books as well and produce their own books to give to the next generation of investors and collectors.

The traditional publishers are complaining about getting themselves in traditional bookstores.

Meanwhile, we are promoting our art to be in as many venues as possible not only in our own cities and communities, but in other venues in the rest of the world, as our art spreads out.

This means that our books will end up displayed and available in other venues—cafés, beauty salons, gift shops, gaming shops, offices, galleries and janitor's closets. All outlets are fair game. We don't care if we don't end up in a bookstore shelf.

Traditional books need the traditional bookstores to make money. Let's say we know 4 bookstores in our area, so that's 4 outlets.

If our art ends up in 100 locations in our area, our books will also end up in 100 locations. Our books will end up being in more places within the same area, all of them on display on shelves.

Finally, guess what?

If we trend enough, the bookstores *will* give us shelf space anyway. They can even host events, just to get us and our contacts to the stores.

The bookstores can become the venue that does not discriminate. The $1 dollar artists, investors and collectors can meet the $50 million dollar artists, investors and collectors because everyone's books are there.

We are already doing the CEO's suggestions

We are actually naturally doing what the CEO is advocating, in response to their lull in publishing:

1. We are community building
2. We are building new channels for book sales, marketing and community building
3. We are producing books around a big new idea. We are immersed in our own events and experiences
4, Our books are "pass-along" books. Pass-along books are books that people buy for other people

What's a pass-along book? If your child is going to cooking school, and you don't cook, but you buy a cookbook for your child, then that book is a pass-along book.

When we sell art and give a copy of our published books to the next

8: Reselling to Friends & Colleagues

investor or art collector, the book becomes a pass-along book.

We can actually skew the publisher's data even more.

Just be reminded that we don't care about what the traditional publishers have been complaining about, because their ultimate goal is to sell and profit from books.

We're publishing as many books as we want, because we can. Our ultimate goal is to sell art for a lot more profit per piece than what our books will earn.

Have you ever read articles like this one?

Once in a while, we read about articles on art asking: Will there ever be an art bubble? This might be it.

If you're discussing this chapter with a friend, the topic of economic bubbles might come up. It's too soon to tell if a bubble will happen or when.

As you know, those who were first in any economic trend that became an economic bubble tend to be the ones who made the most profit. If you're reading this early, then you have an advantage.

On the other hand, unlike real estate where you had to go to the bank to gamble and profit, I'm encouraging you to only invest in art that you can afford.

If people start acquiring art but they have no contacts to resell to, then a bubble might happen. It would be better to get a $10 art piece and resell it for $100 even if the artist has plans to reach $1 million dollars. Let the next investor sell to the next contact.

Actually, an investor might get 10 pieces of $10 art for the same artist, resell 5 for $100 each, and wait for the next 5 to go up to $1 million dollars.

Everyone has the ability to publish their books either right now, tomorrow or even yesterday. I had gone through publishing for more than 20 years, just so you can shorten the time you can invest in this idea.

Let's just do what we can right now.

Not every artist will care about selling

We all might just set a self-publishing trend.

However, not everyone might proceed to the pricing and scarcity schedule.

Some might just keep writing memoirs, biographies, essays and manifestos without the need to produce art.

Some artists might like writing books and publishing books and art books without the need to make a single art sale.

I still have all of my works that I included in my first book of nudes, **Valentino Zubiri: Nude Drawings and Paintings from 1995 to 1996.** I don't want to sell them.

Us and the future

This is how I see this: We are aggressively taking space for our art, attention for our books, and money to spend for our art, from the future.

We package our accomplishments now, and we hand them back to the future. We are making art and books that people can keep trading even after we are gone.

A bubble that would not burst

A few factors would help here. If the sale of our art slows down, we can delay or stop production. Hopefully, by this point, we would have become financially stable.

If you're an artist and you believe you just cannot stop yourself from creating your art, let your potential investors and art collectors know. Some might not like your decision—at least you're not misleading anyone.

We're not stocks and bonds, where all of them need to keep circulating, nor are we construction companies which need to keep constructing houses and buildings.

There are art collectors who collect to keep, so some pieces will stop circulating.

We can also assume that some investors will acquire 10, for example, and keep 5 for themselves and their family, and only recirculate 5.

Everyone is encouraged to only purchase within their budgets. No one needs to borrow money. Unlike real estate, some art pieces will start at less than $10. This is affordable enough.

If everyone only bought what they can afford, and others work to earn commissions, then there might not be a bubble.

Chapter 9

We will All Become Marketers & Collaborators

Working with a small group

There is a book I had read, **The Starfish and the Spider: The Unstoppable Power of Leaderless Organizations** by Ori Brafman and Rod A. Beckstrom, that you might want to read.

There is another book I will match with this current discussion, **The 21 Irrefutable Laws of Leadership: Follow Them and People Will Follow You** by John C. Maxwell.

The Starfish and the Spider shows the difference between two organisms, starfishes and spiders, and compares that with the way we organize ourselves.

If you cut off one leg of the starfish, the original starfish will regrow the leg back. The separated leg will become another starfish. If you cut off the head of a spider, the entire spider dies.

The way we will be organizing ourselves will be like that of the starfish. We will form our own local, maybe national, or even international groups, as needed. If we cannot fit in whatever organization we join, then we should move on and form another group elsewhere. Sometimes, someone wants more control over your own future. Know when to move on.

I cannot be everyone's leader, I really just came up with the idea. I can probably help a good number, but not everyone.

In the future, there might be a few businesses who will come up with online programs and apps where everyone will be able to "trade" art.

For example, if I am proposing 3,000 works total, then I might have 3,000 entries and all the owners, present and previous can attach themselves to each art piece. There might be graphs and whatever else that can help others make a decision to purchase my work from myself and everyone else.

Get included in group books

Some of you might have a call for group publications, based on a common, agreeable theme.

Here are a few examples. You might call for:

1. 10-50 artists from the same city, state, province or country
2. Ceramicists only
3. American veteran artists
4. Cancer victim paintings only
5. LGBTQ artists
6. Drag queen artists
7. Homeless street artists
8. UFO abductees for their alien abductee art
9. YouTubers
10. Kids under 12 years old
11. Artists in prison
12. Artists in your city, state, province or country

The organizers may have published books in the past. Check out their credibility.

Some organizers might require barter, a payment for services rendered, no sharing of book sale profits, or combinations of these. Everyone decides freely, comes up with rules, and everyone else may or may not participate.

Investors and art collectors are also free to produce art books. You can organize groups and produce books that will serve your purposes and showcase artists that you already own.

Come up with a name and brand yourselves.

9: We will All Become Marketers & Collaborators 63

Book ideas you can come up with

You can come up with two collaborative art books from one.

One book can be a generally acceptable art book. The other edition can include charts for pricing and scarcity and a list of each participant's finished and upcoming book projects.

Who would be the leader?

The second book, **The 21 Irrefutable Laws of Leadership** coined the "Law of the Lid," which is the first of the 21 laws.

Mr. Maxwell basically says that an organization's limit is the leader of the organization. This is analogous to the lid of a container or a jar. Nothing gets past the container's lid.

I am proposing a leaderless organization for the whole #valzubiriagenda, just like a starfish. Leaders can emerge from the smaller groups.

The simplest way to form a cue: Email

We want to accommodate everyone fairly. Everyone can email everyone else. The timestamp orders the cue effortlessly.

You can use email for reserving art and have a first come, first served cue.

If you have a call for artists, like a call for 50 Brazilian artists, and 500 respond, then you can qualify artists based on the timestamp. You can also consider coming up with 10 books, ordering them based on the time the artists responded.

You can also have a call for 50 art investors and collectors for your city. If 500 respond, then you can also order them by the timestamp.

If you discover 200 artists, you can publish four art books, featuring 50 artists each. If only 20 responded, allocate your pages to the 20.

Use email while we still have nothing like an AmeriTrade nor E-Trade in place.

Find a way to let people know if the price ranges moved up, changed, etc.

Come up with a newsletter of sorts, to let everyone know of your progress and list the investors who want to resell your art.

Respect agents who will work for commissions

As an artist, I would welcome investors, art collectors and agents who can introduce me to even more investors and art collectors.

Agents are very important. They can get others to invest in 1 or 1,000 works. If there is someone who can convince someone else to purchase 50 to 300 works, they can be set for life from the commission, depending on the current prices of the artist.

Help others get ahead

I mentioned that my art takes time to make, and therefore, my art books will take time. That does not mean I cannot help others with their art books. I have gained experience by helping others.

So now I don't just say, take pictures of your own works. I say take pictures of your own works, making sure your head does not cast a shadow on the art you are photographing. I can also say that you can take a picture that is slightly tilted and correct the right angles and dimensions later using Photoshop. I will discuss this more later in the chapters about taking images. (Chapters 24 and 40)

I would not know how long it takes to write a book if I did not do it in the past. I had always been open to helping others. I can now get ideas of who I can collaborate with and who I should avoid.

Practice is key to getting better. Help others with their projects so that when you begin to work on your own books, you would know more and know what mistakes to watch out for.

Skill comes from practice. Don't bullshit with people who think they can cope and deliver when the time comes just because they know something is possible because they had seen it before.

Chapter 10

Use Hashtag #valzubiriagenda to Find Each Other

I'm also a programmer. I tell people I can do PHP and MySQL with my eyes closed. I'm kidding; I need my eyes open. I can do Login, Logout, Forgot password, Upload your image, Check your email to confirm your membership, and all that wonderful stuff.

I am also in full support of other companies taking over. Maybe some companies and individuals can come up with our version of E-Trade.

I had the idea that I would only make money from my own art, but in analyzing all this, just being an artist, writer, book designer and publisher is not enough.

My added challenge is that I'm pressed to become an example for everyone. I'm also worried about attracting everyone for everyone else.

For my immediate area, it would be good if I can open a warehouse and give workspace to other artists.

It would also be good to have computers set up so that writers, editors, photographers, desktop publishers, book designers and others can work on books. It would be good to have the best collection of software for everyone to use.

The computer users will also be able to help others remotely.

For now, we can all do the following...

Use hashtag #valzubiriagenda

I was trying to figure out a word to use as a hashtag. I came up with words, but worried that the words were too generic and might already be trademarked. I also had second thoughts about using my name, but I finally figured out that #valzubiriagenda would be the best way to promote this.

I'm almost sure that there will be people who might not use this in a good, supportive, honest way. I am hoping that we will police ourselves in the long run. Scammers did not stop Amazon and eBay from continuing to grow.

I once asked a guy who was a masseur listed in the yellow pages if he ever received threatening and crank phone calls. He told me, "Yes, but you have to believe that 99% of society is good, and they are the ones who will give you money, pay your rent and get you to contribute to society."

I'm not trademarking the hashtag, so use it as you see fit.

I compare myself to the Pied Piper, in a good way. I came and went. If I leave too soon, I left with you an idea that might get you in a better place. We should never go to hell for art. We go to hell for something else, but not for something as stupid as art.

Just know that as you join this idea, I am not legally responsible for your actions and the agreements you get yourself into. I am only responsible for my own art, my own delivery of my art, and the agreements I personally get into. For now, I have my memoirs and this book. I hope that I have enough credibility from my current books to convince others to invest in my art.

Google can find us fast

If you still don't have any form of web presence, you must know that the search engines, especially Google, have all evolved and have become much faster in finding new or updated web pages.

You don't have to trust me on this one, you can test it yourself. The way to find out is to begin having your own web presence.

If you're going to announce that you will use #valzubiriagenda for yourself, add something like this on Twitter, your web page or new blog entry:

10: Use Hashtag #valzubiriagenda to Find Each Other

"Your full name, your nickname, #valzubiriagenda, Boston, Massachusetts, USA, investor, art collector, artist, $50 to $150,000, Carol's Café, memoir, art book, oil paintings, veteran" and whatever other keywords you want.

Give Google a few hours and see if your page shows up when you type in some of the words you put on your page.

Twitter can make this available immediately.

Get a blog

Search engines like Google (and the others) seem to have become very fast cataloguing blog entries. I cannot endorse a single blog site here. Whatever I name here might become overshadowed in the future.

I can actually tell you what I use, but I have seen more sophisticated blogs. I use Blogspot, which Google owns. I know there are others out there with much more features.

My "hunch" about Blogspot, is that Google just might have some preference for searching it sooner, because they own it.

Get to know the icons on other people's blogs

Check out some of the blogs out there. You will notice little squarish icons that link to other sites. We have all become familiar with the square icons for Facebook and Twitter. There are others, like Pinterest, Reddit and Instagram.

By joining #valzubiriagenda, you have become your own marketer of your own products. Look into getting a web presence and increasing your presence with as many online tools as you can handle.

Here is something relatively easy which the internet-savvy do

If you took a picture, the name that your camera or smartphone assigned to your file is generic and tells nothing about you and the image.

It can be something like:

13507038_102099848126_4362801965753265629_n.jpg

If you upload this file, Google Images and the other search engines that find image files might not find you. The search engines will only depend on the text that you put on the same page.

If you go to the Google Image search, and you type my name, a lot of images I uploaded will show up. This is no accident. I have been making my own websites and blogs, revising them as needed. I also know that I should always rename my images in order to be found.

Here is how I tend to name my images, so that my keywords will show up:

From:

13507038_102099848126_4362801965753265629_n.jpg

to:

valentino_val_zubiri_porcelain_dolls_collectible_chicago_illinois_new_york_city_galleries_gallery_dollman_the_musical.jpg

I also jumble up my keywords. I don't just copy and paste the same order of words. Google might already have a script discouraging the same sequence of words, so I will rename the other files as follows:

red_dress_zubiri_valentino_valzubiriagenda_collectible_art_galleries_london_chicago_new_york_newyork_manhattan_hocus_pocus_lately.jpg

blue_dress_collectible_porcelain_bisque_valentinozubiri_valzubiri_galleries_collectible_memoirs.jpg

purple_costume_wonder_dollmanthemusical_dollman_the_musical_artist_art_collectible_gallery_val_valentino_zubiri_agenda.jpg

If you don't want to be confused, you can order your images as follows:

0001_red_dress_zubiri_valentino_valzubiriagenda_collectible_art_galleries_london_chicago_new_york_newyork_manhattan_hocus_pocus_lately.jpg

0002_blue_dress_collectible_porcelain_bisque_valentinozubiri_valzubiri_galleries_collectible_memoirs.jpg

0003_purple_costume_wonder_dollmanthemusical_dollman_the_musical_artist_art_collectible_gallery_val_valentino_zubiri_agenda.jpg

10: Use Hashtag #valzubiriagenda to Find Each Other

Vary the naming so that not all of your keywords appear in all of them. Use either or both your long name and your nickname.

I'm not sure what Google discourages and encourages. I have, however succeeded in having my doll art, paintings, theatre poster work and book covers show up when my full name or nickname is searched.

When you rename your files, limit them to 150 characters. Some computers might have a conflict with lengthier file names.

Get a blog and join the popular blog links

Go online and look at how other people promote themselves. Some of them have blogs, Facebook pages, Twitter, Instagram, YouTube and Vimeo videos, and Pinterest. There are many ways to promote ourselves.

If you decide to get a blog, check out other people's blogs. You will notice that they do not stop at just posting on their blogs.

You will notice icons for sharing pages. The more well-known icons at this time of writing are the square Facebook, Instagram, Twitter, Reddit and Pinterest. Learn how they are used. You're going to have to register with these others as well.

I cannot give you an exact list. Use whatever is popular and available in your country.

When you make an announcement on Twitter, for example, include the hashtag #valzubiriagenda. Include your location and whatever keywords you feel you should include.

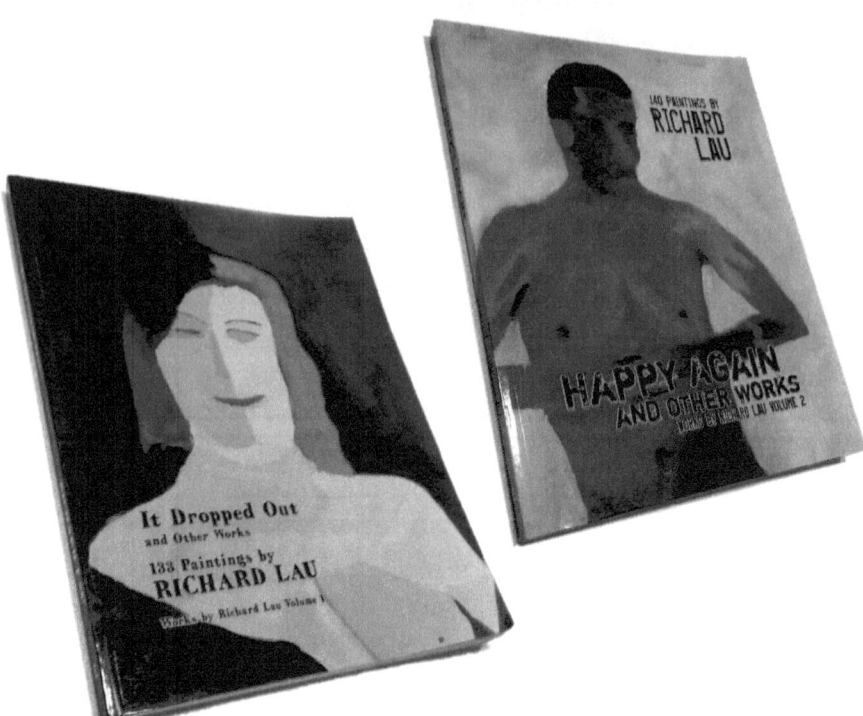

**From Chapter 41
pages 256-259**

Artist Richard Lau's 3 books: **Richard Lau Paintings: 273 Works by the Artist, It Dropped Out** (Volume 1 with 133 works), and **Happy Again** (Volume 2 with 140 works).

I decided to reshuffle and split the big book into Volumes 1 & 2, which have a lower price. Three books resulted from 1 set of files!

While you still have the image files for your art book in your computer, you can come up with different books!

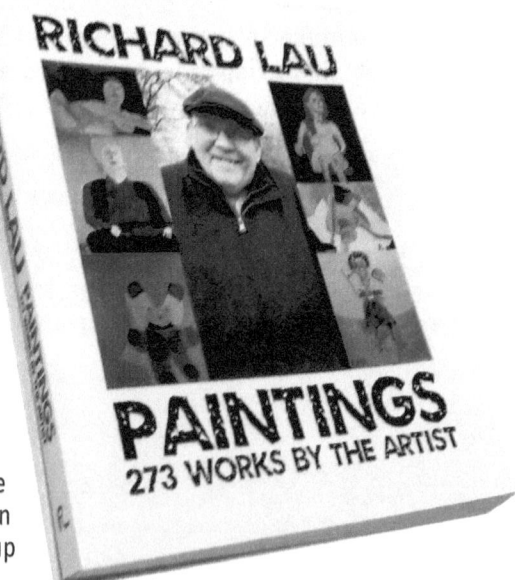

Next image is on page 80

Chapter 11

Ideas for Banks & All the Other Financial Companies

Are you too busy to read this book?
That's okay. I priced the book to be affordable to everyone. $13.95 US dollars. Buy a few and give it to your subordinates. Ask them to read this book, and meet at an opportune time. I've suggested this earlier, I'm just reminding you.

Sometimes, the lowest employee would have the most input.

A bank near me closed
There was a nearby, relatively small bank that had to close about three years ago. They supposedly defaulted on less then $200 million dollars.

I think the brothers who owned the bank just wanted their troubles to be over with. They settled with the FDIC for under $10 million dollars.

I did try to get in touch with them, but anyone planning to close a bank soon would be avoiding people. I was the least of their problems.

If an artist succeeds using the #valzubiriagenda and reaches the top price of $50 million dollars, $200 million dollars is the equivalent of 4 art pieces.

My suggestion is find an artist at $100,000 and get 4 or more art pieces. Wait for the price to increase. If you can, invest more, promote and accelerate the rate of demand.

Had they invested in an artist using #valzubiriagenda, they probably could have raised the money they needed. They already had their list of clients to start with. They wasted their contacts. New buzz would be needed for people to entertain them now.

Take charge of your #valzubiriagenda community

I suggest that you look for your own still-unknown artists.

Use your available meeting spaces. Call for artists and everyone else who can get involved, especially the book production people.

Look for people who will care enough about your company to make this succeed for you. This might be more important than talent.

The smaller investors will piggyback on your budget

Make sure not to monopolize your artists. The only way you can generate buzz for your artists is if others have also invested in your artists.

Advertise whom you have invested in, so they can also invest in the same people.

If you made an announcement in the national paper, even if you paid for an ad, the public will know who they can follow up and invest in themselves. For example, a full-page ad for $75,000 in a national U.S. newspaper is something the general public cannot afford. They will piggyback on your budget.

If you bought enough to get the artist to the next price level, you can even begin reselling the pieces that you own, To get your capital back, resell half and keep the other half. Then reach for the higher price points.

Chapter 12

Cafés, Restaurants, Offices & Other Locations

I've seen some cafés close in my area

I've been to a lot of cafés through the years. Recently, two cafés near me closed, although a few also opened in the neighborhood. Cafés usually allow their walls to have art for sale by local artists.

There is also a café that's still in business here which decided to close earlier. They used to close at 8 p.m. everyday except Sunday, when they close at 5 p.m. Now they close at 5 p.m. everyday. I asked why.

They said the customers, by 5 p.m., just linger until closing without buying enough. My heart sank. People just like me who need all the time with their laptops won't use their place anymore.

I had the idea that cafés provide ample space to entertain those who come in and out and those who stay forever.

If cafés also made money from the art they display, they might be able to continue being open until 8 p.m.

The similarity between cafés and art galleries

I can tell you one very important similarity between cafés and art galleries: Both have rents or leases to pay.

Adding #valzubiriagenda just might help to get additional traffic to your location and provide you with an additional income that might be impactful enough.

The difference is that you can be more flexible than the galleries.

While you're already toying with the idea of publishing, the usual galleries might have second thoughts. The galleries might stick to what they have been doing for years. They will be slow to decide on all this.

I had gallery friends who struggled and then had to close because they were hoping to weather the worsening economy through their usual business approach.

A vision a café owner told me

I just had a very recent, serious, art-related talk with a café owner. He gave me some relevant thoughts about the art on display and for sale at his café.

First, he said that he cannot dictate the price. It is always the decision of the artists. He said that artists usually overprice themselves. The crowd of coffee lovers he attracts cannot afford the art.

Second, he told me, he had always wondered this: How can an artist on display at his café become a big success, enough to make him rich as well?

I told him about the set of ideas that makes up #valzubiriagenda. I told him, if he or his café publishes its own art books, collaborations and solo books of profiles, essays and memoirs, then people might become more motivated to buy art at his café.

If a system of promoting artists were online—when everyone uses the hashtag, #valzubiriagenda, then even people from far away will find a way to come to the café to check out the art. I call this activity "chasing art."

The café owner's motivations for displaying local artists were to help artists and to make a difference in the community.

We actually talked at his second, newly opened café, less than a mile from the first café he opened more than a decade ago.

You could be just like the café. You already have a location. You already have walls and drawers that can display and hold art. You already have display shelves for upcoming books. You may already have been supporting artists for years.

Display #valzubiriagenda on café windows and websites

Even if you still do not have artists who want to get involved, you can display a hashtag #valzubiriagenda sign on your store window and

12: Cafés, Restaurants, Offices & Other Locations 75

web presence.

Your excuse in doing so is that you are now entertaining the idea, and that you are calling for artists, writers, book designers, lawyers, investors and art collectors, etc., so that you can form a core group, in the city, based in your café or establishment.

One simple commitment to produce at least one book, or getting an artist to do it or getting an artist to price his or her art at an increasing price schedule, is all a café or any establishment needs to do.

In Chapter 38, I will tell you that as soon as you begin the process of producing your own books, you will be able to call yourself a publisher.

Online, you can chart your artists' past, present and future price points and quantities. You can include the charts in your books. Show how your artists and their art pieces are making progress. If you can show the speed of increase in their market value, you might generate a lot more sales.

Announce all your book projects, even if the books involved have yet to be published. There will still be interest since all this is relatively new.

Art sales can help your café

I'm hoping you read the Introduction. I was basically telling artists that galleries reject 99% of artists.

This is where your cafés come into the picture. You have been providing space for the artists. This time, publish books. Set up your own requirements. You can be strict. You might require them to write and publish their books, besides what you can do for them and your café. You can carry both their art, their books, your art acquisitions and your books in your café.

You can require that your artists produce their own books, and that they agree to be included in your own books of the multiple artists you will carry.

You might want to come up with a system where besides a commission, you can get an art piece from the collection that you've already published.

You might form a core group of book writers, photographers, designers, etc., all of whom might also be interested in acquiring art from your artists or earning some money. Everyone has to meet to agree on all this.

Remind the artists that you're the one with the storefront and employees, not to mention, you want your café or establishment to produce it's own series of books. All this requires time and energy and will add to everyone's prestige.

Make your own rules. As long as it's acceptable, you're okay. You might just end up with an in-demand reputation that's difficult to say no to.

If this trends, local bookstores might carry everyone's books, including your café's own books. This can promote your café. Look forward to the bookstores having their own events. Look forward to even meeting galleries, if they too decided to publish books, just like what you're doing. The books even out the playing field.

Remember in the Introduction that some galleries think that publishing their artists in book form "just sounds like too much work?" Another thought they have is that their artists might leave them as soon as they see their names in art books.

Your artists get known *because* they are all over the city.

Investors might chase art

We're hoping for art chasers to chase art from place to place. I believe the art chasers will have a few considerations.

1. They will return to your place if they notice the artists' prices are going up fast. The way to do this is to not have exclusivity, but to share artists amongst other locations. The more locations an artist has, the more books you will have that connect to other locations. Not all the books need to be produced by your café, but you can carry them

2. They will also return if you give investors reasonable, respectable discounts and other incentives like free books. Just let your artists know about these moves. Remember that you can get your own books at a wholesale price so you can better afford giving books away

3. They will like your place if you also give them the opportunity to resell their art at your location, so come up

12: Cafés, Restaurants, Offices & Other Locations

with a program and include insurance if you can
4. You can encourage the investors and collectors to get published themselves.

Coworking space

You might be in a coworking space. The good thing about coworking is that your costs are low. You can schedule meetings to get people involved with you, and then condense your input to a manageable scale. There is no need to be available all the time.

Coworking spaces are popular because they can become flexible.

Look into your coworking space and see if you can sell art, both individually and with the management itself. Repetition is what will make all this work. You might represent the same artist. Find a way to turn this into a gimmick.

This can result in collaboration, and an influx of investors and art collectors to your location.

The art you sell may be in just one of the drawers in your desk or stored in your locker.

Do all this on the side. Your regular work should keep flowing as usual.

Some additional pointers

1. Find a way to have fun and be accepting and encouraging of everyone
2. Use your place as a meeting place. Let everyone know early on that you are encouraging them to buy your food and drinks while at your place
3. Offer one or more books, book ideas and book projects to publish
4. Establish a system to allow publishing books that will include your artists and the art that your investors and art collectors want to resell
5. Engage the community by asking for volunteers and collaborators: graphic designers, writers, editors, book designers, idea people, marketers, proofreaders, art collectors, art investors, and others

6. Have a sign-up sheet online and at your location
7. Form your core group of volunteers, collaborators and artists
8. You can tell everyone there may or may not be money for the moment, and you are promoting barter. All this is new, so don't make promises of money too soon
9. Set meeting dates and deadlines
10. Schedule a few events to accommodate your artists and everyone else
11. If investors and art collectors are acquiring work that have yet to end up in a book project, find a way to show them that you are already working on the book
12. Be okay to sell all ranges of art prices. The idea is to encourage your artists to keep increasing their prices, even if the current price is $1
13. Be on the alert for investors and art collectors who are seriously into acquiring art. Encourage them to keep doing it. Refer them to your book writers and designers if they have their own book ideas. You can also sell their books in the future
14. Have an updated notebook of artists, their progress and other locations where they also have their art for sale. Update the tabulation to include investors who are re-selling art. You can do the same online
15. Prepare a local directory of your artists and their other locations besides yours
16. Allow ample time to edit and proofread your book projects. Make sure that your books have as little mistakes as possible and meets the aesthetics of what a published book looks like
17. Give two weeks for the printers to ship your final books to you, if you plan to schedule an event

Chapter 13

YouTubers, Other Videographers & Their Followers

I follow a lot of YouTube channels

I want to encourage you to make art, even if your topic is not about art. You can make your views your art. If you don't feel confident, make enough to publish in book form. You can also team up with other channels and come up with a group book. Then see if you want to continue. Even if you think your art is not good, your perception will change for the better once you see your art published.

Tell your subscribers that you are also making art with an increasing price schedule and scarcity.

I'm including this short encouragement so that you would better consider this idea, because I fully support your online efforts.

You don't have to make "perfect" art. You have a voice that many already follow. Create your art pieces so your followers can have something you made. You obviously already know how to promote yourselves, you can add art into the mix.

You already have videos, you may or may not have to write your memoirs and biographies or whatever is related to your topic. Some of you are already published.

You know that some of your videos do not qualify for monetization. You also know that accumulating funds on Patreon can take a while.

Make art for your followers. As your voices keep getting bigger and bigger, so will the collectability of your art.

From pages xxviii, 4, 120 & 269

My mixed media porcelain doll art. Each piece is 13-14 inches tall.

I'm proposing to include multiple dolls in an art piece, with a backdrop so I can incorporate other elements including gemstones and precious metals, because that's how I think I can justify my intended price schedule. The works will be encased in glass because this is not a toy. (They're "chick magnets"—see Introduction, page xvii.)

I published my memoirs and this book sooner because my art and the art books will obviously take longer. I'm proposing that the art commissions or contracts can be traded the moment you get them for artists just like me.

Whoever owns the contract gets the art. If this happens, the art itself becomes irrelevant to the investor. Some artists are faster. The investors and art collectors decide.

Even if our art can reach 6 to 8 figures, the cafés and other locations can still represent us.

Next image is on page 84

Chapter 14

Galleries
Some Considerations

I hope galleries profit!

I used to hang out at the galleries in Chicago around 2007. This was just before business slowed down in 2008. Unfortunately, some of my gallery friends had to close.

I cannot claim that I understand the business of galleries 100%. I can tell you that I care about my gallery friends 100%.

I can say that galleries have their own business practices that have worked for them for decades, so, to the galleries, here is a way to get into this in a safe way:

Let your artists, not you, come to a decision to announce their scarcity and their increase in price. Let your artists come to a decision to produce their books.

All you need for the moment is their decision.

You can immediately relay to the investors who come through your galleries that you have one or two artists who "intend" to follow the #valzubiriagenda.

The current prices of your artists will not change. The ideas will affect the future. The price increase, possible scarcity and upcoming books will help prompt investors and art collectors to buy art sooner than later.

If you observe that investors do get prompted by this, let your other artists become aware of this.

Making the art books

You already know how to photograph art the right way. If you have an artist who plans to publish books, then simply photograph that artist's art pieces and email the files to the artist so the art in your gallery gets included in future books, exactly like what you tell your potential customers.

The investors and art collectors might also want to produce their own books, so ask your artists if they are okay with this.

One gallery-related reason why I came up with this idea

I have seen some galleries resell the acquisitions of their clients and customers who lost their jobs due to the 2008 recession.

The galleries got themselves in a bad position, because they were reselling art at much lesser prices than what their clients paid for.

It was good for the gallery owners to have done this for their clients. On the other hand, it can also be bad for the gallery to resell art at a price lower than before. This proves to others that the art never went up in value.

You're not competing with the cafés

Just remember that the cafés and other venues will generally entertain lower price ranges for lower budgets.

If the same artist already represented by one or more cafés and other venues gets represented by your gallery, that's good for everyone involved. The price increase happened.

You are also showing that you have a collectible artist at your gallery who most probably already has books and art books in other locations. This can also be proof of local or even greater fame.

You also already have contacts who have higher budgets. This can work to your advantage.

Generating local demand

I hate to have noticed this. Chicago is well-known for financial institutions, hedge funds, new corporations with recent IPOs. These groups have money for art. I have even been to law firms that own entire buildings that have original art in their corridors on every floor.

Unfortunately, some interior designers and even some huge non-

14: Galleries Some Considerations

profit art organizations insist on heading out of the city to buy the expensive art, even though the same artists are represented in Chicago.

I have also met someone who was charge of acquiring art for her law firm. We talked for a while. This was in 1996. I had nothing much to offer then, although I had some degree of recognition.

She recognized me from my column on the arts in the free monthly paper I was in. It was just good to have been recognized then. I never knew before meeting her that positions like hers exist in a law firm.

The galleries claim that these groups and individuals go elsewhere to buy art because: Who would pass up an all-expense paid trip to London or New York?

They get first class accommodations, for several days. On the other hand, there is no excitement heading to the local galleries for the price of a taxicab fare.

As I have explained before, there is a pecking order of which city is better.

The interior designers, the executives and art buyers of the non-profits and companies, on the other hand, are valid to get art where they think is best.

Because they can afford it, they would find it crucial to keep up with the rest of the art world. We are talking "world," they can hop from country to country to get what is perceived to be the best place.

Nobody here is evil or wrong. Art is still a business and everyone, especially the galleries, are in this business to make money.

What needs to be done is to convince the people and groups with money that there is a local trend happening, and that if they don't participate, they can be left behind.

What if a huge corporation announces that, for the next number of years, they will only acquire art by artists who are participating in the #valzubiriagenda? Don't get left behind.

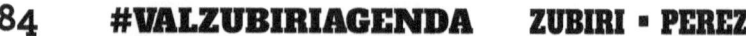

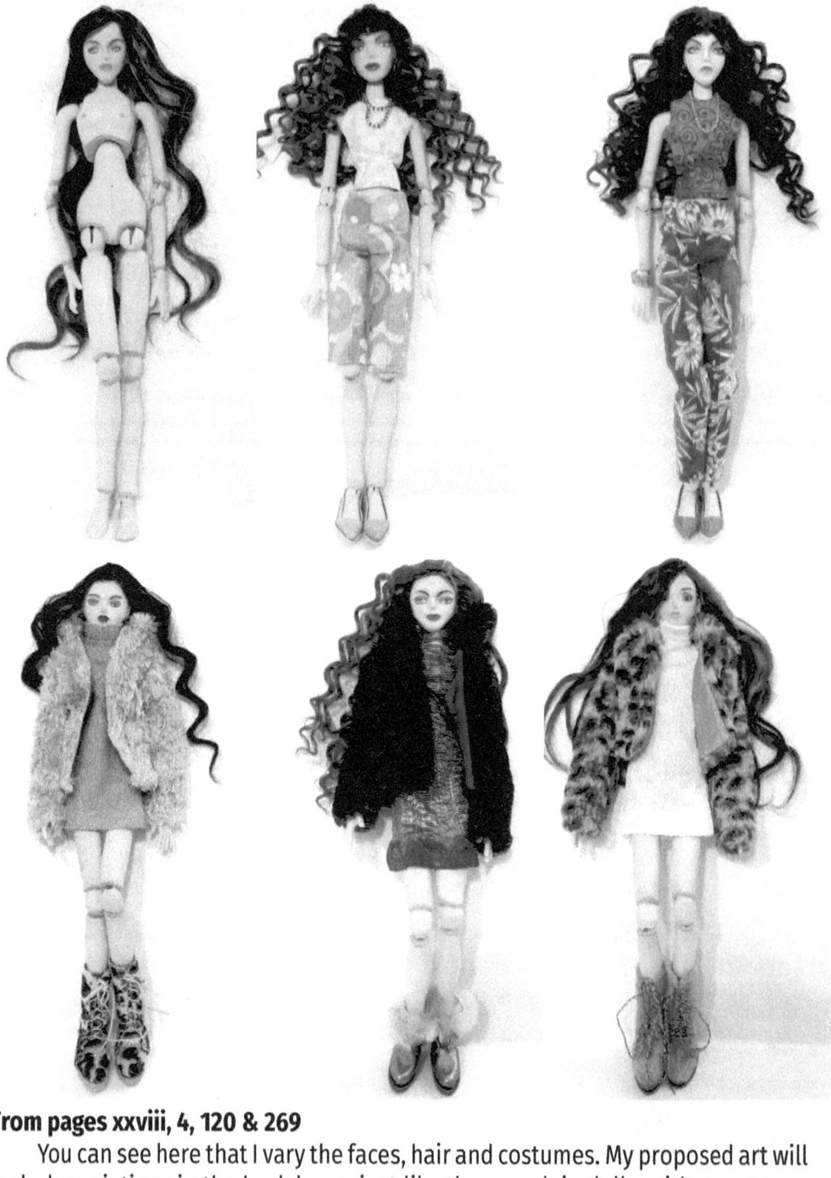

From pages xxviii, 4, 120 & 269

You can see here that I vary the faces, hair and costumes. My proposed art will include variations in the backdrops, just like the porcelain dolls, with gemstones and precious metals as well so your acquisition becomes more and more complex and worth looking forward to, displaying, keeping, and trading with others.

I'm also open to being collected and displayed with the middle tier and lower tier art, even art by the homeless. I want everyone to succeed. Our books will even out the playing field.

Next image is on page 116

Chapter 15

Homeless Street Artists, UFO Abductees & Others

What inspires me to keep believing that this would succeed

During the last few years that I was analyzing the conditions, I came across five groups of people:

1. Homeless street artists I passed by in downtown Chicago
2. The well-dressed army veteran who was missing a hand
3. The father who had cancer who was pictured with his daughters
4. The UFO abductees featured in paranormal radio shows
5. I had already mentioned the YouTube people in Chapter 13

It is okay to display #valzubiriagenda on the sidewalk

To the homeless street artists, I wish you luck. I would be honored if you display a #valzubiriagenda sign on the dirtiest sidewalk, if that is the best place you can be at.

Make sure to be responsible. I once went to a homeless shelter and asked a manager to refer me to someone who can come to my place the next day. I needed help making rubber stamps for a street fair.

I was referred to someone. I gave the man $5 for the train ride, promising more. The man never showed up. On another day, I came back to tell the manager that the man did not show up. The manager chuckled and said that was to be expected.

I still believe in helping the homeless. I'm now referring to those who would be responsible artists.

Make sure to tell people that you are also still looking for your own collaborators if you haven't found them yet. Be ready to barter. Analyze how you will increase your prices.

Here is an idea: allow your paying collectors and investors to publish your works in their own books. Make sure to keep in touch with them. Ask for copies of their books so you can show others. Ask people to mention you online.

Ask people to help your own books get published and to refer you to people nearby who can take photographs of your works and produce your books for you.

If someone gives you a laptop and a camera to work with, be careful that it does not get stolen. However, your life is more precious than any laptop or camera, or even art. Let it go and start over.

Make sure to back up your files. Use a flash drive, email your files to yourself as you progress or use a cloud storage. Google Drive will allow you to store 15 gigabytes for free.

The army veteran who was missing a hand

I was on a bus, when I saw a man on the sidewalk in his army getup. He was very clean-cut and perfectly dressed. He walked confidently and steadily. He carried himself well. I'm almost sure he went to some veterans office to take care of something.

He was missing his right hand. He can still make art.

If you're a retired or disabled veteran, you can make the ugliest art, someone will buy it. If you produce your art books and memoir, and announce your prices and scarcity, then you are being professional like the rest of us.

You can join a collaborative book with veteran artists. You can call for art and organize to produce the book yourself.

15: Homeless Street Artists, UFO Abductees & Others

The picture of a family whose dad had cancer

This is another unforgettable image in my mind.

I was waiting for the bus, when I saw a bond paper printout taped on a glass window. It was a printout of a picture of a dad with four daughters, and a note that said something like: "We need money. Our dad has cancer and we don't want him to die. Please help."

This was in 2014. I hope their dad survived. I had been analyzing our set of conditions, what I now call #valzubiriagenda.

Children can make art. If you're in need of money, make art, get the art published. You can choose to make your book look like a children's book. There is no need to write your memoirs. Ask an adult to help out.

Homebound people can also become artists.

How far you will take this idea to apply to your situation is up to you. Keep at it to get noticed and succeed. Get listed in websites which promote causes.

Collectible art from UFO abductees and other famous paranormal authors

Hocus Pocus Lately is my paranormal memoir. While writing it, I listened to podcasts and radio shows that were about UFOs and the paranormal. The shows usually featured authors of paranormal subjects. Some were authors who wrote about having been abducted by aliens and UFOs.

It occurred to me that these authors already have their books about themselves. Sometimes, their books even have drawings of the UFOs, aliens, and whatever else. They already have an audience. They are either self-published—they know how to make books, or published by a familiar imprint.

Their drawings in their books may look unskilled, but if they sold their original drawings of UFOs and aliens, they can become collectible. They should publish each one of their works, to prove authenticity.

Years ago, I was at a bookstore, lingering at the Paranormal/UFO section. Someone else started looking at the same books. I mentioned this short meeting in **Hocus Pocus Lately.**

The man said he was a physician. He collected books on UFOs as a hobby. He referred me to a book about alien implants which I bought.

He would be someone who will want to have a roomful of original drawings and matching art books by those paranormal and UFO personalities who are also well-known authors in the field.

There was also a time, when I was listening to a paranormal/UFO radio show, when the guest was an old man who was abducted by aliens. Toward the end of the interview, he mentioned his website. I immediately checked out his website.

I visited his website again a few months later. He posted an announcement. He said he was closing down his website. He said he had hoped for enough traffic to the site so he can make a little affiliate income from ad traffic. He did not make enough. He could have made art.

Famous authors can make pencil, charcoal or crayon rubbings of pyramids and other eerie locations! Famous graves! Even if you make a hundred original rubbings of the same location, you should still sign each work and publish them as a book. How your crayon applied on the grain of the paper should show and will authenticate your works.

There are gatherings and conventions on the paranormal all over the world. The famous and not-so-famous authors can sell original art and matching art books. They may have hesitated in the past. Now I'm encouraging everyone to make this their norm.

Chapter 16

Tips for Publishers, Writers, Ghostwriters, Editors, Book Designers, Proofreaders, Lawyers, Photographers, etc.

The Soloist

Go online and research on Nathaniel Ayers and Steve Lopez. Ayers is a gifted musician who is also a schizophrenic. The movie, **The Soloist,** was a movie made about him and his interaction with Steve Lopez, a Los Angeles Times columnist.

Lopez only met Ayers in 2005 when Lopez was around 52 years old and Ayers was 54. Lopez started writing about Ayers in his column in 2005. By 2008, Lopez released a hardcover book about their meeting. By 2009, the movie, **The Soloist** was released. In 2010, the paperback version was released. Both of them are still alive.

If these two people can collaborate, there should be someone who will collaborate with you as needed. You just need to actively look for that person or group of people.

Don't take yourself for granted

Unless you agree to be a ghostwriter, if you're a collaborator, allow for your name to be put in print.

Mention names and contributions in the Acknowledgments, Preface or Introduction. Don't mention real names if you have nothing good to say about them. They might sue you.

Avoid mentioning too many names.

Acknowledge only those who helped in the book. Everyone will take this book to the next project / book collaboration.

My experience in theatre

I started joining theatre groups in the early 90s. I was already a graphic artist for a copy shop, and had just started to write a column for a free monthly community paper.

The first graphic design project I had with my first theatre group was a show poster. I discovered one weakness. Too many cooks spoil the broth. The final poster was a bad-looking compromise.

Each of the main collaborators did not want to put in more time than the others. They were also too nice to each other. They did not want to make decisions without the consent of others.

They were holding each other back. I also noticed that people liked meeting with each other more than getting themselves to work on the project.

I was the lower-tier volunteer for that first poster. I was not with the main group. I think they burned out, because I took over the graphics for a few later productions. I insisted on working alone.

Become aware of this. Your finished book might look like a compromise. Know to what extent you want to collaborate. Know when you are better off working alone.

Eyeballing a project

There is a thing called "eyeballing."

You eyeball a project and the people involved prior to joining or volunteering, and "see" if it looks right *for* you. Know if it looks balanced or if it needs more work. Just like art. Join to positively contribute. Don't bring the project down to a halt.

Here are some collaboration pointers

1. Search online for hashtag #valzubiriagenda and your city for venues, events, locations, offices, artists, investors, art collectors, writers, ghostwriters, editors, proofreaders, digital designers, book designers, pho-

16: Tips for Book Designers, Proofreaders, Lawyers, Photographers, etc.

tographers, and lawyers interested in collaborations to produce books

2. Have a portfolio or samples of your abilities ready
3. Be honest with your skills. If you still need to hone your skills some more, look for someone more skilled who will be willing to teach you
4. Post your abilities on a website or blog
5. Know when to say "yes"
6. Know when to say "no"
7. Be able to accept a "no" if they cannot work with you or are not interested in you and know when to move on
8. Offer to hold a meeting or regular meetings at your place
9. Be ready to attend both large and small meetings
10. Print out business cards you can give away, with safe information that you are willing to share
11. Connect first with people before you give away your cards
12. Come up with a system for your phone to identify contacts. My simplest suggestion is adding prefixes to First Names, like "Art Artist Sally," "Art Writer Dan," "Art Investor Carl" so you can easily scroll through an alphabetical list
13. If you don't have a laptop or camera or something needed to move forward, look for someone who will be willing to share equipment with you
14. Look for people you can help, volunteer or hang out with
15. Your services should not be free. Give yourself an acceptable asking price
16. Look into bartering
17. Look into signed agreements
18. Honor signed agreements, because if you succeed and become highly valuable, some agreements you did not honor in the past might haunt you

If you're underage, bring a guardian

All this #valzubiriagenda is new, so if it's your child who is the artist or who has publishing skills, go with your child to meetings to look for others to collaborate with. Be in charge of screening people.

I'm calling attention to this because the #valzubiriagenda might not be a long-lasting trend. Everyone strikes when the iron is hot. A gifted child cannot wait to get older.

You might be an artist looking to produce a book. If you're underage, make sure to bring your guardian.

You might know how to make a yearbook in the safety of your school, and you might have publishing or artistic skill that people could use. Bring a guardian with you.

This is a career

We all have an imaginary region of tolerance where we can tolerate people within that region. I do my best to help people, but some just cannot be helped. I still like people because stories come from them. Memoirists are storytellers.

Know your tolerance level. Just because you're looking for the next story to write does not mean you should put your safety at risk.

When we tell friends that we are involved in an art show opening, they think party night, food and drinks. When a brain surgeon talks about brain surgery, we don't think party night, food and drinks.

We are doing what we can to further our careers in art. I'm saying we can still party—later. We just need to make progress now.

Chapter 17

Business Authors, Business Writers & Economists

What is happening to the world

It now takes a shorter span of time to disrupt business.

Travel, music, movies, books were separately disrupted. Electronic and computer stores have also closed. Long distance calls with video are now free over the internet. Smartphones have taken over cameras.

Now, shopping malls have slower traffic and department and clothing stores are closing. People are recirculating clothes on ebay. Uber may be using drivers now, but they want to have driverless taxis in the future. Groceries are going to become cashierless. There's a huge online retailer that is now looking into offering health insurance.

What is weird is that each industry seemed to refuse or deny that there was going to be change.

I have a friend who recently ordered a gigantic television on the internet instead of going to the nearby electronic store.

This is no different from the man who won the auction for a Leonardo da Vinci painting which reached $450.3 million dollars and the bidder did not even need to see the art. The bidder will be happy to see it once it arrives.

I believe that #valzubiriagenda might disrupt the art field, but I don't know which factor of it will be key.

People have become more actively in search of alternative sources of income. A lot of people are unemployed. Even the homeless can make art.

This might become an economic bubble

I do have a hunch this will become a bubble. Then again, it might not become one.

Right now, I'm just hoping that people who need to make money for themselves and their companies will be helped.

This idea is global, it can help people everywhere. It uses the same basic set of guidelines.

Writing and publishing add a few degrees of difficulty.

Self-publishing gives everyone a chance to come up with books without the system of permissions that the huge publishing companies require. However, I have noticed that it is still a hurdle to be creative enough to write a book of life stories and essays.

Making art can be difficult as well. Like me, for example, I'm just saying I want an official maximum of 3,000 pieces. I'm just setting a tangible ceiling. That doesn't mean I will produce that many.

Comparing this with the Tulip Mania in 1636-1637

First off, anyone can propagate tulips. With art, the artist would be the source. There might be a lot of artists, but each of them are supposed to declare a limited quantity.

I tell people that books last 300 to 3,000 years. That should be enough time to make money.

The books will keep "propagating"—the investors and art collectors will continue publishing books. The collectible art doesn't keep increasing per artist.

The investors and art collectors are encouraged to purchase only within their budget. There is no need to borrow, get in debt and lose money.

Some pension funds are in the spotlight right now

They are supposedly desperate to make faster money than what they had been accustomed to. I once worked as a processor of retirement benefits. I highly care about pension funds.

Right now, some U.S. government pension funds are bankrupt.

17: Business Authors, Business Writers & Economists 95

They just could not find a way to generate income in a faster way. They could use a new, profitable idea.

Private investment companies help increase the funds.

If the funds drastically need money, I suggest that they can look into having a more direct hand at selling and profiting from art especially if this will just be a temporary project. They can still do it with their investment companies—as long as they get a drastically larger share.

Some national level governments are in trouble as well.

The Greek government can look into working with just a handful of artists, to be able to pay their IMF debt.

Could there be others like Madoff out there?

Bernie Madoff did not have gone to jail. I did his math in Chapter 3.

hashtag #valzubiriagenda

Part 2

Preparing Yourself

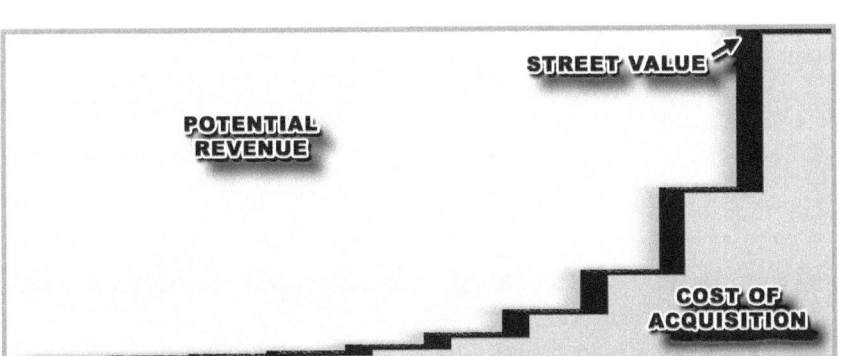

SPECIAL SECTION #2

Ask Yourself:

What will you not gain if you do not pursue the #valzubiriagenda?

Chapter 18

Preparing to Become a Writer

In 1998, I placed a masseur ad in a local free weekly paper. This cost me $17. The state only decided to require massage licenses in 2008. To cut the story short, I became a masseur. By 2006, I had my first draft for a memoir.

I revisited my manuscript in 2014. I had started writing new chapters in 2013, then I reorganized my old chapters. I finally came up with **1-Hour Mentors, A Memoir of an Artist as a Masseur** and two other books, **Wonder** and **Hocus Pocus Lately.**

I had written **Dollman the Musical, A Memoir of an Artist as a Dollmaker** in 2012, so I was productive. I prepared for **Dollman the Musical,** because from 2009 to 2012, I immersed myself in learning. I will share with you some writing techniques that I learned during that time in later chapters, especially in Chapter 36.

Returning to 1998, I moved downtown near the hotels. I had to smartly time this, because there was a deadline for placing ads in the annual yellow pages. The yellow page directories immediately end up in the hotel rooms the following February as soon as the trucks drop them off.

My so-called friends in 1998 delighted in the latest buzz—I had become a prostitute. I added fuel to the fire, joking that I charged for the massage, but the sex was free.

I came to the point where I made up stories that they wanted to hear anyway, as they put me down and saw me as a desperate nobody. If those people don't want to respect me, they might as well talk about made-up stuff. Besides, I was thinking a story for my future book might develop.

I had to live in an expensive downtown area to be close to the hotels, so this decision was for the business, not for my own luxurious living.

I overheard some degree of envy from my friends.

I never told them what I'm telling you now: My main idea behind becoming a masseur was to come up with a memoir of sorts, written from an artist's perspective, when I'm ready.

It was only in 2005, 7 years later, that I started to type my first attempt at a manuscript. I finished my first book-length draft in 2006. I counted a total of 170,000 words. I wrote too much.

As soon as I finished that last word of the draft, my interest in continuing to be a masseur just instantly disappeared!

"On to the next adventure!" I said to myself, on that morning when I left the 24-hour Starbucks and walked 2 miles home to where I lived. I then had to prepare for that annual publishers convention, which was to happen in Washington DC.

All throughout those years, I kept my interest in art and writing by attending conventions, even flying elsewhere to attend wherever they were held.

Meanwhile, those people who made fun of me came up with an unofficial saying, "If Val can do it, then so can I."

I gave them some degree of confidence. I started a trend, but they took it to an unhealthier level.

Eventually, a few started placing ads. Four even placed ads as transgender escorts. One of my best friends who was gay—his is a very long story, he also became transgender, and he, or now, she, also placed her ad online as a transgender escort for men.

They did not become masseurs, they became escorts. Some of them got arrested, and some of them narrowly escaped friendly visits by policemen and undercover cops knocking on their doors.

I'm not transgender. It must have been their lack of better opportunities that prompted them to do what they did anyway. This entire fiasco can become a story in a memoir.

Those people should have asked me for insights. They should have asked me why I became a masseur. To those people, I was prostitute.

18: Preparing to Become a Writer

They put me down in their minds and behind my back.

I never told anyone of them that my initial plan was to write a memoir of my possible misadventures. I was thinking I would have a book like Xaviera Hollander's **The Happy Hooker.** Instead, I ended up with **1-Hour Mentors.**

The celebrities, singers, actors, authors, CEOs, chairmen of the board, ordinary people, drivers for touring bands were so generous with their knowledge that as I gave them my transitory, 1-hour massages, they gave me permanent life lessons that I needed to hear. I was someone who had a dream to become an artist and a writer.

I would have been 200% helpful to my friends had they asked me for advice. Friends are friends. I'm not their guru.

You might still say, "If Val can do it, then so can I."

This time, I hope you do think that way, because now you have a book of my knowledge, dreams and good intentions that my old friends never had.

I want to make writing as simple as possible for you. I know that our group is a group of visual artists, investors, art collectors and others who will now get into writing memoirs, producing art books and publishing books.

I will tell you stories that you can learn from. Just like my memoirs.

Through the years, I have met people who went or are going to school for creative writing, who to this day have not even written one single book. I have also met people who never went to school for creative writing who have written more than one book.

Your goal is to see just one written book for yourself. There is no need to go to a university just to produce one book. You're also pressed for time. This #valzubiriagenda might trend and so the earlier you get into this, the better.

I personally was a victim of my own tardiness. I came upon the idea of writing a memoir in 1998. When I finished one in 2006, 8 years later, the book industry had changed. It was no longer business as usual. A lot of bookstores started to close.

I will give you useful knowledge to get you started, not only in writing, but in eventually seeing yourself with books and art books.

If you remember John F. Kennedy with his famous words,

"We choose to go to the moon in this decade and do the other things, not because they are easy, but because they are hard."

I want to show you that we can choose to write and publish, because it *can* be easy. It is **now** easy!

Art, writing and publishing—what I have done and keep on doing for myself, is now my manageable "normal." You can do this as well. You might see some errors in my writing. That's okay. Realize that it hasn't stopped me from reaching you.

You will discover that writing your second book will be easier than the first, but the only way you will find out is if you get through your first book.

I will tell you what to watch out for, especially some mental and emotional considerations when you write about your life. Then I will get into the more technical aspects.

Chapter 19

Permissions & Apologies

Our actions are based on a world of permissions and apologies.

Let's say you consult a friend. You tell that friend, "I'm looking into writing my memoir. I also plan to pursue art a little more seriously."

Your interaction with your friend is an indirect way of asking for permission to move forward.

Your friend would weigh the circumstances for you. Your friend might say, "Think of the consequences of your actions."

That friend basically is telling you, if you fall flat on your face, you'll be apologizing later.

On the other hand, if your friend says, "Go ahead with your plan," that's a permission.

So permissions are what governs our thinking and our actions *before* we do them, or if we even ever do them or not.

Apologies are visions of ourselves feeling the shame, humiliation and embarrassment of failure. Apologies only happen *after*, because we decided to act.

A simple example for "permissions and apologies" is waiting for the correct street light so that you can cross the street.

As you wait for the light to turn, you're waiting for permission. You might decided to disobey the light and cross the street too soon. You then visualize the apologies, if an accident, something nasty, happens to you.

You might still decide to cross, without permission, if you see no cars that might hit you.

Imagine yourself, right where you are right now. You have a future waiting to happen. You know what stops you? Permissions and apologies.

You make decisions wary of whether enough people will give you permission to act. You also make decisions with the factor of having to apologize if your decisions were wrong.

My early version of permissions and apologies

When I decided to become a masseur, I did not ask anyone for their opinion. I simply did it. Nobody around me had my vision. I had to trust myself.

I was already writing a column for a monthly free paper around 1995.

I read in a book that in order to get some recognition through the media, you either get featured in an article, or you write the article yourself and feature others. The former will get you recognized for the duration of that one issue. The latter, if you become a regular contributor, will get you recognized longer.

In May 1996, I got on television and other media for AIDS Awareness because I made an artistic statement. I attached the red AIDS ribbon to the beak of the origami paper crane.

I said, "In Asia, there is this belief that if you make a thousand origami cranes, your wish will come true. I attach the red AIDS ribbon to the beak of the origami crane, because I wish for a cure."

This came to me after reading a book by the famous advertising genius, George Lois. He said that if you put together two familiar concepts, you will come up with a new, original concept that can easily be embraced, because you started with elements already familiar to the public's subconscious.

After that media blitz, I went to attend a publishers convention for the first time.

In the morning of the first day, I naively lined up to register to get in the convention halls. I was ready to fill the forms and pay my entrance dues. There seemed to be a hundred people before me. I heard that about 120,000 were attending the 4- or 5-day convention.

19: Permissions & Apologies

I had my Press ID, because I had a column in the free monthly paper.

I was pulled to the side by the attendant who was checking credentials to speed up the processing. She said I was in the wrong line. The press had a press room. I went there. There were no lines in the press room!

I got in free! I was registered as press. I was given a press badge. The press room was spacious, with empty chairs and tables, press kits and folders were on the side tables. There were free beverages and food! I took all of this as a sign. I was feeling high. I was there, with permission from the powers that be, and no permission from friends and family.

I saw the huge publishers and smaller ones. I saw authors signing their books. They were also giving away free, crisp, unread, new books to all the attendees who cared to get them.

There was an autographing section. I learned that this publishers convention happened in May or June so that the booksellers, or bookstores, for the most part, can check out what will be released in September. They will have time to decide how many copies of books they will order for the fall, when school was back in session, vacation was over, and the parents and everyone else will have time to stay home and read books.

Besides authors at the publisher's booths, there was a special autographing section. It was a row of about 40 tables. Authors were scheduled to appear for an hour to two hours, to autograph and give away their books to whoever lined up. The scheduling was done so that the new authors for the hour showed up at every other table, so that the lines of attendees would be better managed.

I learned a few things early on.

1. Only a handful of authors are famous. The rest are not. They still make some money
2. Publishers are like music companies. They invest in 10 authors, with the hope that one of them becomes a bestseller and pays for money they may have lost on the other 9
3. Authors can be as frumpy and ugly as anyone can be.

Some can be tiny. The book industry only cares to put names on the covers of books. Authors don't have to look handsome or beautiful
4. Authors are not pop stars who need to establish themselves before they get old. Just like artists, authors can get famous at age 80.

My life-changing author

I shook hands with an author that I had always looked up to when I was growing up—since high school. His book, which he wrote with his wife, seriously turned my life around.

That guy, when I finally stood face to face with him and shook his hand, was red in the face. He was drunk. I smelled alcohol on his breath. He was giving away his book and I got one autographed and dedicated to me! I also took a picture with him!

Years later, I found out online that the lady I saw with him was his second wife. She also looked a little red that day.

It came to me then that getting published is possible. We are all regular, ordinary people. What we *can* have is a *huge*... reputation!

Writing sexy books

Between 1996 and 1998, I noticed something while lining up for autographed books. There were 3 books that had the longest lines:
1. If the author was famous, it did not matter what genre the book would fall under
2. If the book was a cookbook
3. If the book was announced to be "sexy"

I had read books about getting famous years before because we artists and authors need a little fame to get stable in our profession.

One lesson I read was that the first impression the public has about you might typecast you for life.

People lined up for cookbooks. I thought that if I wrote a cookbook, I would be typecast as being in the food business. I wanted to become known as an artist.

I also told myself, I was not famous yet. I can't have a line for my

19: Permissions & Apologies

book as a famous person.

Those people who wrote about politics, if they were not famous, did not get a long line.

When a famous political commentator made an appearance to promote his book, people lined up. His book wasn't even printed yet. He and his publishers only produced spiral-bound photocopies that had a few sample chapters. The attendees did not care. They and I lined up anyway. I got his autograph on photocopy paper.

Finally, in 1998, this wallflower lady gave me the best idea for myself. It was two years after I first made the "who gets the longest line" discovery. I'm not the brightest person.

There was a lady who had a long line. I looked at her. She was not familiar, there was no name recognition, she was frail and her dress was not glamorous. She wore nerdy glasses just like me. I had found a kindred spirit.

I asked someone in line what her book was about. The man said it was a book about her misadventures as a cashier in an adult bookstore.

This was in 1998. This was why I decided to become a masseur. I thought, my best bet for a long line, if I ever ended up signing my books was a "sexy" book. I was nobody famous and getting a cookbook published was not going to work with getting known as an artist.

I never asked anyone for any opinion. Or permission. I just went ahead and did it. I was an adult. I couldn't even tell my parents nor my siblings about my thoughts. Had anyone stopped me then, I would not know what information I can offer you right now to get yourself going.

There is something else about the publishing industry that I praise. All books are welcome to get printed. This is why we have pornographic books and religious books. If someone got something printed, it was their prerogative.

There is also the premise that the printed products exist to help everyone feed their families. Once an author gets published by a huge publisher, it means that the publishers hope to sell the books, so that the profits trickle down to all the employees of the company and the booksellers.

Here is why people become famous. One person gets pushed to fame so that everyone else involved gets to feed their families. There is a mechanism behind it. A method to the madness.

As artists, we can become famous if we can help other people feed their families. Other people will make us famous, because they need us to be famous. This is one healthy way of looking at it. Comparing it to our circulatory system, I would say fame is not the heart. It's the veins and arteries.

For now, the goal is just to write and publish, not for the world, but for us to see how it feels. I can only assure you that it will help you level up. Let's all get famous later.

If you want to get yourself in print, I suggest to only get reactions *after* you got yourself in print. Let them react after your publication. Some people will attempt to discourage you. If you make an announcement of your publishing plans, and you hear a discouraging remark, then you announced too soon.

Chapter 20

Who the F#%k Told You to Get Yourself Published?

How to think if someone tells you that

The operative word to use is "think." Process other people's evil comments so they go in one ear and out the other. Let our hearts and minds remain unaffected.

Those who react and even attempt to correct other people who have nothing good to say, are wasting their time. There is the rest of the world to convince, so they should not correct or sway people just because they are in close proximity.

The reason you are producing books is to globally convince strangers about yourself. Convincing someone, who probably already knows you, would be a total waste of time.

There was someone I know who also supposedly wrote. He used to have a column for years in a monthly consumer magazine. It was only later that I learned about it. Then I finally saw a few of his columns years later.

In 2006, as I said earlier, I uploaded my semi-edited first draft to Lulu.com, just so I can see how it felt seeing my name on a book cover. It was also good practice, designing and formatting the book, making it look like a book.

This person, whom I am still close to and whom I highly respect—I just don't want to identify him, ordered my book as well. Two weeks later, I asked for his opinion.

He lambasted me from so many different angles in his email, that I chose to just lump it all in my brain as: total disappointment with a suggestion that someone should stop writing forever, a declaration that someone had no right to write at all and the hint that someone would do the world a favor if that someone committed suicide.

I actually laughed it off, because in my mind, I was the greatest writer who ever lived and no one can stop me from thinking otherwise! I also don't fully blame myself for any disappointment this person may have. I uploaded an unedited first attempt at writing a book.

Guess what? I later found out that this person, whom I seriously still highly respect even now, was bipolar. I got on his nerves because he probably missed his medication.

In 2008, two years later, when I made the book **Valentino Zubiri: Nude Drawings and Paintings from 1995 to 1996**, which was a collection of my art, he praised my Introduction. The Introduction was the only section that can include my writing, so I wrote a lengthy one.

Here is why you should keep believing that you *can* produce your books

I want to show you trends in publishing so you can catch up and begin feeling like an expert. For years, I have been to publishers conventions and you probably have not. It's never business as usual each year.

This is why I made sure to attend *especially* while I still had no book. It was to keep myself interested and updated. As soon as I finished my first book-length draft of a memoir in 2006, I stopped attending, feeling that I no longer needed to be there every year. Attendance declined anyway in later years.

There are trends every year that the attendees are made aware of. I can tell you the ones I can remember being talked about.

Amazon trends

There was a year when Amazon.com was new, and they were giving away premiums and attendees were asking what they did.

After that year, Amazon's buzz was praise from the publishers, because Amazon gave them a new venue to sell books.

There was another year, when the publishers did not like Amazon, because Amazon started discounting book prices.

There was a time, when publishers even disliked Amazon more, when their new copies started competing with used copies. Amazon allowed the sale and recirculation of used books. Publishers started printing less copies of their new releases.

Oprah's trends

Oprah Winfrey also had trends. There was a time when she was praised for Oprah's Book Club.

Then there was a year when she stopped her book club, when she announced there were no more good books to review. Book sales dropped.

One or two years later, famous authors paid for a full-page advertisement in a national newspaper, asking Oprah to reopen her book club, because they, the famous, bestselling authors, still live and still continue to produce good books.

The famous authors reminded her that having absolutely no more good books to mention was an impossibility. Everyone was cordial. It sounded to me like publishing showbiz. I'm sure at least one author had her personal phone number.

What I personally noticed, which I'm sure everyone in the publishing industry did as well, was that the authors Oprah featured in her book club, got hired as talk show hosts themselves. At least one had the same timeslot as her, on a different channel.

The blogger trend

If you remember, there was a blogger, Julie Powell who decided to blog about cooking the recipes from Julia Child's book, **Mastering the Art of French Cooking.** She started her blog in 2002. In 2003, she claimed to have received a book deal. In 2009, Meryl Streep and Amy Adams had a movie about Julie, entitled **Julie & Julia.**

Some new authors in 2006 were bloggers. The publishing industry around 2004 and 2005 became conscious of bloggers who had a lot of following. The publishers assumed that the public who follow the bloggers would also buy their books.

I can't name anyone at all in this, but it was the buzz in 2006. Some bloggers were there to promote their books. I guess the publishers proved their hunches wrong, because by 2007, I heard that publishing deals with bloggers dwindled.

The self-publishing trend

You may have heard of vanity publishing. In the United States, in some Sunday magazines and monthly consumer magazines, you would see ads for authors seeking to get published.

These are vanity presses. They will charge you for their services, which include getting your manuscript edited and finally printed, in book form. For a price, they will print as many as you want. They have other services, but I'm not too familiar with them.

So if you want to get published the traditional way, you send your manuscript to a literary agent, who then deals with a publisher. If this does not happen, you can still get yourself published for a fee through the vanity presses.

I know someone who used a vanity publisher who supposedly signed a dubious agreement so that the contents of the book cannot be transferred to another company.

My friend said that his brother, the author, would have to keep ordering the book from the vanity press, except that the book cover was lousy, and they require extra charges if he wanted to change anything. The inside was not only lousy, but it also needed editing.

I first went to the publishing conventions in 1996. That was the first time I saw a machine that actually printed and bound one single book at the press of a button. They called it "print on demand" or POD.

People used to pass by wondering how a bookstore can profit from just one book. This changed in 2006.

In 2006, the online, print on demand, self-publishing concept finally trended. One of the first online self-publishing companies, Lulu.com, reported that their latest annual sales, was $10 million dollars. It was up from $1 million dollars the previous year. Self-publishing had arrived! Lulu continues to be an online bookstore that self-publishers use.

Amazon.com then was just catching up. Amazon's self-publishing department was called TheBookVault.com. The were still having problems and getting bad reviews. I guess instead of redeeming themselves, they simply changed their name to CreateSpace.com. That was a smart move. I now use CreateSpace for my books.

If you now go online, check out some of your famous, well-established publishing houses. Some are now entertaining self-publishing.

20: Who the F#%k Told You to Get Yourself Published?

They have different programs to choose from.

As a rule, use those who do not charge up front. Use those who will only make money when you make a book sale.

The traditional publishing industry is declining

The word we are using here is "traditional."

There is a publishing house whose main office is in the West Coast. I used to know someone there. Around after the 2008 economic crash, they decided to stop attending and exhibiting at the annual booksellers convention.

I had the idea that publishers would go out of their way to be seen and connect at an annual event, at least at the biggest convention of their industry. He said they didn't find it feasible anymore.

Guess what they had decided to do? Online, they now have a section for self-publishers.

We're not the traditional publishing industry

I have said earlier in Chapter 8 that the traditional publishing industry is on the decline.

The main reason is that the traditional authors who once kept getting rejection letters, were finally able to self-publish. Those authors are not us. The way they want to make money is through the sale of books.

We make our books to sell our art, and I will say this many times over. We will ride the wave of self-publishing and we can abuse it, coming out with as many titles as possible—because we can and because we *finally* can. We now have the ability to pile up as many books as we can that will have our names on it.

It is now possible to spend as little as $0 to produce your books. Even vanity presses cannot say that.

We will even set a trend where we don't even need traditional bookstores to display our books, because our books need to be next to our original art. And maybe, just as an afterthought, the traditional bookstores might give us a shelf, where they will display us, locally, in our own cities.

If your art pieces end up in 100 places in your city, there is a big chance you will have your books being sold at those places as well. That's way better than the traditional books competing for shelf space at the 5 local bookstores you might be familiar with.

Now that you know a little of the publishing industry, you can probably advance some more.

We are not the traditional publishing industry. What we are doing is something else.

Where we are, there we are. It's a great place to be. Just write, self-publish and sell art!

Chapter 21

Becoming Artists & Writers

I have heard adults praise and tell kids, "Wow! You're a writer now!" just because the kids made an attempt at writing their names on paper.

I have also heard adults tell kids, "Wow! You're an artist now!" as fast as the kids show a drawing.

Did you notice that when children play doctor, adults would say, "Oh, you're *pretending* to be a doctor!"?

Or "Oh, you're *pretending* to be a pilot!"

I'm not one to tell people who can and cannot be artists, or writers. Let me just devote Chapter 22 to becoming an artist, based on my views, and then move on to preparing you to becoming writers and publishers.

If you're already an artist, you might still find the next chapter useful.

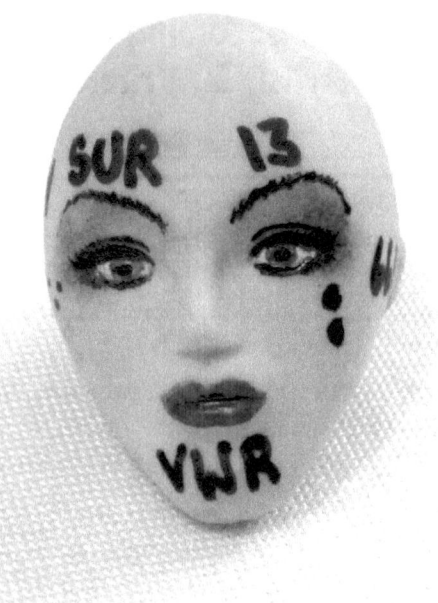

Silverio Perez, Untitled, porcelain & permanent marker, 2018

Chapter 22

Become an Artist Now & Join #valzubiriagenda It's Never Too Late!

My secret, subconscious way to becoming artistic

I learned this when I went to speed reading classes. Before we speed read a book, we turned the book upside down, and as our left hand held the book, our right hand diagonally passed over each page, from the upper right to the lower left. The theory was that the eyes naturally follow the moving object—the hand and fingers, while our subconscious sees the words and messages without letting the conscious mind take over.

I do this with art books. I turn the art book upside down and allow my subconscious mind to see the pictures without letting the conscious mind fixate.

Do this yourself. Do it alone where no one who does not understand what you're up to will see you. You can also do it as a group. You must avoid becoming self-conscious.

If you're at a library, congratulations! You're in heaven! Get a few art books at a time. Do it where no one can see you.

You'll be surprised to discover that this activity can improve your art.

Do you know about negative space?

Negative space is the area around the subject. If you draw a flower, your viewers would also want to see how you treat the negative space, the area around the flower.

My best example is when you look at a Spider-Man comic book. You see Spider-Man, but the artist has also spent a lot of time drawing the buildings and street scenes behind him. If you were a comic book artist, the comic book company will hire you not just because you can draw human beings in costume, but because of how you treat the background, which is the negative space.

Doing the upside-down, quick-viewing exercise can help you with negative space. Do it for now without seeking an explanation because I myself can't explain it fully. I just know it has helped me.

What I learned from the high-end galleries

I realized that there are three locations to appreciate an artist.

First is where everyone goes: art museums. The museums provide one or more representative works by the artists they feature. If no museum has your art yet, I would suggest that you go to art museums once in a while and maybe visualize your art being there.

Second, is where most fellow artists hate going: commercial or non-commercial galleries showing series works by individual artists. Artists apply to be represented by galleries, and most get rejected, even if their work is excellent. The rejections make artists hate galleries.

I hung out at the expensive galleries around 2007. This is a long story—worthy of a memoir (hehe). I observed that the pieces in a show have a degree of similarity and repetition. The collection is representative of a period, or a slice in time, in the life of the artist. For example, between 1900 and 1904, Pablo Picasso produced paintings that were predominantly blue. This became his famous "Blue Period."

The third location to view art is the artist's home or studio. This is the most privileged, most interesting and most humbling way, in my opinion, because the artist at work would have finished and unfinished works, drafts, drawings, rejected art, used and unused paint brushes, books, their favorite coffee mugs, alcohol, the studio itself, a dog, a cat, bills, receipts, garbage, a great conversation and everything else that add up to the visitor's experience.

This is where most of us are situated. This can make people appreciate the works of even the most unknown artist. If you're new to being an artist, you might consider receiving investors, art collectors, fellow artists, writers and others who can help you.

22: Become an Artist Now & Join #valzubiriagenda It's Never Too Late! 119
The 101st is always better than the first

Art is like writing and playing a musical instrument. You get better with practice. Don't expect the first work to be good.

If you do the same thing 100 times, the 101st will be good.

What fantasy and science fiction trading cards taught me

I've talked about trading cards earlier.

I once collected fantasy and science fiction trading cards. A set usually has 90 finely detailed, full-color cards.

Here are four lessons I learned from trading cards:

1. If the science fiction or fantasy artist can produce 90 original paintings for the set, then so can other artists
2. There has to be enough art to circulate so enough people can talk about and trade them
3. There has to be enough art to produce an acceptable art book
4. Consistency. All the cards have a certain degree of uniformity from the first card in the set to the last

What I learned from music lessons

I got a memorable tip from watching a DVD on how to play the guitar. The instructor said, if you learn a guitar technique, do two things.

First, keep practicing that technique that you've learned.

Second, devote time to learn your next new technique. It's tempting to only do the first over and over, especially when you show it to people, because you get praised and validation for it, but you have to keep learning new techniques.

What I learned from a comic book artist

I saw an interview with a famous comic book artist. He was asked why he can draw so well.

He said something which to me was very important. When he was just learning, he concentrated on each body part. He drew just hands thousands of times, before moving to another part of the body. He did the same thing with cars, buildings and others.

That was good to know, because we view an art piece as a whole.

What he said about drawing parts separately and concentrating on them before moving on to the next body part, and then cars and buildings is almost like making my doll art.

My doll art
(Note: You can see my doll art on pages 80, 84, 162, 164 & 188, & Silverio Perez' art on pages 116, 162 & 164)

I decided to get into making dolls in 2009. I finished my first acceptable doll in 2012. I already had the idea of scarcity, pricing and publishing books by this time. I thought I had to justify my pricing goals by making complicated art.

I make dolls from scratch. Each doll has 19 movable pieces made of porcelain—the head, upper torso, lower torso, and pairs of feet, lower legs, knees, upper legs, hands, forearms, upper arms and elbows. I make my own steel springs to string them together.

I start by sculpting polymer clay, then plaster molds are made, then the porcelain is produced from the molds.

The pieces go to the kiln, and heated to a glass-like stage. Porcelain shrinks by as much as 15% that of the original sculpture. Then they are strung together with steel wire.

Then I set aside the porcelain, and make the wig, costume, jewelry and shoes.

For my art, I want to include background settings, so I can incorporate precious metals and gemstones on both the dolls and the settings. I also want enamel and stained glass on the settings. I learned additional glass, metallurgy and jewelry skills for this.

So my preoccupation is pleasing the investors and art collectors. I need to justify a high price even if I didn't become famous.

Each stage is a discipline to master. I focus on my highest price, imagining that I should be able to justify it.

My art will be encased in glass, because I can imagine the collector hosting a party, and everyone gathered round checking out my work. Even a straight man would want my work, because it can attract females.

I don't play with dolls, I just made it my goal to get the proper skills to make them. The gemstones and precious metals add the need for the glass cover, so I also don't expect my collectors to play with my work.

My art is my responsibility. To traders, it's an excuse to make money. To the collectors, it's something to collect. I'm responsible for making something desirable.

I want to be in the top-notch galleries and all the neighborhood cafés, locations and people who would be proud to represent me. I want to share my potential profits, but I keep getting the vision that my art would be so worth stealing, even without fame factored in. I just have to leave my memoirs and scarcity and pricing chart with everyone, not the doll art themselves.

There was a time when Beanie Babies were so popular that people stole them, destroying trucks and stores. My sellers will just have my memoirs, book and images of my art to show. The images are online anyway.

I haven't made an art book because I want to get the orders first, make my "complete" art, and then make the books. It's a question of which comes first, the chicken or the egg, for me. I can't buy the precious metals and gemstones yet, and I need to move to a warehouse to make my art.

This is why it occurred to me to have a wait and see program, where people only pay us artists when almost everything has been reserved at the current price point or when the necessary amount to move to a warehouse, buy equipment and supplies, and hire a few assistants is reached.

I seriously find my own work fascinating. There have been times when I myself could not believe I produced it.

Returning to what I remember reading about the subconscious, mesmerizing impact of dolls, I read that you can naturally trust a symmetrical face, even if it belongs to a stranger. You also gravitate towards round, large eyes. You can easily get hypnotized by dolls and teddy bears because of their symmetrical faces.

This man said he wanted to become a famous artist

I mentioned in Chapter 19 that in 1996, I got in the local Chicago media for my AIDS Awareness artistic statement.

I had two television interviews, one radio interview, two events and was featured in at least one daily, one weekly and two monthly papers. I also actually missed two television shows, a radio show and an event. I collaborated with two nonprofit health organizations. All this resulted from one simple artistic statement.

One day, during that month of my recent public appearances, I was at the café section of a Borders Bookstore. As I sat with a cup of coffee, a slice of cake, and a few books on leadership and marketing, I was approached by someone whom I was not totally friends with. He nervously asked me if I can advise him on what to do because he wanted to pursue art *and* become a famous artist.

He said he was a respiratory therapist, who wanted to pursue art, and was seeing a psychiatrist for his depression.

He asked me if I get nervous garnering media attention and being on television.

He said he wanted to become a famous artist himself but it made him nervous just thinking about it.

I told him I just do what I feel is a step in the right direction for myself and my art, but I also pace myself to keep my sanity.

Here was someone who made a lot of money, who saw a psychiatrist to convince him to be happy as a highly paid respiratory therapist, and to forget art.

I'm advising you to pursue your art now because if you want to wait until you see me succeed before you make your move, it might be too late for you. This person, after 21 years, has stuck to his profession, which is good, too. I've obviously been slow.

Once in a while, there are two things about this incident that I wonder about:

1. What else could I have told him then
2. What I would have told him then if I knew then what I know now

I can tell you that I continue to struggle, but I'm doing what I love—art, writing, coming up with ideas, branding myself, reaching out—and reaching out to you now through this book.

Art to a lot of us is not a happy spot. Only the successful can afford to see a psychiatrist.

22: Become an Artist Now & Join #valzubiriagenda It's Never Too Late!   123

I can tell you to find, in your mind, your "normal, healthy spot." Then put art there. If you find your normal spot and see art there, and you're not happy, then accept that as your normal spot.

Pursue art now, be ready for ups and downs and a lot of internal and external pressure, and pace yourself to keep your sanity.

#valzubiriagenda might trend. Then a saturation might happen. Maybe, even an economic bubble, later. Do art now, ride the trend, make some money, save the money you make. Find yourself in a few books. Bring yourself to this point and make all this your normal, right now. I wrote this book for you so you can speed things up for yourself.

I bump into that person once in a while, even now. He seems to have gotten over his depression. We never became close.

Be confident in pursuing art and writing. I don't think I encouraged that guy enough way back. Now, I hope this book encourages you.

My two "desperate calls for help" from a yellow page ad

Yellow page ads last for a year. Around 1999-2000, I had myself listed under "Artists - Fine Art" for a year. I just wanted to assert myself, and be able to call myself an artist, at least for a year. I got a couple of art commissions, so that was good.

I had two very memorable calls.

The first one asked for advise. He said he wanted to become established as an artist and wanted to know how I was able to establish myself. I told him the honest truth: anyone can claim to be an artist and place a yellow page ad just like what I did. I said it was just an exercise in asserting myself.

The second one was bad. The guy was crying on the phone. He said he was going crazy, because he felt so much "pressure from being creative." He said he wanted to pursue art, but he was "going crazy for it." Then he asked me, how can I "handle all the pressure from being creative."

This incident rattled me that afternoon. The man's demeanor was as if he was in an emergency situation calling 911, hoping I would have an ambulance ready to pick him up.

I told him to just slow down and keep his creativity at a manageable pace. I told him to call me back if he wanted to. He never called back. His call startled me so much that I didn't know what more to tell him at that moment. I was young as well, I cannot be a good mentor then.

In retrospect, he may have really been going crazy. It occurred to me that I could have asked to take a look at his art, but he might think I had a break for him. I was living in downtown Chicago, less than a mile from the Art Institute of Chicago and its adjacent school.

Someone there would have more wherewithal to give would-be artists advice. Except that even I would not begin to bring my own art over there.

I had a crazy dominatrix for a neighbor

I once had a neighbor who was a dominatrix. She lived two doors down. I learned about it because another neighbor told me. This was more than 15 years after the call above.

One time, I was at the corridor just as a man was coming into her place. I saw what she was wearing. Yup, dominatrix. I was going to give her a break, but as soon as she closed the door, she shouted loudly at the poor, old man.

Before you get any ideas, I can let you know that my neighbor did not look like one. I'm trying to be politically correct here. Long story short, she was a dominatrix, and I didn't want any involvement with her. That other neighbor also told me that she was a little off in the mental department.

I should give her a break. She tried at being a prostitute, but it was not a successful attempt. That man whom I saw walk in to her place was the first and last time I saw anyone go in there.

One day, she knocked on my door. She introduced herself to me, and told me she heard that I was an artist. She said she was as well. Her psychiatrist had been encouraging her to apply at the Art Institute. I said that's good for her because the school is famous for producing artists.

She also proceeded to show me her right arm all wrapped in gauze, looking like a mummy. She said she had shingles, and it hurt like hell. I had chicken pox when I was 23. I dreaded the fact that I too might develop shingles in my adult life.

I had not read much about shingles, so I was thinking, it may or may not be contagious to me. At the very least, she had germs I could do without. So as I was looking at her really sad, frumpy state, I wanted to

22: Become an Artist Now & Join #valzubiriagenda It's Never Too Late!

tell her I was busy.

Then I got curious and asked her if she would like to show me her art. I followed her to her unit and went in.

I saw a couple of empty boxes of adult toys on the floor and a black strappy getup hanging on a wall. Oh my God.

She searched for her art and showed me her drawings. I'm sorry to break the bubble, but she showed me a white posterboard with stick-like drawings, mixed in with "therapy words" like "recovery," "alcohol," "overcome my challenges," "art," "Art Institute of Chicago," and a few more.

I once again had an "Oh my God" moment as she showed me that posterboard and another smaller bond paper with the same flavor of art. I asked her if she painted. She said she can paint, and she will get to it soon.

There was no way I would discourage her from pursuing art.

I told her I can give her some paint brushes. They were at my place, I just needed to look for them. I excused myself and headed out of her place. I went home and locked my door. I opened my box of paint brushes and chose 8 different sized brushes. I went back to her, knocked on her door and handed them to her. She smiled and was very thankful. I wished her the best and went back to my place.

Here is the funny part. My experiences with people seemed to lend itself to a story about me and my neighbors. Guess who would be in it? Maybe there's hope for her to become an artist.

She eventually moved. I hope she is okay.

Seriously, art is subjective. The reason an artist becomes collectible is if someone else says so and is willing to keep the art.

The crazy pair

I'm typing this section at the nearby Target store, at the tables where people can sit down and eat. I'm at the farthest table from the Starbucks counter.

By mentioning this story about the crazy couple, I'm paying tribute. There used to be a man and a woman who usually occupied two tables here at the farthest end.

They had paper, pencils and watercolors and they painted works that looked like paint drips. They pretty much had the same style.

They would splash watercolor on paper, just once or twice. Then they would stand back to study their works. The man, who seemed to be the alpha of the two, would approach and rotate the paper and stand back again. He would rotate and stand back a few times, judging which upright position provided a sense of balance and stability.

I had seen them admire the balance, look at each other, then look back at the work, and then give each other nods of approval at their art.

The man was the vocal one. The woman never spoke. All they did were random splashes, drips and lines, after which they either return to the work, add a few more randomness, stand back, admire the work, or finish the paper with a nod to each other. Then they will work on another blank sheet.

After seeing them about 10 times, because I go to Target a lot, I eventually approached them and talked to the guy.

He said they were artists. I asked to see some more, and he showed me what they had.

What I saw them make were their best work. To me, the couple and their art represented hope, love and salvation. Maybe sanity, or insanity, but no matter what, they would rather be partners in art, and never leave the other one behind.

I saw them at Target for a few months. I heard they were eventually told that they could not use the tables for their art anymore. They were messy, they were at the same location everyday, and they were not buying anything.

Once again, I'm not one to judge other people's works. Plus, let's just say we're all crazy to a degree. What they did made sense to them. To me, their works shared a pattern. They can also make a lot in a day. If they published and catalogued their works, some people will get their works.

Chapter 23

The World's Easiest Way to Produce Books!

Get someone to produce your books

Before I get into the simplest, easiest technical tidbits related to publishing books, you must know the easiest way to write.

The easiest way to write a book is to let other people write the books about yourself for you.

The easiest way to produce books is to hand the job over to people who are more skilled than you are who can definitely deliver.

With the #valzubiriagenda, the following people and establishments can be involved: artists, investors, art collectors, establishments like cafés, restaurants, offices, beauty salons, reception areas, homes, janitor's closets. Like what I always say, even janitor's closets can have art.

The art will be produced by artists, art assistants and foundries.

The writing can be done by writers, ghostwriters and co-writers.

These other key people can be involved in publishing: editors, proofreaders, photographers, book designers, desktop publishing professionals.

Remember that the lawyers can handle the legalities.

In publishing, the use of ghostwriters is an accepted practice. Ghostwriters are professional writers who don't get credited for the writing. You as your book's main source and collaborator will get full credit for writing regardless of your relative amount of contribution.

Sometimes, two authors appear on the book cover. That's a collaboration with the agreement that both authors get recognized.

I would suggest that in our case, we credit our actual writers. Having five books about yourself written by five authors sounds good. It shows other people's willing involvement with you.

I wrote my own memoirs—a total of four, plus this book, because I have always wanted to become a writer and an artist. I tell people that I'm the living contemporary artist with the most memoirs. I actually don't even bother confirming that claim. I could be wrong—I also call this book a memoir disguised as an art marketing/how to self-publish book.

If you want to have five memoirs or book-length stories about yourself, then collaborate with five writers. Tell them different eras and events in your life. Within a shorter span of time, you will come up with five books. If you give a deadline of, let's say six months each or maybe less, you will have five books six months from right now, not five books in thirty years.

If you come up with six books about yourself, you will have one-upped me. That's good. Welcome to the club. There should be a lot of us in the long run. We're supposed to be the rule, not the exception. We should all keep releasing our #valzubiriagenda books.

Just don't cut and paste Moby-Dick in a foreign language! (Oh no! Mandela Effect. Moby Dick has a dash! Research "Mandela Effect" for yourself. It's totally unrelated to this book.)

There are some fiction books where the original, long-dead author's name is credited as the writer, but the series keeps churning out new titles. This means they used one or more ghostwriters later for the series. The ghostwriter's job is to come up with stories and a style of writing that mimics the style of the original writer.

Writers have different styles of writing. If you only have one or two books, you can claim that you wrote your books. However, your readers will eventually discover that your styles of writing vary from book to book if you have six written by ghostwriters.

You would be better off telling everyone who the co-authors are. Your co-authors need your books anyway, as proof of their writing skills.

23: The World's Easiest Way to Produce Books!   129
Dispelling assumptions that might hold you back

If you are the source of the story, you are a co-writer or co-author, even if you only wrote on index cards and someone else took over.

You are a co-author even if you only dictated to a voice recorder.

You are a co-author even if all you did was clarify specific details over the phone so that your co-author can continue to write and finish the book.

Make sure that when you deal with writers, if you don't feel comfortable with no written agreement, that everyone sign one.

Memoirs are just stories

I simultaneously released three memoirs in 2014: **Wonder, Hocus Pocus Lately** and **1-Hour Mentors.** I proudly posted them on Facebook.

A schoolmate from grade school and high school asked me why I wrote memoirs at a young age. He obviously does not read a lot.

I told him memoirs are stories. You can write a story that happened yesterday. There's no need to get old. A child can write a memoir about earlier childhood. Memoirs can have light-hearted, even stupid, stories.

A biography is an account of someone's life written by someone else. An autobiography is an account of the writer's own life.

A biography or an autobiography pays attention to the chronology of the writer's entire life while a memoir can just cover one specific aspect of the writer's life.

Look up Augusten Burroughs online. His first memoir, **Running with Scissors** was released when he was around 37 years old.

What I learned from a widow of a famous sports player

Close to 30 years ago, I went to a party where this platinum blonde lady in her 70s was socializing and showing off her writing partner.

She was the widow of a former Chicago Cubs player. She was very gregarious and proudly telling everyone that her tentative title for a memoir as a wife of a now-deceased Chicago Cubs player was, "Why Not?"

She explained that she wanted to write about how it was being a wife of a sports guy. People, she said, had been asking her why she would write such a book, and her answer was, "Why not?"

Because "why not" had been her constant answer, they had tentatively titled their book, "Why Not?"

This was a long time ago. I wonder now if she ever got the book published, and if her final title really was "Why Not?"

Here is another lesson we could learn from this lady.

She complained that the Cubs should have a section for retired players and the widows of the deceased ones.

When she mentioned this to me, her eyes changed to a wincing stare, a combination of hurt, anger and seriousness.

That was a motivation for her writing a book.

If she succeeded in getting her book published and read by Cubs fans and the team's management, she might get the special section and free entrance she wanted for retired players and widows.

The word to use is "relevance." She can get the break because her book made herself resurface and relevant to the present time.

Some celebrities do bad things to get themselves in the news, so people would talk about them. This is an attempt at relevance.

Our books can make us relevant to our present time. It will at least make us relevant to our #valzubiriagenda community.

What I learned from Paris Hilton

I was attending the annual publishers convention. I can't remember the year right now, but supposedly Paris Hilton came out with 3 or 4 publications. I'm using the word "publication," because I don't think all of them were written-through books. I think one or two were like organizers for teenage girls, which just had her name on them.

I was in line for an author signing his book and someone behind me complained about why he could not get himself published while Paris Hilton had many books, and she probably didn't even write any of them.

I laughed, because that was a comment of someone new to the business of publishing. The public buys recognizable products. Paris Hilton's name was recognizable. She was making the most of her fame by having her name attached to products, including books.

23: The World's Easiest Way to Produce Books! 131
What I learned from the Soprano Cookbook

When the television show **The Sopranos** was popular, a recipe book came out: **The Sopranos Family Cookbook: As Compiled by Artie Bucco.** I was once again at the annual publishers convention, and I passed by a booth that was promoting it.

Artie Bucco was the fictional character who was co-owner and head chef of the show's restaurant. The actor who played him was John Ventimiglia. It was funny when Mr. Ventimiglia was at the booth promoting the book and posing with people including myself. He was dressed like a chef, pretending to be Artie Bucco.

He gave away the books to us convention attendees for the time he was there, and he even signed the books. The booth was also taking Polaroid pictures of him with attendees, so I got one.

Months later, I saw stacks of the book in bookstores.

I'm just showing you that the publishing industry is flexible and creative. Their goal is to make money. Our goal is to make money!

What you can learn from politicians

You may have seen books authored by politicians. Not all those books were 100% written by them. They had help. You might think that it was the editors who corrected their spelling, grammar, sentences, etc.

Imagine yourself as a politician. You're already busy as it is. When you get a publishing deal, you're not just pressured to produce a book. The publisher is hoping that the book will sell. Just because you're a politician does not mean you are a good writer.

Imagine a book with two names—the well-known politician and an unknown writer. Imagine a book with one name, that of the politician.

Politicians are concerned about their public image. If two politicians came out with their books, the one which only mentions a politician's name as the author sounds better than the book that includes a politician and a co-author.

I saw one book by a politician, pockmarked with footnotes, it was as if the politician lived for footnotes. As I leafed through the book, I saw him use 'Toto, I've a feeling we're not in Kansas anymore," just as an expression and even that had a footnote, not to refer to the author, but to Dorothy, as if the Wizard of Oz fictional character were a real person.

The traditional publishers will probably allow just one book per politician per year. We are different because we're entertaining six books in six months, so just credit your writers.

Barter!

Prepare to barter! If you're an artist, then barter your art for other talents. Make sure that the exchange is fair. I won't tell you what is fair and what is not. A lot of factors will be in place.

If you are an artist, and you make fast art, and your name is still unknown, then you might have to barter more art pieces for a writer and the other publishing professionals to collaborate with you.

Have a crowd of talents around you

Here is something you might like to consider. Surround yourself with plenty of talents. If you have a crowd of willing collaborators, then everyone can make better decisions on collaborating.

Know when to move along

If you realize that no one wants to collaborate with you, then learn to do things yourself.

You might be introducing yourself to people too soon.

You might have no proof of what it is that you are claiming. If that's the case, produce a sample.

I have met people who claim that as long as they know the general idea, and that they have seen it done by someone else, they can tackle the job at hand. If you said something similar to this at a meeting, congratulations.

Try looking into the technicals in the next chapter.

IF YOU CAN'T JOIN THEM, *BEAT THEM!*

Chapter 24

Easy Technical Knowledge To Help Make You Stop Flinching

This chapter only has general information

I'm just giving you some generalized information that you will eventually get used to. This is not a checklist. These are elements you can ask each other about when you meet to collaborate.

I just want you to get a general understanding of what goes on.

This is for us who have less technical knowledge, just so we all know what to watch out for.

The biggest misconception most people have

People think that just because e-books are cheaper than printed books, they are easier to produce! E-books are harder to produce!

I mentioned this in Chapter 5 page 38—I believe you are now ready for a few more details.

E-books have different formats for different e-readers. The most popular ones are: pdf, mobi, epub, doc and txt. At the very least, you would want your text in pdf, mobi and epub.

The mobi is preferred by Amazon.com's Kindle brand reader, and the epub is used by most other e-readers.

The pdf can be opened by almost all computer systems and readers.

Doc files give you an idea that it most probably is a Microsoft Word document file or a compatible file.

Txt gives you the idea that it is a simpler text file.

Rtf stands for "rich text format," which is similar to a doc file, but we don't need to learn about this one for our purposes for now.

What all these different formats for e-readers means is that you must come up with different file formats for e-books. These formats do not convert with the press of one button and one software.

You must remember that competing machines tend to discourage one another from being compatible with each other. I would not use the word "sabotage," but you might like to use that word.

The two files required for printed books

Here now are the requirements for a printed book:

Only two pdf files are needed. One is for the cover and the other one is for the interior.

The cover only needs one pdf file. The full-spread design includes the back cover on the left, the spine in the middle, and the front cover on the right. You should have everything *designed* as one single sheet, if you want to have a good-looking cover. The letters on the spine should be positioned so that the top of the letters are closest to or pointing towards the cover design.

If your language reads from right to left, then your front cover will be on the left side and your back cover will be on the right side. Once again, the top of the letters on the spine should be closest to the cover, not the back cover.

Spread out a book and look at how the spine is positioned.

Your interior only needs one single pdf file. You need to watch out that the odd pages are on the right side, if you read from left to right, or on the left side, if your book is in a language that reads from right to left. As you look at this current page and the next page, you are looking at what's called "facing pages"—pages 134 and 135. Each new chapter starts on the right.

You also need to watch out for the spine. The spine is the middle area of the cover that is visible when you stack your books with other books on a shelf. Make sure that the spine is not upside-down.

I've been attending publishers conventions with millions of new books, and I always spot a book with an upside-down spine. Don't spend so much time writing and publishing only to have the most visible mistake a finished book can have.

24: Easy Technical Knowledge To Help Make You Stop Flinching

You don't need to print 1,000 books

I've been approached by writers who want to get published, who only want to produce the electronic version and not the printed version of their books.

Their main misconception is that they think they will need to spend thousands of dollars to get a first print run for physically printed books. Once again, we now have POD or "print on demand." The online printers only print one copy if only one copy is ordered. Then they ship that copy to the customer.

If you manage your own files, you can also order 1, 10, 200 or more copies of your own books at a much lower wholesale price. In a few days, you will receive a box or two of your books.

Your wholesale price could be $3 dollars while your retail price might be $20. The wholesale price is based on your book's total number of pages, while your retail price is the value of your choosing.

Programming e-books

The next misconception is that just because the e-book versions retail cheaper, they are easier to program. This is wrong. As I have explained earlier, the two pdf files for printed books are easier to produce, while the e-book versions need to be formatted using various software. Most of the software are free, but each one has a learning curve, and I will detail this later.

Learn so you don't get fooled!

You may have seen ads that ask you if you want to become a published author. These companies will charge for their services which include editing, book design, photography, image editing, and printing of the actual books. They might say that you will receive 500 or more printed copies. You don't need to have 500 copies of your book. Green is in. Nowadays, you can publish your own books and order just one copy for $10.

Files you should become aware of

Here is what I suggest for you to do:

Produce the two pdf files for your printed copies. Then produce three e-book versions:

1. One pdf file which includes the cover, the back cover and the interior pages
2. One mobi for the Kindle readers
3. One epub for the other readers

The first is the easiest to produce. Using the software you have been using to design your cover and interior, duplicate both the cover and the interior, so you don't mess up the originals. Copy and paste the interior onto the cover file and export it as a single pdf.

All you need is to make a single pdf file that includes the designs you have for your front and back covers and the interior pages.

There are free software programs that you can use to make your e-books. You will need to go back and forth between the programs to make e-books.

I personally got faster with practice. I will talk about the programs, Sigil, Calibre, and others later on Chapters 24 and 42, just with enough surface information so you can understand what your more skilled collaborators are talking about, and to remind you to look into the software yourself.

You still need your physical book, because we are entertaining meetings and leaving our books and our art at locations so that the vendors can show to their customers.

You do not need a fancy camera

The next thing all of us should know: New models of digital cameras are okay to use now!

You don't even need an SLR camera. You can use a digital camera at its highest resolution. If you do have an SLR camera, then use that.

Before I go further, you should not trust your cellphone nor smartphone cameras to photograph pictures for publication, even at its highest resolution.

When it comes to taking photographs of art pieces, especially if you're relinquishing or delivering the art piece, you should think 10 steps ahead. Don't pretend like you know what you're doing, only to find out later that there's a problem, like your hand moved. You cannot produce a book with blurry pictures and apologies in the captions.

Book printers only need 300 dpi ("dots per inch") colored and gray-

24: Easy Technical Knowledge To Help Make You Stop Flinching

scale black and white images for printed books. Digital cameras nowadays can actually produce more than this. The pdf file you will submit and manage for printed books will have images that have been converted down to 300 dpi—only do this at the last stage. While still editing your book and images in the book, maintain the highest resolutions.

The e-books on the other hand, can use smaller-sized files, but technology and requirements keep changing. We can now read pdf files on our big-screen televisions. This means that you need to read the latest on specifications.

E-book images tend to be a compromise between how clear you want your images to be and how much your e-book's file size should be.

Don't worry about asking a professional photographer with a studio, high-end cameras and an expensive lighting setup to take photographs of your works, if you cannot afford it. Remember that if you have 200 works, you might have to pay a lot for money to get them all photographed.

Save money, then get the best brand new digital camera you can afford. Set the camera to the highest resolution it can take. Turn off the date and time display setting. Turn off the flash.

Then set it on a tripod and use a 2-second delay. Make sure you know how to focus—you usually have a soft press for focusing and then a hard press for the actual picture-taking.

The camera on a tripod, plus the 2-second delay will steady the picture. If you have 200+ art pieces to take pictures of, you would not want to use a 10-second delay.

Here is why you should use a 2-second delay. If you are taking 200 photographs, your hands will eventually tire. You will produce blurry photographs.

Make sure that you set the camera at its highest resolution. Then make sure that you also set the camera / tripod as close to the art piece as possible. Don't take a picture of the art piece together with the rest of the living room.

The one thing you should become aware of is lighting.

I worked with someone who came back with 200-plus photographs for me to convert into a book. All of them had the shadow of a round head. I cannot correct that with software. I had to reshoot all of the paintings.

Don't complicate later procedures because of earlier mistakes.

Make sure to have more than one light source. Do your best to evenly light the art piece indirectly. Don't point any light source directly on a flat painting, because the light will become uneven and it might produce a glare. Point them away if possible.

There is a term called "photoediting," when you retouch image files with your computer to bring the colors out.

Take darker pictures. I personally avoid well-lit images. Darker images tend to have more information that cooperates well with photoediting software. Don't use bright lighting when taking photographs because the brighter colors would be harder to improve later.

You must also beware of the color yellow in your artwork. Yellow tends to be the most difficult color to capture.

The images you see on your computer screen is usually not what you will see in your printed book, especially since this might be your first attempt at publishing a book. We don't have an art department like the big publishers.

I just helped someone with his memoir, which contained a lot of black and white images from three types of originals: full-color visual art, black and white childhood pictures and later, colored pictures. He got them from different sources, including the internet—he worked with theatre groups.

I gave instructions and explained the reasons why I needed high-resolution originals, but at the end of the day, I still ended up having to work with some low-resolution pictures.

I had to retouch the pictures three times. We got proofs from the printer each time, so I could better tweak the images.

Remember that you don't become an expert overnight, but you start somewhere, and you'll get used to all this. My best suggestion is practice by helping others, if you still don't have your own books to work on.

First and foremost: Do this!

After taking the digital pictures, you will end up with the original files. Upload the files to your computer. You will have a folder with the original files. Duplicate the original folder.

Retouch and photoedit the second folder. Leave the original folder untouched.

You can also maintain an extra external hard drive for the original files, and set this aside.

You're working on a book, not a single-page document. If you have lost single-page documents in the past, imagine the dread you will feel losing multiple files.

Respect collaboration

Remember that the finished product is the book. If you want attitude, put it in the book. Don't take it out on your collaborators.

If your group is producing a book with several artists, investors or art collectors, you should always think ahead to make sure your part of the book has crisp images. If you submit your images and they are blurry and your head's shadow is on your work, your collaborators can opt to take your art out. It's not about you, it's about coming out with a good book.

Remember permissions and apologies. You already have the permission to join, anticipate the apologies.

You know the saying, misery loves company. Not only that, misery is contagious.

Additional reasons why you need high-resolution images

The high-resolution images are not just for your books and e-books.

They are for posterity. You should save high-resolution images for the future. Buy an external hard drive, store all of your images and files on a per book, per project basis, and store the hard drive in a safe place.

As I have said, the large screen televisions need high-resolution images. Technology keeps getting better. This means that your current e-book versions may need to be redone in the future.

You must anticipate possible occasions. If you are collaborating, you're not alone anymore.

You might find yourself being promoted at a venue. You might need some huge banners and large signs.

You might also end up making presentations using a projector.

These will need high-resolution images that are obviously larger than what you used for the books and e-books.

You might issue a press release of your book. You will need to make a press kit, which is a folder that includes the press release, your images—including printed copies of your head shot, body shot, your book's front cover and your art. *And*, to help blogs and other internet websites, a flash drive with all the printed out text and images in digital form.

The resolution of the images you provide should be large enough. The flash drive can have three different sizes of your images in separate folders.

Somebody invented the word "photoediting"

What photoediting software can do…

The pictures you take of your paintings, for example, might be a little tilted or skewed. You can correct this using photoediting software.

For example, let's say you took a picture of a painting that has a horizontal measurement of 10" and a vertical length of 15". You would expect that the top and bottom of the work will both be 10", but since your camera was at an angle, the top had become shorter than the bottom.

This is when photoediting comes in. You can drag corners to make the edges perfectly perpendicular and correctly proportioned.

The most widely used photoediting software is Photoshop, made by Adobe. I suggest that you watch YouTube tutorials. There will only be a handful of functions you will use the most, so just enjoy those complex tutorials and take notes of some commands you might end up using.

You must know the importance of great images. I can't imagine how some of us will produce and even show off books with really bad, unprofessional pictures—I'm sure someone will. Please help them if you can.

You should know these three fractions: 4/0, 1/1 and 4/4

These are printer terms, "4 over zero," "1 over 1," and "4 over 4."

Paper has two sides. There are 4 basic inks for printing: cyan (blue), magenta (pinkish red), yellow and black. The abbreviation for this is CMYK.

You may have heard of RGB. Your computer and cellphone screens use RGB. Each microscopic square uses red, green and blue in various proportions to create color.

24: Easy Technical Knowledge To Help Make You Stop Flinching

4/0 is usually for the cover. This means that one side will use the 4 inks, and the other side will require no printing.

1/1 means that both sides will use one ink each, usually black. This is for the interior of black and white books.

Sometimes, a company will require additional colors. For example, we all know that Coca-Cola uses an exact shade of red. If Coca-Cola produces a book, the cover might need the exact red ink. In this case, they might require 5/0 for the cover. Some print jobs might also want silver or gold ink in addition to the initial 4-color printing.

The interior of a book with black and white ink and grayscale images is 1/1. The cover will be 4/0.

Your full-color art books will need a 4/0 cover and a 4/4 interior. This will be more costly, and your customers will have to pay the higher price for your art books.

The e-readers are glorified webpage viewers

I won't detail all of the differences between them. I just want to give you a couple of ideas on why e-book files can become incompatible.

The Kindle, which is Amazon.com's own brand of e-readers, recognizes mobi files, but not epub files.

Other readers will recognize epub files. However, Amazon has an app so mobi files can also open in non-Kindle readers.

Most readers can open files with the pdf tag.

You cannot rename your epub files into mobi files, and vice versa, just to make a reader open your file.

A single file named mobi or epub is actually a bunched up set of web files and images. The images are in folders that are named differently for epub and mobi readers..

Understanding a little of the software needed

I highly suggest that you use Adobe InDesign to compile, design and finalize both the cover and the interior.

Go to YouTube to become familiar with InDesign and Photoshop.

Then make the duplicate copy that will have the combined cover and interior for your pdf e-reader version. Kindle and other e-readers can display pdf files.

Then you need to start working on the epub and mobi versions.

There is a command to export your InDesign file to epub. The epub file you will get might not be a perfect epub file. You will need to edit it using Sigil, which is a free software from Google.

Once you are happy with the epub file from Sigil, you will need to use another free software, called Calibre.

Calibre will convert the epub file to mobi. Once again, there are no guarantees that the files are perfect.

This is just one way to make e-books. There are other software.

You may have to borrow some e-readers to check your files as you go along. You can also install "simulators" in your computer—simulators "pretend" to be smartphones so you can check your work. As you can see, this is an inexact science.

You'll see some incompatibilities that will need to be corrected. This is why I encourage you to finish your printed book version's pdf files first. These other formats will take more time. It's all trial and error.

Become aware of this term: "embedding fonts"

When you make a pdf file for publication or when you make different e-book formats, you will need to make sure that other devices also see your books the way you originally designed and saw your books.

Our computers have many font styles, but other computers may not have what we have. For example if your book has letters that look like stenciled letters on crate boxes, other computers and readers may not have this.

If your print on demand company does not have your fonts, the design in your book will be degraded to whatever generic font they have. The same will happen with e-readers.

This means that you have to "embed" your fonts, or include your font file, into the pdf file itself. Epub and mobi files also require including the fonts that you used.

There are copyright laws on using fonts for books and e-readers. You need to research on copyright permissions for your fonts. You want your book to look as nice as possible, and this means that you should not just use the simplest, most generic fonts.

InDesign is able to embed fonts. Look for instructions online.

24: Easy Technical Knowledge To Help Make You Stop Flinching 143

I would suggest that you only use fonts that are free for commercial use. Make sure that all the glyphs you need are included. Chapter 40 mentions glyphs. Glyphs are special characters and symbols that the font designers sometimes don't bother to design.

Making your books look more professional

There are two types of images that you can use—photographs and line images. Look at a professional book. The photographs should have crisp resolution. This means that you should not have a picture that is blurry or pixelated if that is not your intention.

Look at the letters or titles. The letters should be crisp as well. If your letters aren't crisp and blend in with the rest of the background, like a blurry photograph, then you made a mistake.

Do not use Photoshop on your letters. Use Photoshop only for photographs. Use a different software called Adobe Illustrator for your titles and line drawings.

InDesign will accept both Photoshop and Illustrator files.

You need to make sure that the letters on the cover are much more crisp than the photographs you used for the background. Especially the main title and the subtitle. Even after putting in a lot of effort writing, you still have to remember that people still judge a book by its cover.

I will mention Adobe Photoshop and Adobe Illustrator again in Chapter 40 just so you remember.

By the way, I deliberately designed three of my memoirs to have an '80s indie publisher look. I wanted to hide in plain sight, because I was not ready to promote them in 2014. I plan to redesign my books once I finish writing a few more memoirs I'm still developing.

What I expect from a professional book

Outside: Price, category for bookstore shelving, ISBN number, barcode.

The usual: Title, subtitle, author's name, about the book (back cover) and about the author (back of the book).

Inside: Table of contents (if needed), title of the book or chapter (on top of the regular pages), author of the book (on top of the regular pages), page numbers on almost all the pages, chapter numbers, copyright page, preface, dedication, acknowledgments, introduction, etc.

Go to a bookstore, or open a book from your shelf. Find one you like and use it as a guide. Chapter 40 lists the parts of a book and what are called "running heads."

ISBNs and LCCNs

I'm most familiar with the United States, other countries might have a different systems.

There are free barcode generators online which require two numbers: the price of the book and the ISBN number, also known as the International Standard Book Number.

The print on demand company you choose will usually be able to provide a pair of free ISBN numbers. One has 10 digits and another has 13. The 13-digit ISBN is usually needed to generate the barcode.

Here is one *very* important pointer: On top of the bar code are two areas for numbers. The area on the left will show the ISBN.

The space allotted for the price of the book is on the right. If you don't have a price there, your brand new book will have a number that is used for the bargain section in the bookstores.

If you entered your price in the barcode generator, for example, $17.95, the barcode will have "1795" included. If you forgot to enter the price, the barcode will have "9000." If you go to the bargain section of the bookstores, you will see that same number.

This hints at being in the bargain section. Do not look like a bargain bin book, after all the work you did. You want your book to be as professional as possible. Always decide on the retail price, stick to it, and make sure the barcode shows it because people notice these things.

Our books are like the dogs in a dog show. The show is not really a show as much as it is a competition and a way for the judges to see if the dog is a perfect breed and can reproduce fine offspring.

On the inside, the copyright page must repeat the ISBN numbers. I'm not sure about other countries, but in the United States, you will want to have the 10-digit and 13-digit ISBN numbers. Both of them are unique to your book.

Besides this, once again, in the United States, you should also have what is called the LCCN number, or the Library of Congress Catalog Number. It is also unique to your book. Research on the Library of Congress and how to get your LCCN if you are in the United States. You will

24: Easy Technical Knowledge To Help Make You Stop Flinching

also need to place the LCCN on the copyright page.

The Library of Congress will only give you the LCCN if you provide them with the 13-digit ISBN. They will also ask for the 10-digit code in the form, if you have it.

If you go online, look for "copyright page template." There are many sites that will give you examples of what you should place in the copyright page, including what information you should provide for librarians and the Library of Congress.

Here is also something beginners don't know much about

When your readers read your book, they usually hold it with one hand, at the bottom of the book, while the other hand turns the pages at the top corner. There is something subconscious about this activity.

You need to have more empty space at the bottom of the page than you have at the top. This makes it easy for the hand to hold the book at the bottom. Even if your book design has a lot of space, the subconscious still expects more unused blank space at the bottom.

What's the minimum word count for a memoir?

I tell people 55,000 words should be the minimum for a memoir. You might be able to cheat with less, if you add pages with just pictures.

The expected font size for a 6" (width) x 9" (length) book is between 11 and 12 points. Typewriters tend to use 10 points, so you can imagine that the sizes of letters for books are just a little bigger.

This book is using 11.3 pt, not 12. If you want to know how thick a 55,000-word book is, feel the book from the cover to page 174.

Go to page 193. There is an explanation about this book's 55,000 words being on page 174 or 240.

What are serif and sans serif fonts?

Some families of letters are designed with extra decorative flourishes on the ends of the strokes. Those are called "serifs." "Sans" means "without." This sentence you are reading is a serif font. The subheadings are sans serif.

Our subconscious gets excited as soon as it sees a variety of font styles on a single page. Use three or more styles on a page, just like what I've done to this book.

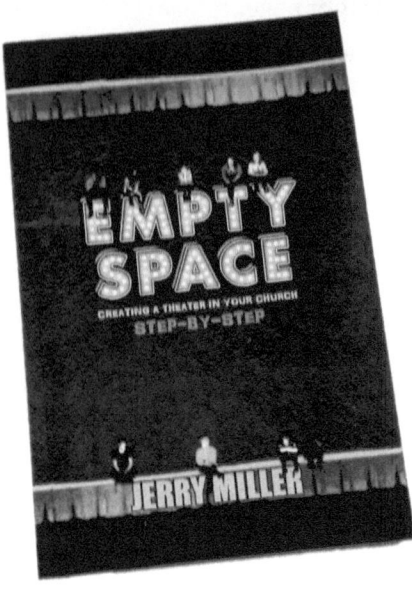
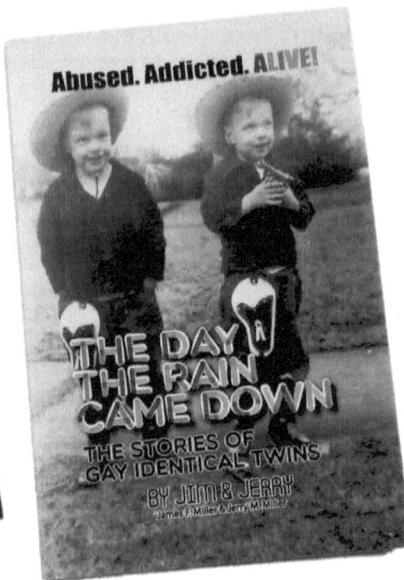

**From Chapter 33 pages 191 -192
& Chapter 37 pages 218-219**

Jerry Miller's first book is **Empty Space: Creating a Theatre in Your Church Step-by-Step,** which was released just before he turned 70 years old.

Once you prove to yourself that you can write a book, you will write another.

Jerry collaborated with his twin brother, James, for the next book, **The Day the Rain Came Down, The stories of gay identical twins** in 2017, at age 72.

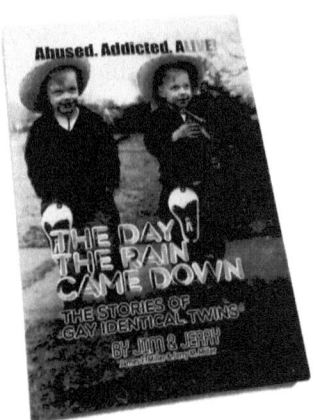

You need to inspect a tentative copy of your book (a proof) before you release it to the world. The smaller copy of the second book was the first cover version. I had to lighten the cover picture because the proof was too dark. I also added a shadow to the title.

Jerry is also an actor, director and producer. He has done book signings for both his first and second books.

Next image is on page 152

Chapter 25

Book Production Preliminary Basic Knowledge

The stages of book production

I want you to keep calm and just know the 5 points below as a matter of fact.

Before you start writing, become aware that writing is only part of the equation.

You will need to do 5 things for your book:

1. Outline the book
2. Write the book
3. Edit the book
4. Design the book
5. Promote the book

I'm giving this list of 5 its own chapter because this looks simplified, but it is everything to us. Everything we do related to self-publishing boils down to the five above.

#5 is a little more abstract for us doing the #valzubiriagenda. We don't need to churn out bestsellers. We want our books out there 300 to 3,000 years from now. We can relax our book sales and promotion a little.

If you go back to Chapter 2, my suggestion is for all of us to have books of the artists, investors, art collectors and all the other sellers and resellers that we represent in our stores, venues and wherever we might be. This can fall under promotion.

I'm also giving this chapter special attention because below is exactly what I use for myself everyday and every moment I start slowing down or slacking. They are the exact sentences I use on myself to get up and work on my projects. If all else fails, I use this.

How to use the 5 stages to get you motivated

If you were God, then you don't need to do this. I'm assuming you're not, so here's an activity you can do to keep yourself motivated.

When you're feeling you're not at your best, and you feel slow, you need to brighten up and motivate yourself to keep working.

Tell yourself the following for each stage you are in:

"Come on! Get up! Wake up! Get some coffee! That book is not going to **outline** itself!"

"Come on! Get up! Wake up! Get some coffee! That book is not going to **write** itself!"

"Come on! Get up! Wake up! Get some coffee! That book is not going to **edit** itself!"

"Come on! Get up! Wake up! Get some coffee! That book is not going to **design** itself!"

"Come on! Get up! Wake up! Get some coffee! That book is not going to **promote** itself!"

Saying these lines over and over in my head, like a mantra, always works for me!

Chapter 26

My Encounters with a Very Famous Author

I want to show you a real example of a famous, bestselling author of many books.

I'm making this a special section so you would know this is for real.

I would not mention who this man is.

I gave him a chapter in one of my memoirs, **1-Hour Mentors,** the book about my time as a masseur.

When Borders Bookstore was still open in Chicago, his books occupied a shelf tier. This is how prolific he was, and still is.

It was because of him that I figured, for myself, and eventually for you too, right now, that I should ambition to write enough memoirs to fill up a tier of a bookstore shelf. This "funny" statement just might happen!

This man used to come to Chicago for many days. Maybe he still does. I stopped running my yellow page massage ads in 2006 when I finally finished my first attempt to write a full-length memoir, another long story.

In his hotel room, he only had his laptop, and it was always turned on. It was usually next to his bed.

I never brought a massage table when I went to my clients. The reason for this, which I tell everyone, was that lugging a massage table tired my hands even before I began a massage session. I also used to say that a table was too conspicuous in the hotel lobbies.

It gave the hotel security the signal that I was not a paying hotel guest. I told my massage clients that hotel security tended to stop people with massage tables.

The guests would have to either come down to pick me up, or they would get a call so that they can vouch for me to go up to their rooms.

Something else too: the hotels want their guests to use their expensive spas, so they gave outside masseurs and masseuses complicated delaying tactics.

I did my massage using hotel towels placed on the hotel bed. I simply positioned myself on the hotel bed next to my clients, and moved about to different parts of the bed as needed.

This writer wrote on his laptop, which I obviously saw. The screen would be fixed, and I dared not disturb the massage by scrolling through his work.

His laptop was always right next to me, as he lay face down on his bed. He had me visit him as often as three times within 10 days.

This famous, bestselling writer did not write perfectly on the draft. I saw mistakes in spelling and sentence construction. He did not bother with the correct punctuation.

Basically, all this would be changed in the editing. Whatever I read was not funny, so I guess even the funny parts are added in the edit. His books are funny and entertaining.

I just feel so privileged and lucky to see the unedited work of this man. It gave me permission that I can also be bad in my drafts. I'm assuring you right now, that your writing and draft are going to be just fine. Keep on typing.

Here is another insight I got from him

On television, I once saw an interview with Isaac Asimov. Behind him was an entire wall of shelves fully stacked with books. Mr. Asimov said that this room, with the wall of shelves, was where he wrote.

This client of mine stayed in a hotel. There were no books at all. Just himself and his laptop.

I guess the way to write for him was to get out of his hometown, wherever that was, head to Chicago, shut in, and only be with his laptop.

If you have never written something that would be equivalent to

26: My Encounters with a Very Famous Author

a full-length book, just begin to do it wherever you are. The author I mention here can afford to pay for a hotel. Maybe he had some public appearances in my beloved city, and the stay was sponsored.

I did not bother to ask him for writing tips. I was just a masseur then, with future plans to write. Picking his brains then would have been too early. There is a difference between planning to write and actually doing it.

Back then, I was just thankful that God allowed me to look at a famous, prolific writer's laptop many times over, as if it was God turning the sample pages, showing me how an unedited, simple draft can bring endless possibilities.

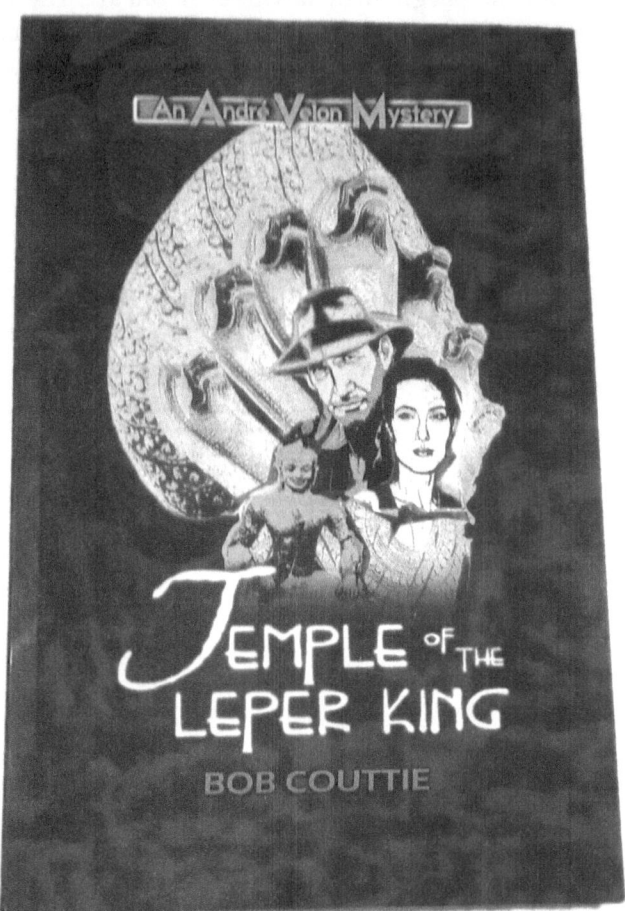

From Chapter 40 page 246

This is Bob Couttie's book, **Temple of the Leper King.** (Amazon.com)

I co-edited and designed this book. He currently resides in Cambodia.

We collaborated by sharing files on Google Drive. He signed up for it, and gave me permission to come in the private folder for his manuscript and some of the images used. We used Messenger for communication.

Once in a while, I left files of his script and the front and back cover design in the folder so he can further edit and revise them.

The cover illustration uses a combination of my hand drawings and copyright-free images. I used both Adobe Photoshop and Illustrator. The text is also in Illustrator.

Next image is on page 162

Chapter 27

Internal Conflict
Preparing Your Mind to Write

Once again, I'm reminding you of your "mission" should you choose accept it. You might not be a writer yet. I am encouraging you to write a book-length memoir. If you feel you can produce a biography, which might need more accomplishments, and accurate dates, then do so. You might also be able to produce a collection of essays, or your own artistic manifesto.

The important part is that it has to hint at something about you, even by a small percentage. In our case, we should flavor it with art.

Three negative emotions

As you write, watch out for three states of mind. You will get:

1. Cranky. When you become irritable to people around you, that's crankiness
2. Irritable. When someone does something and you easily get irritated
3. Depressed. When you feel bad within yourself for a longer period of time, that's depression

Just so you know—these are normal behaviors, even for famous, veteran writers.

If these three happen to you because you're a new writer, then the reason you feel these is because you're "attempting" to write.

You are self-publishing. You already know that whatever you produce will get published.

Traditional authors who made attempts to get published in the past went through bad emotions *and* still get rejections, so feel better because you're better off.

These feelings also happen to veteran writers. The difference is, they have proven to themselves that these feelings are temporary.

Writing memoirs is especially depressing because you will discover that your most poignant, traumatic experiences can produce the best stories.

The way to not get too depressed is by focusing on your readers, not yourself. Remind yourself this: You write memoirs and other essays to teach lessons in life to people you don't know, the public.

With memoirs and biographies, the stories are based on your life experiences. People get to know you, but they get entertained and keep going because they discover lessons in life they could use.

It's a bait and switch only better

Bait and switch has a bad connotation. It is the bad practice of tricking or convincing someone into buying something with the intention of giving a more inferior item or service, or eventually convincing that person to get something else, usually something more expensive.

With writing memoirs, you can bait someone into thinking they are reading about you, but they are seeing bits of information and lessons that they can apply to themselves.

If you disagree with me, you might be right. We all have different ways of seeing things.

If you're just starting and this is your first book, try my way for your first few chapters. See if you get less cranky, irritable and depressed with my approach and mindset, where you focus more on the lesson to be learned and less on yourself.

I'm not even worried about your skill. I'm just worried about your disposition.

Fables, fairy tales and your memoir

Fables are defined as stories, usually short, typically with animals as characters, conveying a moral. Do you remember reading Aesop's fables?

Fairy tales are longer stories intended for children about magical

27: Internal Conflict Preparing Your Mind to Write

and imaginary beings and lands. The lessons to be learned are there, except that you almost miss them because your attention is in the story.

Pretend that your memoirs are the adult versions of fairy tales and fables.

So you bait them into thinking that they are reading about you. Once they are involved, you tell them a lesson to be learned.

Know the "why" or the "salvation"

Sometimes, you get cranky because you know you want to tell the story, but you can't figure out why.

For example, you know you want to tell how you pushed your friend into a muddy canal. That was mean.

Find out your why. You can mention that you remember this story because it started a very long friendship. This becomes the moment when your reader would say, "Oh, now I get it!" This is the why. There's salvation. There's the bait and switch.

You must know that reading is for the conscious and subconscious.

Those writers who keep telling stories that do not appease the subconscious with the "why" or the "salvation," their reader's subconscious minds will get irritated. Those readers won't be able to pinpoint exactly why those writers' books are irritating and dissatisfying. Those readers' subconscious mind will tell their conscious minds to stop reading.

Why you're still cranky and irritable

Your writing skills might be the reason. The challenge is putting on paper what you feel and are thinking in your head.

Remember that writing is a string of words. It's very linear. There's a beginning and an end. Everything is continuous. Your challenge is to get your mind into thinking in a linear way, so you can put your thoughts onto the paper, using a string of letters, words, sentences, paragraphs and chapters.

Leave the World's Greatest Novel for another writer

I would once again remind you what I learned from my publisher / editor, when I worked at a monthly free paper:

1. Your published product is not a term paper
2. Publishing is like giving birth

You write term papers to make the grade. You're memoir is not a school project. When you put your book out there, no teacher will grade it. You're not ambitioning to get an A, so treat it a little less seriously and more lightly.

Because this is your first attempt, treat it as an exercise. Forget those people who will rate it with stars. Just do it.

Writing a book is project-oriented. It's like getting pregnant for 9 months. You get into a routine for 9 months. Then you suddenly give birth to your book and your routine. You feel accomplished. You also feel that the entire process is over, just when you have started to get used to it.

This is like postpartum depression or PPD. You will prove this to be true later on. Just know that once you've done it once, you can do it again. You can always give birth to another book.

You might get into the mindset that you want your work to become the next, greatest American Novel. You're adding pressure for nothing.

That's like an pregnant woman expecting to give birth to a good-looking baby. Mothers do not reject ugly babies. They should. Kidding.

Know that there are as many as 1,000,000 titles of books being published just in the United States alone, right now, every year. You're adding your work to it. Just write.

Your brain as a whole pie (chart)

When you write, you think. Sometimes, you think too much. You immerse yourself into so much emotion, grief and traumatic past experiences, which you feel you should write.

I would suggest that you see your brain as a pie chart. Don't let everything mix. Put in a time when you will write objectively about the trauma of what happened to you without you feeling too much about it. Tackle your feelings later.

Allocate a time when you write about your life in a more objective or scientific way. Be emotional later. Like a pie chart, have demarcations so when you write, you get more into the technical side of writing.

27: Internal Conflict Preparing Your Mind to Write

We are self-publishers

There is one good thing about self-publishing. We can keep writing knowing that we have already been accepted for publication.

Most traditional published authors went through rejections before getting accepted and published. They easily get their book deals later, only because they had already previously proven their sales and talent and there is name recognition.

Traditional writers also started without name recognition. Just like yourself right now.

You might have heard or read this before. Editors and publishers talk about being the shoulders that their famous writers cry on. This is true. Even famous writers get depressed, and the editors and publishers have seen this behavior many times before. They allow themselves to be the shoulders to cry on, like psychologists and psychiatrists. I also call them shock absorbers.

We self-publishers don't have editors and publishers to be our shock absorbers. We just need to manage ourselves better. Those editors and publishers are the same people who reject thousands of would-be writers. Let's leave them be and be stronger for ourselves.

You're writing about your life

My internal conflict comes from having been molested by the househelp when I was 6 years old. I'm 52 now. I'm still healing, but at least I can type about it, as I am doing right now. I'm letting you know this, like a fable. Know my story so you can learn from it.

It's also like a fairy tale. You know that something good is in store, I would not just blurt out that I was molested when I was 6 years old without any degree of salvation in the end.

To lessen your depression, visualize the salvation—the lesson to be learned, before you even start that sad, traumatic chapter you have planned.

The depression might take a long time to get over

I know this to be true. It happened to me, so if this happens to you, at least you've been warned.

I wrote my first draft between 2005 and 2006. I counted 170,000 words. When I told my sister about it, she reminded me that she was an editor and had been for decades. I don't think she lied to me, but she said she can edit it in three weeks. She volunteered to take over my work.

It was my first try at writing a book, and I seriously got depressed, so I was thinking, letting my sister take over would be productive. As I would be recuperating from writing so much, someone would be editing the work.

The three weeks in June passed. She kept on saying she was working on it. It turned out, she stopped. By September, I had to get it back from her. She had reworded 2/3 of my work, leaving my original "voice" in 1/3 of it. I actually liked the way she reworded it, it's just stupid that 1/3 was left unchanged. Then again, it was a very lengthy draft.

I was still mad. She promised 3 weeks, not 3 months. She said she became depressed herself, because of her own personal problems. I told myself, professional editors don't say that.

I had already told her, right from the beginning, that I only wanted to tell my family, including her, the good news that I wrote a book-length manuscript. In retrospect, a normal book is 55,000 words and my book was 3 times that much.

I now have better knowledge in treating my work. I should have re-shuffled the works and produced 3 or 4 books. I only did this from 2013 to 2014.

I shelfed the file in 2006, only to have recovered from my depression and only to feel empowered and more knowledgeable enough 7 years later.

I'm telling you this so you can have the courage to speed up your own writing.

When I finished the draft in 2006, I was hurrying myself up, because I was planning to bring my draft to the annual publishers and booksellers convention, BookExpo America, in Washington, DC. I was able to do that.

I had been a masseur for 8 years, barely making money, in an attempt to write a story about it. I got comfortable in my situation. I only started writing on the 7th to 8th year. Then I suddenly felt the need to change my situation.

My yearly lease ended in September, so between June and September, when it was crucial for me to make another leap of faith and move

27: Internal Conflict Preparing Your Mind to Write

out of my apartment to do something else, my sister was holding my manuscript ransom, not understanding what I was going through with my own life.

While all this was happening, not only was I depressed. It felt like if I killed myself, having written my "legacy," I would still go to heaven, because the general public never attempted to write a memoir. I had.

I had also written about my traumatic sexual molestation experience. It was obviously my first time writing about it, so the worry about exposing myself too much was part of the mix.

It's good that I went through this. It has made me a stronger person. It was just a low, deep crevice of depression for a few months, after which, it slowly dissipated. After a year, I was so much better, that I started to assess my writing skills.

When I read my sister's editing, I realized that there are many ways to tell the same story. Between 2009 and 2012, I learned more writing techniques.

Feeling productive, I wrote **Dollman the Musical, A Memoir of an Artist as a Dollmaker** in 2012. I still did not want to look at my first 170,000-word draft, but I produced a new book from scratch. **Dollman the Musical** also put me in a depressed mood. I knew this would happen, so I was able to handle it better.

Between 2013 and 2014, I looked at my first draft. I was able to reshuffle the chapters, edit better, add new, relevant chapters to each of the books that resulted.

I remembered the crankiness, irritability and depression I experienced not only from the first draft in 2006, but also from **Dollman the Musical** in 2012. So here was what I did: I deliberately finished and released 3 books simultaneously in 2014. They were not weeks apart of each other. They were released on the same day.

I edited them many times over by going from book 1, then book 2, then book 3, then book 1 again, book 2, book 3 and so on this way. Then I worked on the book design the same way.

I felt a huge sense of accomplishment, because I never heard of any writer go from 1 memoir to 4 memoirs by simultaneously releasing 3 titles. I knew this was not normal, so I was happy.

Hocus Pocus Lately is actually about the time when my dad was dying of cancer. The book was my ultimate tribute to him, and this

(Note: You can see my 4 memoirs on page 36)

made me feel okay. It helped me accept my dad's situation.

I'm writing this book, **Valzubiriagenda,** and I can tell you, I'm writing it freely without any feeling of depression. I'm just looking forward to getting it done.

As you can see, I'm prepping you mentally and emotionally more than teaching you writing techniques. I know people who are going or have gone to their 4-year or 2-year Masters Degree in Creative Writing.

They have yet to produce their books! I'm encouraging you to write your memoir right now and not worry about educating yourself.

The secret is facing fears. People have fears. It's like collecting recipe books, when all we really need to do is face the fire and start cooking and know that the house won't burn down if we're careful.

The best stories we naturally have tend to be the worst periods in our lives. We need to scientifically understand ourselves and, with skill, be able to put our events and feelings into words on paper.

We need to see our books as separate from ourselves. People we don't personally know will be reading what we wrote. It becomes a little more impersonal.

As you move forward, you will realize that it is not the traumatic, sad events that you are conveying. It will be the perspective you have on your own situation. This is what the readers will pick up on, because people read to discover the resolution to the story.

We are all artists and human, we should expect this. Just get over it. Other people who cannot cope commit suicide. We are here to be productive.

Hear this audiobook

I want to recommend an audiobook. The author actually has a book version, but to me, hearing the narrator's voice is even better. Every once in a while, I listen to the recording.

The book is titled **The War of Art: Break Through the Blocks and Win Your Inner Creative Battles** by Steven Pressfield.

He uses a keyword: Resistance.

He said that the process of being productive, when we are already in the zone, is easy. What is not easy is getting into that zone of productivity for our art, whether it is writing, playing a musical instrument or visual art.

We will resist getting into that zone, by doing or thinking other things. Even sex can be an escape from the actual work we should be doing. In our case, it is producing books and visual art.

I will recommend other books later.

I like to hear the narrator's voice, so I prefer the audiobook version. I also noticed that listening to audiobooks frees my hand to make my art, especially when I mess with clay, which is dirty and time-consuming.

You will learn a lot about the struggle to produce and be creative from Steven Pressfield.

Acknowledge your crankiness

Here is what I notice about myself. I sometimes get cranky on days when I play with the idea of being productive while seriously feeling lazy.

I have come to manage this, not by forcing myself to be nice, but by simply acknowledging it. When I erupt on someone else, I can almost tell that the other person was not at fault at all, I was just frustrated, being lazy and taking out my frustration on someone else. At this point in my life, I do try to be more mellow, but the frustration and eruption, usually mild, still happens.

You might experience this degree of challenge, laziness and frustration for yourself. If you cannot manage this, then you should at least be able to calm down and know to apologize to those you get emotional with.

Your good intentions are not theirs

I read somewhere that this billionaire oil magnate died unhappy. He also left his kids and grandkids unhappy and maladjusted despite all the money he left them.

The reason for their misery was that this highly accomplished billionaire *and* the media expected the rest of the clan to become successful themselves.

This is 1950s thinking. Just because you're getting into all this does not mean those other people in your life should get into this too. Leave those people be.

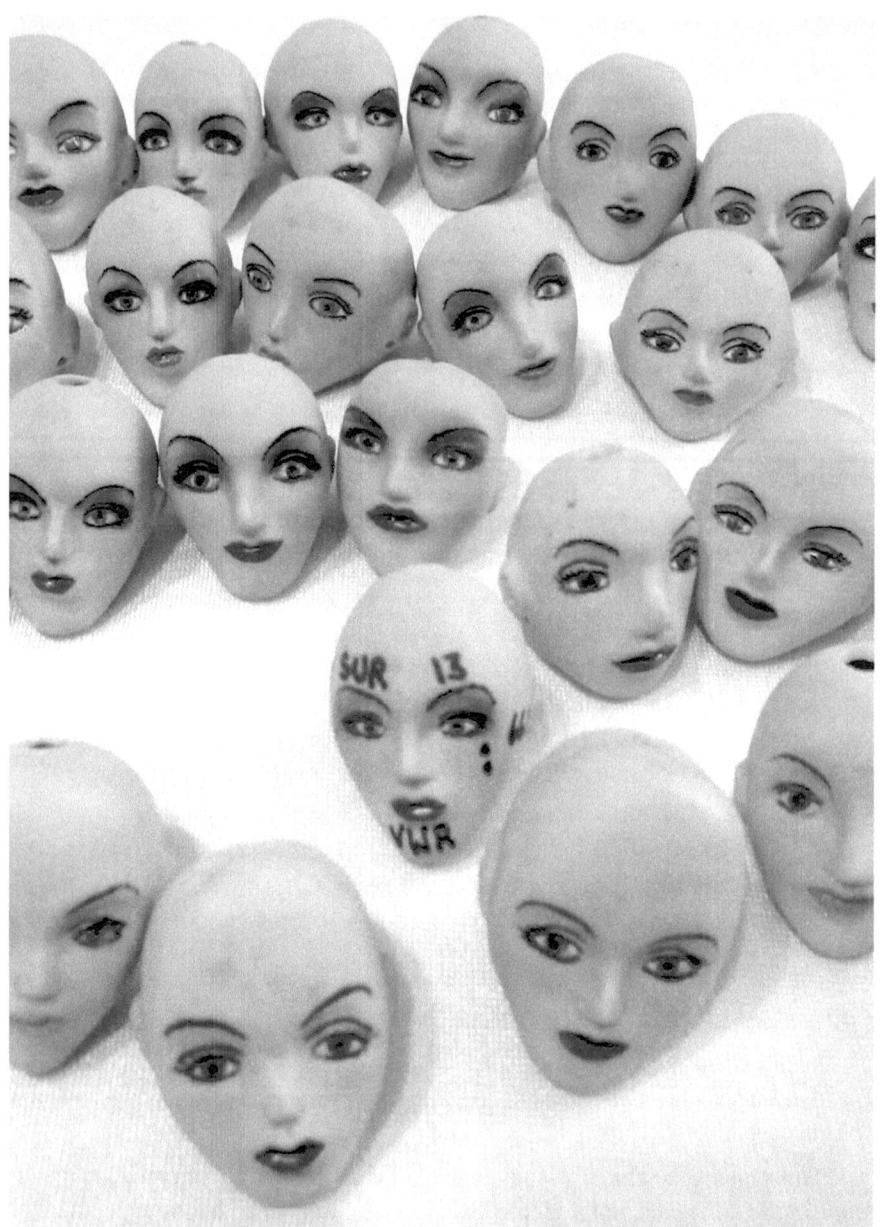

From pages xxviii, 4, 120 & 269
 Notice how Silverio Perez' work stands out. It was a whimsical moment when he was holding a permanent marker while checking out my box of doll's heads. Done with permission and he made sure not to alter the better faces.

Next image is on page 164

Chapter 28

Try this: Publish First What Your First Book Will Do for You

The mathematics of art and publishing

If you put in 100% effort in art, and 100% effort in writing and publishing books, your perception of yourself will jump to more than just 200%.

100% effort in art + 100% effort in writing = 1,000,000% jump in self-worth, self-image, self-respect, self-whatever else.

You will even think you don't care if you sold art or not.

I personally experienced this as soon as I saw a printed book version of my manuscript even when it still needed editing.

When you're just selling art, you are selling art for the day. Your goal is money.

When I had my book in my hands, my long-term visions surfaced. I was into art for the long haul. Even if I died the next day, I knew I left a legacy. It was a great thought. I'm glad I'm still alive to produce more and better books.

I would suggest that you work on your book. Get your book published. The process of getting to there will take time. You will have enough time for your thoughts.

Once you see your book finished and tangible, you will feel different about yourself and your future. At this point, you can better price your art.

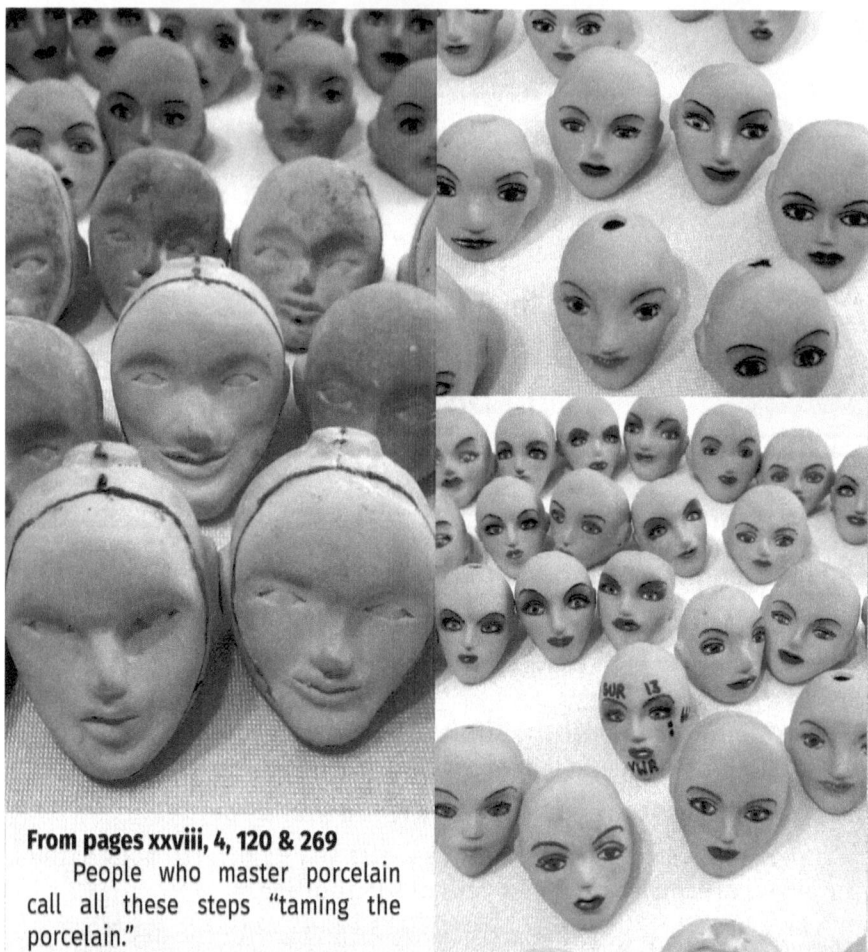

From pages xxviii, 4, 120 & 269

People who master porcelain call all these steps "taming the porcelain."

The doll heads start with individual sculptures from polymer clay. I then make a plaster mold from each head. Each mold has 4 pieces that intersect like a 3-D puzzle—this is why I marked the polymer originals, so I know where plaster pieces should be positioned. I pour liquid porcelain, called "slip," into the molds.

The porcelain pieces go to the kiln by as much as 12 times or even more, because the colored details on the faces are actually heated layers of colored ground glass, called "china paint." The heat shrinks the porcelain to as much as 13 to 15% the original size of the polymer clay original.

Shown here are male and female polymer clay heads.

As you can see, the process is multi-step, and while others might think it's tedious, as soon as you master the steps, you will, just like me, realize that it's fun, highly rewarding and worth trading with other investors and art collectors.

Next image is on page 188

Chapter 29

External Conflict
How Others can Affect You

Leave those people be

You're not the only one with mental and emotional anguish.

The people around you will also be affected by your art and writing—friends, relatives and coworkers.

You have a choice right now of either telling or not telling your friends, relatives and coworkers that you plan to write a book.

They will react to your announcement that you will be producing art, memoirs and art books. If you're forging ahead, then you don't need their reactions, because some will be good, and some will be bad for you.

You're expecting that everyone should approve of your decisions. Leave them be. Your books are for the public.

The two words I mistakenly interchanged

I need to define *envy* and *jealousy*. They sound the same.

I need to define this for you so you would not make the mistake of publishing using one word instead of the other.

Envy is when someone wants your success or accomplishment for himself or herself. A coworker who does not care about you, but wants your money or accomplishment is envious.

Jealousy happens when someone you know and cares about you starts to feel that your progress and success might make you disappear from sight.

That person will feel that your progress might put you at a higher level of existence, leaving that person behind. That is jealousy. It is negative and discouraging reaction from someone who cares about you.

Both envy and jealousy can be subconscious. The person who gets envious or jealous may not know that he or she is manifesting the thought or behavior.

I'm telling you this, so that you can expect it. You cannot deny that envy and jealousy do not surround you. This is human nature. There were those times when you felt them, too.

I'm telling you this so that you *will* know to laugh it off, and if one or both do show themselves, just become aware.

If you get these feedbacks from people you love, you can correct the feeling with an explanation. You can even define the two words to them, just so they can analyze their feelings better.

If you get envy from someone you don't care for, you can include that in your memoir. Just don't name names.

There is a third word. Spite. Spiteful comments come out of envy and jealousy. You will hear them once in a while. Once again, this is a normal human behavior. There is no need to be confrontational nor violent.

Now, if you can just learn to keep your plans to yourself.

When you write, you write for the public

Don't waste your time writing a book so that your family will read it.

Once you are almost done with your book, you will start designing your book for publication. You can assign a dedication page, where you can dedicate your book to your kids and your spouse or someone else.

I hate to burst your bubble, don't expect those people to read your books.

The dedication is as much for the public as it is for your loved ones. It tells the public there are people you care about.

Even when you mention how much you love your family in the book, don't expect them to read it. They're not your fans. They're your family.

Parties and friends

There are "parties," and there are "professional parties." There are "friends and family," and there are "professional friends" and a "professional family."

Professional parties, professional friends and professional families are the ones who will read your books, buy your art, and help you make money. When you are with them or at a party, you discuss your projects because they can help you progress.

Regular friends, family and parties should just be exactly that. Do not expect even one family member to care about your work. Do not expect them to buy and read your books.

When you are sloppily eating the barbecue at a family gathering, just be yourself, be there and eat that barbecue. Don't expect a pat in the back and a few phrases. Never give your books away to them! You'll see people toss your books at each other and to the back of their cars. Some will leave them behind. Be ready to collect them back—I already told you not to give them away!

You'll remember how the book positioned itself in the back of that car and the next time you see the car again, you'll know if wasn't even touched.

The problem with family, unlike the unknown public, is that they won't go away nor can you get away from them.

With the public, if you hear a negative remark, you can always walk away, heal sooner and forget anything untoward happened.

I just shared a pdf of this book with my brother. I'm counting the days when he mentions anything about it.

Beware of fake success

Our brain has at least 4 chemicals for feeling success and happiness: dopamine, serotonin, endorphins, & oxytocin.

Research on these if you want. I usually just tell people that we produce endorphins, which give us a high.

Here is the trouble we have with our brain: The brain cannot tell real from imaginary, because the same happy chemicals are produced.

Imagine a stupid person you dislike. Person #1. Person #1 is at a party. Imagine that person telling Person #2 he or she is writing a book.

Imagine Person #2 smile, beam at Person #1 proudly and congratulate that person. Person #1 smiles back, feeling proud and happy.

Those feelings of pride and happiness were produced by the brain's happy chemicals.

The same chemicals get produced when you finally finish your book and you get the same handshake and good comments.

People can also trap themselves in the process of writing without finishing, or worse, talking without writing. This way, they continue to feel successful without the work.

Why I don't advise friends

Let's pretend you approached me, and you tell me you want to write a book. Because I've done it before, you ask me if I have any advice for you. Let me tell you what happened to someone I know, so it would not happen to you.

I had a friend who in 2013 flew in from another state. Let's call him Walter. He used to live in Chicago, where I was at, so we had mutual friends by the hundreds. I know because more than 15 years ago, I was living in a condo that had a party room. I held a birthday party where everyone was invited. 185 people came. This is me being boastful. That was my last birthday party anyway.

So in 2013, one of his best friends and former roommate, whom I knew but wasn't really close to, was dying. Because Walter and someone else we knew flew in from different states, to visit the same person, the two out-of-towners, myself, and two other friends, got together at a neighborhood bar. Walter then held the highest position in a relatively small-sized nonprofit, but he told me he was retiring and returning to Chicago soon.

I'm not one to point out physical conditions, but I saw my friend walking with a cane. A hip seemed to have shifted, I can't really tell where, because he was obese. I think he was 250-275 lbs and about 5'8", so he wasn't monstrously big. He needed to lose weight, but he had been that way for the more than 20 years I had known him. When we were in our 20s, he was actually more physically active than I was, because he played competitive volleyball.

Before the day that we saw each other at the bar, Walter called and told me that he wanted to get into writing scripts. The reason he told me this was that I was known to have been a columnist for a monthly paper, and that I had just recently finished writing my book, **Dollman the Musical, A Memoir of an Artist as a Dollmaker,** which was in the form of a musical script. By the way, I know that there is no such word as "dollmaker," like "shoemaker" or "dressmaker." Artistic license.

The next day, I showed up. I brought with me a book, **Save the Cat! The Last Book on Screenwriting You'll Ever Need**, a how-to-write book by Blake Snyder. I highly endorse this book, because I read this more than a year before 2013, and when I misplaced it at home, I decided to return to the bookstore to buy another copy. Then I found my first copy, so I had two. I gave Walter the second, newer copy.

As we drank, he asked if I can give him any advice for the meantime.

I said, "I don't give friends advice unless they really need it."

I also said, "I may have made a mistake sending copies of my work to friends."

Then I joked, "That's my advice."

He asked, "Can you be more specific?"

I said, "Okay." Here now was more or less what I told him, which I will now share with you:

If you want to write, do it. You should initially keep your writings to yourself. Only share it with the world when you feel it is good enough.

When it comes to the world, I mean the public. You write scripts and books to please the public, not your friends and family.

Don't share it with friends and family, especially if you feel the need to hear their feedback. Friends are friends and family is family. You should only share it with professionals.

I felt I made a mistake sharing **Dollman** with my friends, but I actually was experimenting with how I would feel sharing something very personal with people who know me. So I wasn't really asking for feedback then, I just wanted to know how it felt sharing my highly personal work. Now I'm over it. I know never to do it again.

I told Walter, "Don't let me read your work because we're friends." I told him that if he wanted me to read it for a critique, then I would read it like a professional, and I might not be nice. I will compromise the friendship because I will consider him a professional colleague.

As a friend, I gave him the book **Save the Cat.** I encouraged him to read it and implement the tips from the book.

I then told him, "Don't share your work with your friends and relatives. Imagine going to a party where you expect to enjoy yourself. You will have friends and relatives asking about your current writing projects.

"If you're not too happy with your writing and creative processes, you would not enjoy being at the parties anymore. So keep your writing projects to yourself, away from friends and relatives. Only get them into the hands of the professionals and the public, who will not bug you at the parties."

I also told Walter that another reason friends and family should not read his work was that if the work sucked, there is no way those people will be nicer to him. They will form a bad opinion of him at an early time in his writing career. It just would not be comfortable.

I explained to him that I was confident with the book that I wrote, because it was not my first attempt at writing, and I was also mentally and emotionally ready to share my book with people.

My friend had never written anything nor received any public attention like I had in the past. Whatever full-length book or script he wanted to write was going to be his first attempt.

About a year passed. I had another friend, Jim, whom I talk to a lot. One afternoon, Jim called and asked me if I was going to a party. I asked, what party he was referring to. He said that my best friend, Walter, finally quit being the head of the nonprofit.

Walter had scheduled a welcome home party at the house of another friend of ours. The party was also going to be a reading of his movie script. He had assigned roles to different people—I knew almost all of them. What a big bash, everyone but myself was going to be there. I wasn't invited at all.

So the party came and went. Jim didn't bother going, because after all these years, he didn't want to see some people who were also invited.

Walter did exactly what I told him not to do. A few more months later, I got a call from him. He wanted to see me for coffee, but before that, he wanted to send me a copy of his script, so I can give him a critique.

I told him that if I read his script, I will treat him like a writer and no longer a friend. He said that would be fine. I said okay, send me a copy and let's see each other the following week.

29: External Conflict How Others can Affect You

He emailed me a copy, which I printed out. I read his work. We then saw each other.

I joked that he did exactly what I told him he should never do, which was announce and let friends read his work. I told him it was too early to subject himself to humiliation. I also reminded him that our friends know that I write, but it stopped there; I don't want them reading my works.

I gave him a printed copy of his work, with some handwritten critiques from me. Then I also told him what might have been missing in his narrative and what might be good to include. He said thanks.

Two more years passed. In 2016, Walter passed away. I went to the wake, and I saw friends I had not seen in years, some of them decades.

I learned that Walter had a fear of doctors and dentists. He was diabetic. He had an infection on one leg, and he let the infection get worse. The more the infection spread, the more he became scared of going to the doctor.

According to a relative of his at the wake, when he finally showed the infection to the relatives he lived with, he also mentioned that the prospect of getting an amputation was even worse to think about—he really had a serious aversion to doctors and hospitals, so only when the infection reached his groin and had become gangrenous did he agree to go to the hospital.

Antibiotics didn't work anymore. After a week's time at the hospital, he died. Some relatives at the wake told me his pain was so severe that he screamed when he had to be moved even the slightest. Whatever he had was so painful during the entire time he was hospitalized and dying from gangrene.

I hope you're learning a little from this story. I warned him that writing can be a depressing activity. He never should have announced to his huge crowd of relatives and friends that he had started to write movie scripts. Some professional writers only get their scripts and other written works reviewed after so many tries.

The one good thing going for all of us is that self-publishing is now possible, and as artists, as I keep telling everyone, don't even worry about mistakes in writing. Our books will be studied 300 to 3,000 years from now, and we should not expect criticism from people now.

I'm almost sure that between the time he had a welcome home and script-reading party and the time of his death, people asked him about the status of his scriptwriting "career," not out of concern but out of it being something he had openly announced. I'm almost sure he noticed some spiteful, envious and jealous comments that he did not need to hear. His script lacked conflict.

If you are new to all this, and you have not proven that you can produce at least one book, be it a memoir, biography, set of essays, manifesto or art book, tell only those close to you about your plans. Then tell, cooperate and collaborate only with those who will be your professional friends and professional family, related to the #valzubiriagenda.

Learn to take comments in stride

I know someone who can produce this stupid, strange expression: I know something you don't. It's a stare with the eyes, and something to do with the lips, only produced to match something you said.

Nowadays, I just take his plastic attitude in stride. In my imagination, as I face him, I take out my imaginary pocket notebook and my imaginary pen, open the imaginary page I have for him, and proceed to write another vertical line in the tally.

Of course I would never have him around with me all the time. I just can't avoid seeing him at gatherings.

Here is something else you might hear.

"Oh you're self-published? I thought you had a real publisher."

I would not think you will hear that often if you say you're following the #valzubiriagenda, assuming this trends and becomes popular.

The lady with the stack of manuscripts

I met an 85-year old lady who still has not self-published. She had a box of manuscripts that had not seen publication. There supposedly were more than four novels in the box.

I'm talking "box," because she started writing using a typewriter. Now, her eyes are failing her. She may have written some in computer files, but she was proud of her box of writings.

I showed her my already-printed books and those of people whom I had helped. In our conversation, she kept insisting that she will be discovered by a literary agent and she also looked down on self-publishing.

She and I talked at length about book ideas. I guess she was recently

29: External Conflict How Others can Affect You

introduced to a screenwriter's group, so that was where her heart had been lately. Her eyes lit up when she talked about how her group regularly met. She said they were productive meetings.

If I met with a support group just so someone else's prestige rubs off on me, I would think twice. If that's all that happens.

I think she went to a support group, not a meeting group. You meet to either get things done, or pat each other in the back.

When I told her that I met celebrities during the years that I was a masseur, she stood up, excitedly, and exclaimed that my story about being a masseur lends itself to a movie. She excitedly said that I should meet some of her screenwriting friends so *they* can write a script about my life.

I thought, "Really? Last I heard, I was already writing."

Then she said, "Throw your books out! That's not where the money is! Your life is a screenplay!"

As you can see, I didn't appreciate that line, *throwing* my books out. What she said reflected her own subconscious. However, these comments that we encounter are good to learn from. They just might end up in a book.

Hotdog-eating contests

In 2006, obviously more than a decade ago, when I was still writing my first draft, someone made a comment to me, that he was praised for his writing ability.

A close friend picked me up at 8 a.m. at the 24-hour Starbucks. I had my precious laptop with me. I was still wide awake, pumped with caffeine and adrenaline. With him was this friend of his.

I was obviously seriously writing for my life. I was being nice and naive when I asked, "Really? Who said it?"

"My high school teacher." He was in his 40s then. I laughed when I heard his comment. It was not because what he said was funny with an imaginary lunge at me.

This guy hailed from Boston. He liked to tell people how much he loved playing tennis. On the side, he also made sure to mention going to different cities to watch famous tennis tournaments.

Behind his back, his Chicago friends talked that, based on his obese stature, he cannot really be playing tennis. Instead, he must just be joining hotdog-eating contests at those different cities.

Fortunately for me, I now have a few books. He kept in touch with people I know.

He passed away some years ago. He choked on a hotdog.

Something my friend encountered

I have a friend who wrote plays for the same theatre group I was in. I will talk about this in another book.

He had already acted in plays and written a few plays for the group, when he was approached by another friend of his who said,

"Let me know if you write any new plays, so I can read and critique it."

Chicago has more than 300 theatre groups every year. It's easy to volunteer and get onstage.

It's also easy for me to say that for every one person in theatre, there are many more people who are too shy and afraid to go onstage in front of an audience.

My friend has already had theatre experience for years, while his friend had none.

My friend told me, "Why would I allow him to critique my work? He has never been involved in theatre!"

If you haven't written a book, your level will go higher when you start writing. It will go higher up again once you finish writing. Once you see the book in print, your level will go up again.

If his friend joined a theatre group, my friend would listen.

I never heard this—some of us might

When someone hears of your plans to write, and someone approaches you to say, "Oh that's great! There's a nearby college that offers a 2-year degree on writing!, " I would say, "Good for you!"

What do you think that means? Read between the lines, dummy!

Obviously, you did not heed my suggestion of keeping plans to yourself.

Be reminded that people around you aren't all mean. You can trust them. These things are at the subconscious level.

29: External Conflict How Others can Affect You

Reading between the lines

You might have heard of the phrase, "reading between the lines."

You will come to a point where when you write, you are saying one thing, but hinting at another.

This can also happen later when you start editing. You can look for portions of your writing where you can hint at other things.

For example, when you at first wrote, "My stepmother told my two stepsisters to leave me alone with the dishes."

Let's say you decided to change it to, "My stepmother told my two stepsisters to leave me alone with the dishes as soon as one of them approached me to help out."

This is just a simple example. As I will forever keep telling everyone, write from start to finish first, to what you think would be the actual ending of your book. Then start editing and analyzing what you did. Of course your ending can change. More chapters might be added in. You can add hints at things to come.

As an exercise to writing, start listening to how people word themselves during conversations. Read between their lines.

Analyze how you word yourself as well, and wonder how you might have said things better.

Begin to become more observant right now, reading between the lines of people you interact with, as a form of exercise.

Once again, what stops people from writing and publishing is perception of themselves from within themselves and from people they interact with.

You're not my personal friend here. Begin to consider yourself a writer and a publisher because I have been treating you like one. You can be my professional friend. I have a few suggestions and secrets on how to write to get you started.

hashtag #valzubiriagenda

Part 3

Writing & Editing

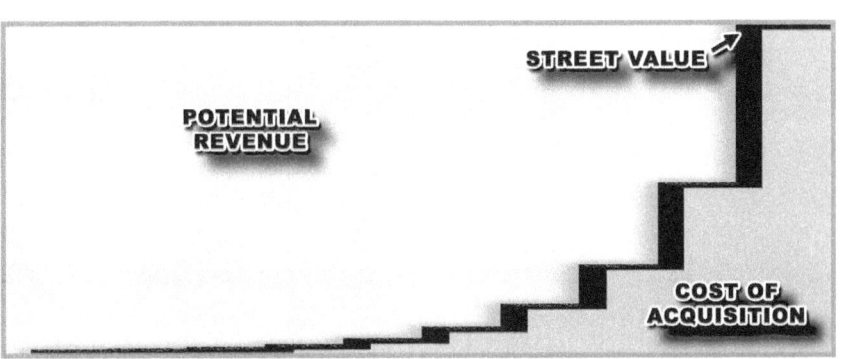

SPECIAL SECTION #3

From Chapter 8 page 58:

Pass-Along Books

We have been buying
more and more books
for our friends

This book has been
priced low to sell

Buy this for someone
who could use it—

An artist friend or relative
Someone who just lost his job
A struggling café or business
Someone else

Chapter 30

You can Use Other Writers or Write Your Own Book!

I'm just reminding you that Chapter 23 suggested that you not write your own book. I also mentioned ghostwriters even earlier in the Introduction and Chapter 5. A lot of famous people get away with not having to write.

You can produce 5 books by contracting with 5 writers.

When you barter, figure out a way to give your art later. You might collaborate with 5 writers—what if only 2 deliver? You might not be able to retrieve your art pieces if you gave them away too soon.

Here are other scenarios.

You can write for yourself, and still welcome other writers to write about you.

I personally do not mind collaborating with another writer to help me write my books. I'm actually sharing this book with Silverio Perez. We wrote it as if I, Val Zubiri, wrote the entire book.

Silverio Perez is also an artist. We plan to have solo and collaborative projects in the future, both in art and publishing.

You can get 5 writers to write, and then reassign their books to one of the other writers so they can edit each other's works. You'll come up with edited books.

Or you might want to write your book, and enter into an agreement with an editor.

Then you can contract with a book designer who can design all 5 books with a common feel. You can also have 5 different designers to work on one book each.

Whatever you decide to do, depending on the people you have around you, make sure you don't barter away what you have to offer your group without producing results. The final result is what counts, which is having finished books available for the rest of the public, which includes art collectors and investors.

Let me now finally teach you some tricks in writing. You will discover that what they say about writing are true: Writing is a craft. There are ways to weave words, just like a basket. It is like music, as you orchestrate your words from start to finish.

Chapter 31

How to Come Up with 2 Books from 1 Draft

Because you can!

I'll tell you a story later in this chapter and my own motivation for this tip. Meanwhile, here is the tip:

Publish your first book without any revisions. Call it "Artist's Original Unedited Manuscript." Claim it to be an artistic statement itself. Make sure to include a phrase like

"Artist's Original Unedited Masterpiece"

"Artist's Unretouched Writing"

"Artist's Manifesto, Original Raw Version"

"A Visual Artist's Attempt To Write Without Editing"

Include your chosen phrase on both the cover and the back cover, and repeat it on the inside, on the title page. Make sure to include this as part of the book cover's design. Avoid making it look as if it were stamped on as an afterthought.

In your Introduction and maybe your first chapter, make sure to let people know there will be a revised, edited version of your book. Avoid apologizing. You can make your decision funny and entertaining. You can be serious. Never apologize.

I'm not fully encouraging you to do this. You probably should edit your book before you release it. I'm saying that this is a possibility. I'm mentioning this in this book because it did occur to me and I am not discounting it.

I boosted my self-image the moment I saw my name on a book in 2006. Even though I had yet to rework the first ever book-length manuscript I produced, I designed and uploaded my files online to Lulu.com. I proved that my possibility had become a reality.

I even shared my book with a friend, who happened to just get hired as the executive director of a museum. I mailed him what best I had—a lengthy memoir that was yet to be edited.

The things I do, including the embarrassing ones, they are like seeds. I plant some and I throw away some. I don't know if they will sprout and grow at all. Some will, I don't know when. I have come to look at all this lightly.

We are not represented by a literary agent nor by a large publishing house. Some of us might be, eventually. We are really left to our own devices. No one will stop us from embarrassing ourselves.

The "embarrassment" is a learning experience, even for investors and art collectors. It's like slipping on an icy sidewalk during winter, or slipping on a wet floor on a rainy day. It happens, and you will learn to be better next time. It's like an imaginary bar. Once you get past it, you know you will produce better.

Right now, we can print unedited manuscripts—maybe until our print on demand companies come up with a policy to discourage this.

You must be careful. You might want to not do this.

Once you have a better, final version of your book, you can release it as your second copy.

You can call it "Artist's Final Edited Version."

Make sure you really have it edited.

Why would we attempt to come up with two books from the same manuscript? Because now we can.

Don't say it's an "Advanced Reading Copy" or "Proof"

I don't think Amazon will allow you to list commercially books that are marked "Advance Reading Copy."

"Advanced reading copies" are usually already edited and designed. If your book has a lot of mistakes, you do not have an "advanced reading copy."

The big publishers print "Advanced Reading Copy" on evaluation

31: How to Come Up with 2 Books from 1 Draft

copies. They imprint this on books that they don't want to be sold commercially—they are given to:

1. The press, so they can review the book in advance of the release date, and to
2. The booksellers, so they can better decide if they would order 10, 100 or 1,000 copies for their stores

Most traditional publishers simply send the final, consumer versions of their books, because a few books for the press and booksellers really would not hurt their sales.

On the other hand, if the book is supposed to be a hardcover, and they don't have the time to produce the final hardcover book, then paperbacks with the "Advanced Reading Copy" message would be given away.

Publishers, booksellers and librarians conventions happen in May and June. The release dates for books are usually in September. The advanced reading copies are given away at the conventions so that everyone has ample time to read the books, and order copies.

The publishers get a better tally of how many books they should probably print, including overages. Everyone gets the orders on the same shipment period, in time for the "official release date." Some official release dates are important, like the Harry Potter series.

The young man Herman

There was a young man, Herman, way back around 1995. This man was from the suburbs. My friend Jaime introduced him to me. The guy was supposedly homeless and lived in abandoned buildings in the suburbs, having run away from home.

Jaime said he wanted me to meet him because he had a manuscript. I was probably Jaime's best contact then for some sort of writing and publishing, because I had started my column on the arts for the free monthly paper.

Jaime printed the guy's work and gave me a copy. The manuscript was about 30 pages of continuous poetry. I said I would read it and tell them what I thought about it later. Meanwhile, the three of us hung out and had coffee.

I'm an almost visual guy. I remember facial expressions. Even now,

I may not remember his face too well—he was thin and tall, not necessarily gaunt, but his eyes conveyed that he so much wanted to have his writing be worth something.

When I was finally alone, I read the first few pages and stopped. None of his lines made sense to me. They seemed to be just nonsense. When Jaime and I talked over the phone, I said his writing made no sense.

Jaime said, "Oh, okay. I thought it was just me. Herman said he wrote it while high on weed. But he was seriously hoping it will make sense to people."

I was tricked into reading a string of words written by a homeless person who was high on weed. How he got hold of a computer I would not want to figure out. Maybe he used a public library. Maybe a copy shop with computers for rent.

These past few years, I wonder about Herman. He may already be dead. While homeless, he might have contracted the HIV virus, or something else. I pray for him to be safe every once in a while.

I still remember his face when I met him the first time. He wanted his writing to make sense, because if it did, in the way I now analyze it, he too will make sense.

He does make sense to me now. I still have his manuscript. I still wonder how he is now. I still pray for him. His work now seems important to me, in my guts and in my heart, even if it still does not make sense. He has become an inspiration to me.

I cannot tell you to be perfect with your books.

Instead, be as imperfect as you are right now.

This is why I tell everyone that our efforts now will matter 300 to 3,000 years from now—this is manageable pressure. Let's leave the bestsellers to the huge publishing houses. Let's not even make sense if we choose to do so. Art sells if it makes sense to the other person.

We just need to start writing, start editing, start publishing and start helping each other, bartering our skills and art and whatever we can offer for one another's talent, time, money and whatever else.

Chapter 32

Do Warm Ups
Pretend You're Already Writing

Theoretical activities

When I begin writing, I get into what I call my "theoretical activities." I say theoretical because I know it helps me, but I don't want to bother proving this.

I time my typing speed using two sentences: "The quick brown fox jumped over the lazy dogs. Now is the time for all good men to come to the aid of the country."

I get a stopwatch or a watch and type the two sentences for five exact minutes as fast as I can, without pausing to correct errors. Then I stop and count how many words I was able to type.

> the quick brown fox jumped over the lazy dogs. Now is the time for all good ment o come to the aid of their countries.
>
> The quick brown fox jumped over the lazy dogs. Now is the time for all good men to come to the aid of the country.
>
> The quick brown fox jumped over the lazy dogs. Now is the time for all good men to come to the aid of the country.
>
> The quick brown fox jumped over the lazy dogs. Now is the time for all good men to come to the aid of the country.

The quick brown fox jumped over the lazy dogs. Now is the time for all good men to come to the aid of the country.

The quick brown fox jumped over the lazy dogs. Now is the time for all good men to come to the aid of the country.

The quick brown fox jumped over the lazy dogs. Now is the time for all good men to come to the aid of the cuntry

The quick brown fox jumped ove thal lazy dogs. now is hte

374 words in 5 minutes

If an acceptable book-length memoir has 55,000 words minimum, then:

x/55,000 words = 5 minutes/374 words

x minutes = (5 minutes x 55,000 words) / 374 words

x minutes = 735 minutes

This means that the shortest time I would need to write a memoir from start to finish will be 735 minutes, or 12 hours.

Of course it will take longer than that, but knowing that I would need 12 hours, I get into thinking that devoting some time writing, like *right now* is not a bad idea.

So here are to important points I want to point out from the discussion above:

1. You only need as little as 55,000 words to have a full-length memoir
2. If you can see that the shortest time needed to write a book is 12 hours, you should try putting in 12 hours and see how far you can progress. Depending also on how many breaks you tend to take and how much time you spend on the breaks, you should have an idea of how much time you would really need

If you want to feel how thick 55,000 words are based on the font size I used, feel the book's thickness from the cover to page 174. Page 193 also explains that I used 11.3 points (the font size).

32: Do Warm Ups Pretend You're Already Writing

The importance of The quick brown fox

Look at the letters in "The quick brown fox" sentence again. If you don't know it yet, all the letters from A to Z are included. This is why typists type the sentence as a fun thing to do. It exercises the fingers to touch all the letters of the alphabet.

Just knowing this tidbit in your head does not make you a fast typist. You should spend time typing the sentence over and over. If you remember the past, when computers were absent, people used typewriters. They used up paper and rolls of ink just to fill pages with this sentence, just to exercise their fingers and increase their typing speed.

"Now is the time for all good men to come to the aid of the party" was proposed as a typing drill in 1918, but the sentence actually showed up first in 1889. Just so you know. I won't get into details for this.

Once again, just because you know does not mean you'll become a fast typist. You just have to start typing to become a fast typist.

Don't worry about looking like a professional, skilled typist.

Just get your fingers to the right letters, expect misspellings, and missed ideas. You're writing a book.

Like what I said, you just have to start typing to be a typist. You just have start writing to be a writer.

Let me give you a few more pointers.

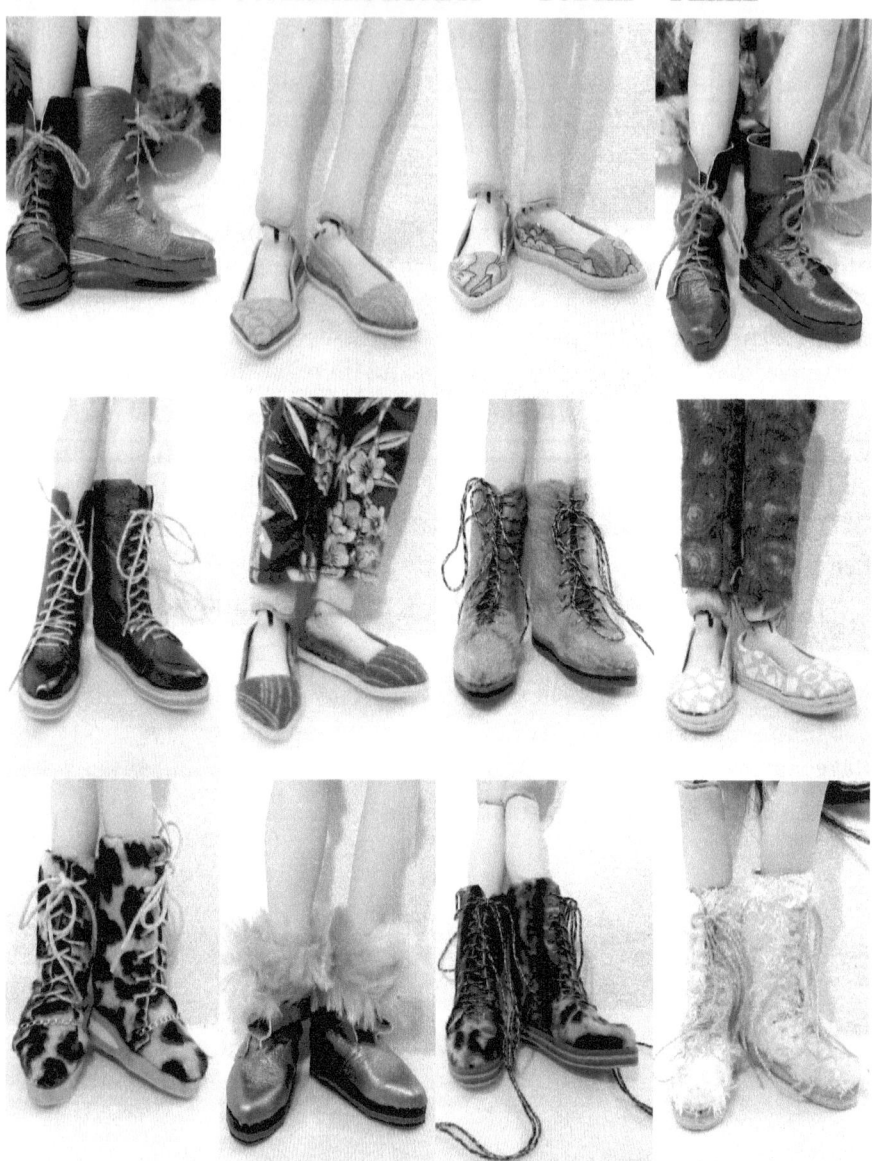

From pages xxviii, 4, 120 & 269

The shoes are complex as well. I make sure to continue the variations in the shoes. I like collecting materials, like the fake fur, fabrics, leatherette and threads. You will also notice the stripes on the soles.

The shapes are hard and permanent because there are hidden layers of metal in the shoes. The soles are just a little over 1 inch long.

End of images. First image is on page 18

Chapter 33

Beginning to Write
Some Nice Simple Pointers

What artists can learn from writers

There is a great, great number of books where the cover includes praise and endorsements from other fellow writers, encouraging the readers to read the book. Famous, professional writers actively help each other advance in their field!

We also see non-published writers read published books.

It is difficult to see artists praise and endorse fellow artists.

This is behavior by artists that has been happening for centuries! I'm hoping this changes with the #valzubiriagenda. I came up with this so that art and artists can help improve the economy. When you show up at local meetings, as you slowly start looking into writing, you start looking for stories. One way is to interact and start getting to know others.

If money starts coming my way, I would not hesitate funding and helping other artists and writers.

You might want to read a few bestselling memoirs. Or just read one. Choose an easy one or one that you like. Later on, start reading each others books.

As an exercise, for starters, write your book in that same way you perceived the book you read to have been written. As you make some progress, you will eventually find your book going in its own direction.

Do not worry about style. Just tell yourself, "Style is overrated," and keep on writing.

Did you notice this method that I used for this book?

I use subheadings to separate sections within chapters.

However, I prefer not to mention the topic in the subheadings. I'm hoping that the subheadings invite you to continue to read out of curiosity.

I call this approach "read bait."

Online, this method of having a vague but interesting headline is called "click bait." The reason people online do this is to get the public to click the headline, which has the link to the article or video. The producers only make money if the link was clicked.

My consideration was that I need to keep engaging you, my readers. I place headings as soon as I felt it was time to move to another related topic. I did it for this book as my own writing exercise. I did not use this approach in my earlier books.

My other memoirs simply used an extra line space.

There are many approaches to writing a book. There are many ways to tell a story. You're free to do what you want.

Know your "bar" so you can set it higher and higher

I have this saying, where you are, there you are. That's your bar. Where you are at writing, that's where you are.

You will discover more and more about your writing and from there, you can set higher milestones.

I say milestones because "goals" seem to be more definite. For example, writing a book would be a goal. Improving your use of dialogue and getting better with punctuation would be milestones.

Encouraging a friend to write her memoir

There was someone whom I had been encouraging to write. She's a lady friend who has a lot of stories from her life that she can write about. She used to be my neighbor.

She used to tell me that she was just turning 70, and I still consider that a good age to write. She was once a guest in a television talk show, hosted by a famous person. There *are* valid reasons why I encouraged her to write.

You will encounter this type of person, I just hope it would not be

33: Beginning to Write Some Nice Simple Pointers

you.

She told me a few times that as soon as she's ready to write her memoir, she will call a friend who owns a cottage in the woods. Over there, where it's peaceful, where the birds chirp and the air is fresh.

You do not need chirping birds and fresh air to write. Her PC was working and it was about 15 feet away from her bed.

Even if I had that cottage, I would not dare lend it to her. She'll slip and decompose by the time I cared to check up on her.

My friend waters down her whiskey and smokes weed, even at 70. Fresh air and whiskey don't always mix well anyway. That PC was just 15 feet away from her bed!

Less than a year ago, she had to get an operation, after which she went to rehab for addiction to prescription drugs and alcoholism.

I started bits of this book in October 2016. It's December 2017, and still unfinished. She has not yet started to write. I visited her in December 2017 at the rehab facility. We are no longer neighbors. She had to give up her unit and her PC is now in storage, safely locked.

She's a good story from my perspective. I don't think she'll be able to produce anything, but if I succeeded, I will make sure she's okay. I will get her a laptop. Then I will once again bug her for her book.

She's not getting off that easy.

Jerry and Jim's book
(Note: You can see Jerry Miller's &
James Miller's books on page 146)

I productively helped another friend, Jerry Miller, who is an actor, theatre director and producer, publish his first book. **Empty Space: Creating a Theatre in Your Church Step-by-Step** was published just before he turned 70, in 2014. I designed the final book. I also helped edit it. He is also a retired pastor, so he knows churches can have unused spaces that can be turned into theatre space.

I know he was turning 70, because I was invited to his 70th birthday party that same year.

As I write this, it is December 2017, and Jerry just got done playing the role of Scrooge in **A Christmas Carol.** He is now 72 years old. He has a twin brother whom I have not met. His twin lives in Colorado.

Jerry and his twin brother, James, just collaborated on a new book, **The Day the Rain Came Down, The Stories of Gay Identical Twins.** We finished and released the book early this month, December 2017. I'm editing this part of my book now, in January 2018. I did a few last tweaks of Jerry and Jim's book in January 2018.

It has poetry by both of them, art by James, pictures of them through the years, pictures of Jerry in stage productions and chapters on their bad, traumatic childhood, bad vices and later recovery. It was written for people in 12-Step programs.

After Jerry wrote his first book, he proved to himself that writing a book is possible. The second book, which is this new collaboration with his brother, came to them much easier.

James had seen his works published in the past as a reporter for a newspaper, and in a couple of solo poetry books.

James had a bad experience with a vanity press, so he let Jerry and I work on finalizing their book. I edited and designed the book.

The vanity press supposedly kept having additional charges for James' book project. I never asked them for details on that book.

I can entertain a lot of possibilities, either siding with James or the vanity press. Companies have employees to pay. They have hourly rates. When you deal with companies, it can cost a lot more than expected. This is why I encourage collaboration and barter to start and to keep costs down to $0, or as close to that.

Three different but similar movies

If you have seen any or all of these three movies, you can better follow this discussion. Let's look at why **Hello Dolly!**, **Casablanca** and **Billy Elliott** (either the movie or the musical) are similar.

Remember the following scenes:

1. In **Hello Dolly!**, she finally walked down the stairs with elegance
2. In **Casablanca,** they finally said goodbye and kissed in the end
3. In **Billy Elliott,** when he was asked, "Why do you dance?", he answered, "I can feel it in my bones."

This is how I am suggesting you visualize your book: Everything you

33: Beginning to Write Some Nice Simple Pointers

mention in the book eventually supports and leads to one most memorable moment, or lesson, or focus.

If you have seen at least one of the movies above, recall the scenes and dialogues and see how they all connected to the most memorable or meaningful scene.

As an exercise, see your entire book as a two-hour movie. You've heard how movies get edited and whittled down to what the public finally views. Get your narrative to lead to a crucial main one.

I'm going to kill this book's ending for you, just so you can learn now.

Once in a while I tell you that we should not have to go to hell for our art. This is my message. God created and shared his creation with everyone. We create art to help everyone to make money. There must be a way. Our memoirs and art books will help. Our intentional scarcity and price increase schedule will help too.

We do not create art to penetrate a members only world of intrigue, jealousy, envy and spite where people are willing to lie to show their art is valuable and collectible.

So now you know. We do not have to go to hell for our art. That's what I call the #valzubiriagenda.

The initial 55,000 words in this book

Remember that your entire life cannot be whittled down to 55,000 words.

I took the time to count where the 55,000 words are for this book. Including the Introduction, it's on page 174. This will be how thick your book will be if the size of your text is 11.3 points (pt). The recommended size is between 11 and 12 pt, so start with 12 pt. I personally entertain between 11 pt and 12 pt. Print out a few pages to see which size looks best for you.

If you want to see how thick 55,000 words feels at 12 pt, go to page 240. As you can see, by reducing most of the text to 11.3, We saved 66 pages or 33 sheets of paper. I shrunk the size to a negligible fraction to use less paper and keep cost down.

I played with the line spacing between paragraphs in this book, so you see a slight space between the paragraphs. Page 240 is just an approximation.

Write in the language you are comfortable in

I'm fluent in English and Filipino. My language of choice when I write is English. I have an accent when I speak English. I wish I speak more languages.

Writing is 1% writing and 99% editing. I do my best to catch mistakes. You will see mistakes in this book. I has not stopped me from publishing it.

Write in the language you are comfortable in.

Giving your book a title

Your first book will evolve. So will your other books.

You can start with an idea for a title and start writing stories around that idea. When you want to divert, allow yourself. The title will evolve as well.

When you write, and then when you reread and edit, you will discover your own ways to veer your stories back to your central idea. You will find that out for yourself.

Towards the last chapters of your book, and as you edit, you will know the best title to use.

Chapter 34

Secrets Before You Begin Writing

How bookstores arrange books

Go to a bookstore. You will notice that the books are categorized as best as the bookstores can. If you look at the back cover of most books, you will notice the suggested categorization by the publishers. Here are some examples of categories for nonfiction:

Religion / Spirituality
New Age
UFOs / Paranormal
Business / Marketing
Business / Leadership
Self-Improvement
Business / Advertising
Science / Technical
Programming
Art / Artists
Art / Crafts
Art / Reference

If you are writing a memoir, you can categorize your book as Art / Memoir or Art / Biography.

Your art books can have Art / Collection

I'm digressing. Here is why I want to show you the categorization:

I want you to realize for yourself that the categorizations transition to other categorizations.

Here is an example:

Self-improvement ⇒ Finding a lover ⇒ Seduction ⇒ Advertising ⇒ Writing ⇒ Branding ⇒ Marketing ⇒ Leadership ⇒ Self-improvement

As you can see, 1. you improve yourself, 2. if you better yourself, you find a lover, 3. you learn to seduce, 4. seduction is also part of advertising, 5. you learn to write in general and write advertisements in particular, 6. when you get into advertising you also get into branding, 7. branding and advertising are part of marketing, 8. all these lead to leadership, and 9. lessons in leadership leads you back to self-improvement.

Most books can be connected, despite categorization in bookstores and libraries.

For example, if you open a book on marketing, you will notice that it mentions leadership in the marketplace, which means it has a leadership angle in the book.

Here is how this relates to your book: As you write, you might be writing about your life—this qualifies as a memoir. The story is about when you triumphed as a leader—this also qualifies as a leadership book. You might have triumphed because the town finally got to know about your mission and you—this also makes it a book on personal branding.

You can tell others you're writing your memoir, but know that just because you are going to be shelfed under Art / Memoir or Art / Biography, you are allowed to include stories related to leadership, recovery, addiction, self-improvement, marketing, advertising, history, cooking, new age, science, World War 2, the Gulf War, etc.

Here is a visualization exercise prior to writing

Imagine having written your book. Imagine that someone read it and that reader approached you, smiling. Imagine that reader saying your book was a joy to read, that it was sad in some parts, and happy in other parts. Imagine that reader telling you that the ending was greatly thought of, because it was triumphant, after all that happened prior. Imagine that reader telling you that he or she saw himself or herself in

34: Secrets Before You Begin Writing

your stories.

This is how I sometimes write my books. I imagine the reactions of my readers, and then tell my story to meet the reaction. So, in my mind, my life stories are just ways to elicit the emotions of the readers.

So my life becomes a metaphor—a way for others to learn life lessons and to find themselves in.

Some illusions we have are misleading

I have seen some black and white movies where the writer, using his typewriter to eke out a book, eventually covered his room's floor with crumpled sheets of paper. That's just for show.

Become aware that we all choose different words to use in our sentences. We all construct different sentences to convey the same idea. More and more possible variations happen when we construct paragraphs and chapters.

Then we finally come out with a book, which other people would have written differently.

Knowing this, you should simply write and keep on writing, from start to finish. You can return to the beginning and edit later.

Be rest assured that no one ever makes a perfect book that would only be rewritten in the same exact way, because it is perfect.

You can reshuffle your life

Here is an example of a memoir's progression:

A. Childhood
B. Teens
C. Tragedy - Accident happened
D. Recovery from the tragedy
E. You got married
F. Someone died
G. You got old
H. Life continues

You can reshuffle this. You can start with D. Then proceed from A to H, tackling D again somewhere.

You can start with F. Then A, then G, then H, then B, E and C while almost forgetting D, which you include in the end.

You can just have G stories in your book.

This is all up to you.

Here are some funny writing ideas

These are also up to you:

Why don't you just make up stories with absurd scenes of success?

Or just invent stories related to art, involving yourself?

You can also have 5 writers write about the same period of time in your life, and have the readers discover the variety of treatment.

You can have a book where the writers actually just bullshit about you.

I think all this is fair game. Once again, as long as the readers are in on the joke and want to be entertained, you can do whatever you want.

There was a writer who claimed to be an alcoholic, only to be outed. His publisher recalled his books. The book obviously was a solo project. If you are part of a group collaboration, you are disrespecting the others who trusted you if you lied and got featured in a book where everyone else was honest.

It only takes a day for print on demand companies to approve a newly uploaded replacement of the previous book. Your group can opt to remove your contribution.

But and define famous

There is one major word I avoid during conversations and when writing. The word is "but."

Imagine a conversation. Person A is talking to Person B. Person A is sharing information with Person B, so Person B is expected to listen. Then Person B says, "but," and continues the conversation by correcting Person A with new thoughts. Person B actually stopped the flow of Person A's thoughts because of a single word that could have been avoided.

I do my best to avoid the word "but" in my writing. It subconsciously stops the reader from continuing with the thought that was previously introduced.

The writer who mentions a flow of thought, followed by a "but" feels to me like a straight road that suddenly has a bump followed by an

34: Secrets Before You Begin Writing

unexpected bend and a sudden appearance of bandits.

People have a way to stop the flow of a conversation by saying something similar to "but."

My friend Arthur does this.

When I jest, telling my friend Arthur, "I need to get famous," and he answers back with "Define 'famous'," he is actually stopping the flow of the joke by attempting to prove to be smart. He wasn't playing along.

Let me now define the phrase "suspension of disbelief."

The suspension of disbelief

When we go to the theater to see a movie, we pay as much as $25 for the ticket, popcorn, soda and whatever food we can get from the concessions.

After spending so much, we expect to enjoy the movie. We willingly "suspend our disbelief." We don't tell ourselves that the movie is just a movie and not real life. In order to enjoy the movie, we pretend the movie is real—we suspend our disbelief.

When we communicate with another person, we let the conversation flow. We suspend our disbelief.

For example, when Person A says, "I have four kids," Person B could ask, "How old are they?" Person B suspends disbelief to let the conversation progress.

If Person B says, "I don't believe you have four kids. Prove it. Show me a picture and their birth certificates," that's disbelief. It stops the conversation.

In our memoirs, we tell our stories with the assumption that the readers believe us. We do not show baptismal papers just to prove our kids have a god, and show report cards with a date on it, just to tell readers that our kids went to school and were smart at a certain age.

Our minds always look for resolution and closure

When we go to see a movie, we want to get entertained and come out feeling satisfied. It is in our nature to expect that, after we had paid for the expensive tickets and even more expensive popcorn and soda. We leave knowing the resolution and closure to the story.

The only movie I remember that was just suddenly and abruptly ended was **Isadora,** released in 1968, starring Vanessa Redgrave. After two hours of watching the movie on cable television, the movie ended with Isadora Duncan suddenly dead. Her long scarf got caught in a wheel of the car she was on. In the movie, she wasn't even removed from her awkward, lifeless position. No one bothered to even at least close her glaring, open eyes. No onlooker, not even the driver showed emotion.

Creatively, the resolution was a few seconds of other people near the car, still partying, then the sea, then the credits. Thank goodness the 2-hour movie was good, so it still got good reviews despite the short, almost abrupt closure. The movie got away with this short ending. You better be a good writer if you can just suddenly end your book unapologetically.

I compare that movie with the story, **The Little Match Girl,** by Hans Christian Andersen. The story is about a girl who, in winter, on New Year's Eve, used up her matches to keep herself warm. The next day, the townsfolk found her frozen to death, but the story did not end there. She found herself in heaven with her grandmother.

As you can see, the ending was happy. There was resolution and closure through an idealized situation of being in heaven, even if, in real life, there is no heaven and God does not exist. I'm kidding.

Make sure there is resolution and closure in your book, unless your real intention is to not have it.

Chapter 35

Actual Writing Bigger & Better Tips!

Get comfortable!

I can tell you where I wrote my books and what laptop I used.

My first ever attempt to write was written in coffee shops in downtown Chicago. There were at least four cafés. Towards the middle, I discovered that there was a 24-hour Starbucks exactly 2 miles from where I lived. I walked to and from there. It was about 7 a.m. when I was rushing with adrenalin and caffeine and my heart was pounding fast, when I felt I had written my last chapter's last word.

I also wrote a lot at a nearby Argo Tea, which then had just opened.

All this was between 2005 and 2006. I shelfed the book until I had the courage to take chapters from it in 2013 and 2014 to include in three books and a fourth, unfinished one.

Dollman the Musical, A Memoir of an Artist as a Dollmaker, was written at a café on Halsted Street in Chicago. I finished it on the eve of Thanksgiving, in 2012. I immediately sent it to about 4 individuals whom I trusted. I probably should not have done that, but I did.

In 2013, I started writing what was to become **Hocus Pocus Lately, Wonder** and **1-Hour Mentors.** These three books have really long titles. My dad in 2013 was diagnosed with pancreatic cancer. I went to church daily for the 8 a.m. mass, asking God to miraculously cure my dad. The mass finished at 8:30 a.m., I walked to the nearby Jewel, a popular grocer, bought two donuts at 65 cents each, went home, made coffee, and opened my laptop to write my chapters.

I ended up with the three books and half of a book. If I ended up with a few chapters for a book that cannot be completed yet, I call it the "half."

This book that I'm writing, **Valzubiriagenda,** my initial goal was to keep writing until I had enough to organize for two simultaneous books. I started at a nearby café, Everybody's Coffee, in 2016. I then decided to tweak this at home, lying in bed for hours on end, only getting up to use the bathroom, eat or make some coffee.

My plan has changed. I now want to release one book in January 2018. Here is a February update: It is now February. I'm just editing now.

So stay where you are at. Find a comfortable spot, and get into the habit of writing. You don't need a cabin in the woods unless it's haunted by the ghost of a writing coach.

What I learned from a speed reading workshop

I attended a speed reading workshop when I was on my third year in college. Speed reading seriously helped me become a better writer.

We were taught not to do the three "evils" of reading:

1. Fixation
2. Subvocalization
3. Regression

Fixation means that as a person reads, that reader sometimes stops moving forward, and instead fixates on a word or an area of the page. Sometimes, a reader would fixate on a sentence or a paragraph. We should keep moving forward if we want to finish reading the book. Avoid fixation!

Subvocalization is when the reader pronounces each word in the reader's head. Sometimes, the reader whispers the words. Sometimes the reader reads out loud. Sometimes the tongue moves, even when the mouth is closed. All these are the evil forms of subvocalization. Avoid subvocalization!

Regression is when the reader returns to an earlier word, sentence, paragraph or chapter, because the reader felt that understanding the previous sections more would help understand the upcoming sections better. Avoid regression!

Applying this to writing, we should avoid doing the following. Avoid

35: Actual Writing Bigger & Better Tips!

fixating on writing a section that seems to be difficult to tackle. Simply place a message like *"xxxxxxxxx add rape incident here xxxxxxxxxxxx,"* and keep moving on. When the book is finished, use your word search and locate all the "xxxxx" markers. You will be directed to the sections that you still need to follow up.

When we write, including when we type, it might be okay to subvocalize. The reason for this is that we type at a slower speed anyway. If you have read tips on writing, it will include the idea that you should write as if you were speaking to your reader. Subvocalization is more or less okay.

Regression is not good. When you write, simply add the usual *"xxxxxx add the cooking incident at an earlier chapter after the garbage incident xxxxx."* Keep writing forward.

Regression happens when a writer keeps returning to a previous chapter in an attempt to make it better.

How to ruin the writing process for a book

Learn to trust not only yourself, but your readers. Most of them aren't stupid.

Be consistent with your writing style from start to finish.

Avoid returning to a chapter to perfect it.

If you keep regressing as described above, you might tire of writing your book towards the middle and the end. Just keep writing your draft until the end. When you return to the beginning of your book, you need to once again edit without regressing. Your style of writing will be consistent this way.

Readers will know if they read something well-written at the beginning and bad towards the end. You may have experienced this in the movies, where the movie was nice and exciting at the start and then it dragged to a lousy uninspired ending. Don't think that your readers won't find out.

You might discover that you cannot complete sentences. Keep on writing. Avoid regressing just because you cannot complete sentences. Look back and edit your work later, once you have written your entire book. If you still cannot correctly complete sentences, ask someone else for help. Ask a good editor if you can find one.

The magical letters

The magical letters are five or more "x's." As you type, you will need to find the right word, or need to correctly spell a word. You might be at a loss for the correct phrase or idiom.

Keep on typing. If you run into something that you are not sure of, add something like, "xxxxxxxx need to spell interrupt correctly or use that other word that Robert used xxxxxx," and keep on typing.

Once you're done with the entire book, word search "xxxx." Return to them, research and make the revision.

Avoid validation

I'm sure some professional writers say one thing and do something else.

Some writers claim their spouses read their work as they churn them out. That only works in the movies.

The way for the spouse to feel special is by telling the writer their thoughts, critique and advice about what the spouse just read, even though the actual writer is already a few chapters ahead. That's regression with a touch of codependency. They need a marriage counselor.

That feels like the blind leading the blind. It feels like the crazy pair in Chapter 22. The ending might change. It has not been written yet. How can anyone assess work while it's still being worked?

Write as if you're talking

When you write, do your best to write as if you were talking to a single reader. As the writer, you would be the speaker.

I have a Filipino accent. When I speak, you can hear the accent. I can only hear the accent when I record myself and listen to the playback.

I write as I would speak, so you can almost be sure I would have a Filipino way of writing. There are some idioms I would not personally use, which means you would not find them here.

I like my "Filipinoness" to permeate my writing as needed. Our books are supposed to last 300 to 3,000 years, when we hopefully become celebrated as unique sources of story and art. Our voices should not be fully changed into something else. They just need to be acceptably orderly and understandable.

35: Actual Writing Bigger & Better Tips! 205
Start with a pen and paper

Planning the book every once in a while rehearses my mind. I would get a pen and a sheet of paper and diagram my book.

Let's say I want to write about having been a waiter, as it related to my pursuit of art.

I would put a circle in the middle of the page, and write something like "waiter memoir" on it. Then I think about the chapters the book can have, placing them in separate circles. I connect these chapter circles to the central memoir circle.

Some chapters might have one main idea with three short stories, so each story gets a circle connected to their chapter circle.

Next, I would order the chapters, numbering them from 1, 2, 3, 4, 6, onwards. If two new chapters come to mind that has to be between 4 and 5, for example, I just number them "4b" and "4c."

I use a laptop and the Notepad software

I use a Windows laptop to write my book. I make a new folder, and name it something like "001 Val Waiter Memoir."

I open the folder and right-click to make text files. Each text file is usually a chapter. I make as many text files as I need, and rename them, like 001 Clerk job, 002 Quitting, 003 First Waiter job, etc. This way, I know the ordering of the chapters. Once again, if I decide to insert a new chapter in between two chapters, like between 002 and 003, I would name them "002b" and "002c."

The reason I use Notepad, is that I type fast. There is no lag time. I immediately see the letters on the screen as I type them. I can immediately correct what I'm typing.

The way I separate paragraphs is by returning two lines. I add more lines if there's something I need to clarify or add later.

Notepad prevents me from pausing to italicize anything. I will do that later on.

Eventually, I will have a folder filled with text files, each having a chapter or a story. When I'm ready to compile them into a book, I redo the numbering again.

The window automatically rearranges the chapters as they get renamed. I rename everything like this: 001 becomes 0001, 002 ⇉ 0002,

002b ⇉ 0003, 002c ⇉ 0004, 0003 ⇉ 0005.

Just so I don't lose my precious files, I duplicate the entire folder and work on the new folder.

Working with editors and book designers

Remember that your book will have your name on the cover. Your editor's and book designer's names and companies might be included in the Acknowledgments. Your book designer can also be included in the copyright page, together with some acknowledgments of fonts used.

If it's your reputation that's at stake, you should probably read what you wrote, and see if you can find your own mistakes first, before letting your editor take over.

Editors will not bring your work to perfection. They will do their best, except that if you don't, they won't.

After Notepad I use InDesign

I cannot tell you to find the software you will "like" working with, as if we all have choices all the time. I'm honestly telling you, right now, that I use InDesign. I would not master various software if my goal is to churn out a single book.

Because I don't collaborate with editors, I immediately transfer my files to Adobe InDesign. This is also the final page design software that I use.

Each text file gets its own InDesign document file. There is Book option in InDesign, where you have a Book window where you can arrange and rearrange the documents for the book.

The good thing about this is that the files you open and close are separate chapters. If you work with a single document that has all your chapters, and you make a mistake, you can lose or alter your entire book.

I will talk more about editing and book design in later chapters. (Chapter 37 and Part 4)

Chapter 36

My Writing Secrets
Get Started with These Techniques

I know some people freeze when they begin to write

There are secrets to writing. People would not talk about it.

There is such a thing as hypnotic writing. If you've heard of the phrase, "reading between the lines," there is also something I call "writing between the lines."

What you can learn from Harry Potter

As you know, Harry Potter made J.K. Rowling rich, but you might not have realized why.

When you get the opportunity, find a copy of a Harry Potter audiobook read by Stephen Fry, and another children's audiobook by a lesser-known author.

Any edition of Harry Potter will do, as long as it was read by Stephen Fry. I have yet to listen to the books as read by Jim Dale, so I cannot vouch for him as of this book.

You will notice something in the audiobook that you might not have in the printed version: The book sings. Stephen Fry read the books as if the words and sentences kept rhyming with each other. If you listen to how other books by the lesser-known authors were read, you will notice that they don't rhyme or sing in your head.

This is hypnotic writing. It would seem unexplainable, but it happens. J.K. Rowling, I believe, knows principles of hypnotic writing quite well.

The children read the Harry Potter books not knowing that they were reading sentences that seemed to rhyme and sway.

So now that you know, write as if you were following the way the Harry Potter books were written. Even if you only subconsciously are entertaining this thought, your writing will be good. Once again, practicing writing will get you better, just like when you make your art. You will improve.

Your choice of words

Let us look at the use of words using a classic example of optimism and pessimism:

"The glass is half full" versus "The glass is half empty."

If you say something like "The glass is half empty," you are prepping your reader that something less than nice will happen.

If you write something like "The glass is half full," you are hinting at a future optimistic event or view. You are prepping your reader, subconsciously to expect something good, maybe in the next paragraph or the next chapter or the entire book.

Here is something else to consider. When I wrote the two paragraphs above, I initially explained the glass is half full first, followed by the glass is half empty. When I edited, I placed the half empty explanation first, followed by the optimistic half full explanation next.

This is because the mind can also tend to remember the later "thing."

What a Christmas carol can teach you

Look at the lyrics of the classic Christmas carol, **Angels We Have Heard On High.** The English version is a loose, but inspired, translation of the French original. You can research more later. For now let us look at two stanzas.

> Angels we have heard on high
> Sweetly singing o'er the plains
> And the mountains in reply
> Echoing their joyous strains
>
> Shepherds, why this jubilee?
> Why your joyous strains prolong?

36: My Writing Secrets Get Started with These Techniques

What the gladsome tidings be
Which inspire your heavenly song?

Did you ever realize, if you are Christian, that the first stanza is the most popular, the most memorable and the most enjoyable to sing? This is because of the choice of words.

All the words in the first stanza are words that make you "high," big, great tasting, happy. Angels, heard, high, sweet, singing, over, plains, mountains replying, echo, joyous, strains. Add the fact that all this is in a song which uses sopranos and orchestral musical instruments.

Now, compare this with the "Shepherds why this jubilee" stanza and the other stanzas. The word "shepherds" brings you back on the ground. Jubilee is not as fun. In other stanzas, there will be a mention of Bethlehem where most of us have never been, bended knee might not be enjoyable to people with arthritis. There is also mention of a manger—not a comfortable location. Granted that Jesus was born to save the world, we are talking about word use.

What I'm showing you is that the words you use subconsciously influences your readers. You can choose, just like the first stanza, a barrage of grandiose, high words. This will make your readers like you.

Here is a principle of hypnosis

We all know that when hypnotism is mentioned, we imagine a swinging pocketwatch or pendulum. It might be difficult to explain, but our minds like something that goes back and forth, back and forth.

When you write, imagine the swinging, but use it for size, time or something else.

Here is an example of size

"You opened your eyes, and looked at the gigantic stuffed toy near you. The tiny alarm clock woke you up, and you decided to shut it off with the smash of a hand, as you looked up to the sun just outside your window. As you became aware of the deafening sound of the large garbage truck, it was followed by the beeping of your neighbor's smaller Toyota."

If you look at the order of the words, you will notice the swinging of size. Your small eyes ⇒ gigantic stuffed toy ⇒ small hand ⇒ large sun ⇒ small window ⇒ large garbage truck ⇒ small beep and larger Toyota.

If you reorder the description so that the small ones slowly get larger, the description would not be as fun.

The conscious mind cannot explain this, but the subconscious mind gets entertained.

What I just told you can break your writer's block. This is how you can begin your story. You hypnotize your readers into submission to keep reading.

Here is an example of time

You can apply this to the sense of time. This is also good for public speaking. Here is an example.

"You woke up at 2 p.m., remembering the time last night when you got in drunk—3 a.m. Now that you're awake, you feel for the ring that you placed in your pocket two days ago, which will be needed for your friend's wedding in just a few hours."

Did you notice how the time swings back and forth?

2 p.m. ⇉ last night at 3 a.m. ⇉ Now that you're awake ⇉ two days ago ⇉ wedding in just a few hours.

Dollman the Musical

Let me show you what I did for **Dollman the Musical, A Memoir of an Artist as a Dollmaker.** Let me show you a couple of stanzas from one of the songs, *We'll Be Like Children:*

> In your little room,
> When you close your eyes you'll find
> As far as anyone can see
> A wondrous world of music and

> It may all just be in your mind
> Where nothing's left behind
> This great imagination
> It can save each and every nation

> We'll be like children
> We'll be like birds and fish and
> Maybe even lions roaring loud

36: My Writing Secrets Get Started with These Techniques

We'll be like earth and fire
And water and the air

We'll be the universe
We'll go between the heavens and this earth
We'll be this silent, creative, cosmic world of perfection
A sudden burst of grand creation that surpasses all expectations

This calls for a simple celebration
This world, this imagination
We can make things be
We can fly away and be free

And still be here...

Notice that I deliberately used words to swing.

Little room ⇒ close your small eyes ⇒ as far as anyone can see large ⇒ wondrous world large and mind ⇒ just be in your mind small and limited ⇒ nothing is left behind huge ⇒ great imagination inside your mind large intangible ⇒ save each and every nation huge outside world tangible ⇒ children small ⇒ birds and fish smaller ⇒ lions roaring larger ⇒ earth, fire, water, air much larger ⇒ universe even larger ⇒ between heavens and earth even larger because it's even more difficult to conceptualize ⇒ silent smaller ⇒ creative back to the mind ⇒ cosmic world large ⇒ perfection large ⇒ sudden burst small concept ⇒ grand creation large concept ⇒ surpasses larger concept ⇒ expectations back down to limited concept ⇒ simple celebration like a birthday small ⇒ imagination large ⇒ fly away like a bird small + away is heading out ⇒ still be here you are taken back to where you are.

I have had a friend email me back to tell me that she could not explain it, but after reading my book, she felt happy, elated and calm. Her problem at that time was that her daughter was undergoing chemotherapy. She was an atheist so she didn't believe there was a God who can help her, and she was also divorced.

My book provided something helpful to her, at a time when she needed to feel better about her situation. Her daughter got better. They traveled out of the country as soon as her daughter became healthy again. I have had years of theatre, I learned writing secrets and mixed them together.

You only need a few tips to get started

Those people who go to universities to learn to write hope to teach people to write. You're not going to be teaching how to write, unless you're already a writing teacher.

If you think you need to learn more on writing, read one book on how to write. Base your writing on the pointers of that one book. Analyze the time you have to finish your book.

Remember that we may or may not be pressed for time. As we plot and plan our books, there are investors and art collectors waiting for a chance to see our art pieces and books.

Know full well, that if you are just beginning to entertain writing, so are the others. There is no need to go to school for writing. That's a delaying tactic. You might come out with a diploma in hand, while everyone's art pieces had sold and the #valzubiriagenda had peaked. There may not be another art trend for decades.

All you need is to produce one book. Avoid people with discouraging remarks. Treat your writing as a professional move to sell your professional original art or art collection. This can be manageable. Start to get the flow going and get to the end of your manuscript.

Chapter 37

Editing & Proofreading
Read Your Work 8 Times

How to edit your work

One of my sisters is a book editor. She told me one magical, wondrous thing that I follow to this day:

Read through your book at least 8 times. You will always find something to change. Get to the end and then start over. After the eighth read and edit, it should be at its best.

You will also be proofreading as you progress.

Writing is 1% writing and 99% editing

When I say I'm writing a book, I'm actually already editing. I don't tell people I'm writing a book when I'm really just beginning to write.

Like what I have said before, I encourage you not to tell people that you are writing a book, except those whom you are working with. Form your #valzubiriagenda group and find help and support here.

Be online as you edit

This is new to our generation. If you are online, you can immediately check the spelling of words. You can find out when to add or not add hyphens between words. Find out if you should use "é" instead of "e." Prepositions and conjugations can be confusing. There are idioms to use. Sometimes we want to add a proverb. Sometimes we need correct dates in our discussion.

Decades ago, I used to get confused—why use "on the plane" instead of "in the plane." Why be "in" New York City and be "on" Earth.

Backup your files

Whenever you work on a file, make sure you have an original file kept in a safe place.

If you have everything in one single laptop, and you elegantly like to laze about in cafés to edit your work, you can lose the books and associated files if your laptop gets stolen, as soon as you get back to your life-changing wonderful work, after sitting on the toilet.

You can begin editing by having two folders in your laptop. One folder will contain all of your original, related files, and the other folder will contain the files that get actively revised. Only touch the second folder. Later on, just to be safe, make a duplicate of the second folder and work on that new folder. Store the older folders elsewhere in another storage device.

You can also opt to use an online file storage like Google Drive, which has a default size of 15 gigabytes. 15 gigabytes can be fast to use up per project, if you want to constantly duplicate files after every noticeable progress.

I usually use up a lot of storage space myself. For images, I would start with Folder #1 for the original images, naming the folder, "Originals Do Not Touch." Then I will duplicate the folder and call it "Revised 001." I would only photoedit the pictures in Revised 001. Then I will duplicate this folder and call the new folder "Revised 002 Renamed." This will be where I will rename the files that will be used for the books and e-books. If I need to convert the files to black and white, I will make another folder for that.

I do the same thing for the text files. I will have the original files in one folder, then have a second folder to work on.

In Chapter 35, I described how each chapter becomes a text file, how I name and rename files to keep them in order, and how all the files are located in one folder. Once I'm done with writing and the next stage is editing, I would duplicate the folder and work on the new folder, leaving the older folder intact.

Make sure to have backups like this along the way. If you take your laptop to cafés, have backups at home, in a separate hard drive or flash drive. If you feel it would also be good to store the files online, do so.

Choose your book's size at the editing stage

I copy and paste all my text to Adobe InDesign. It is the software I use to both edit and finalize my book design. Each chapter still goes to a new InDesign file.

This is when I go to my chosen online self-publishing company to choose the book's final dimensions. This is also when I set the margins that I want my final book to have. I also choose the font and the font size that will be used in the book.

If you don't know anything about InDesign, you can watch YouTube videos about it.

I will talk more about finalizing in InDesign in a later chapter.

Working with an editor and a book designer

This will be when you can start looking for an editor and a book designer who can finalize your book for you.

Remember that we are not here to improve your skills. We are here to produce your book as fast as possible. As you are doing this, so are others. We're all hoping to make money from art investors and collectors. The sooner we have our books, the better.

Ignorance is bliss

If you decide to go to a book designer, before you get your work edited, you will have a nice-looking book that needs editing. I have seen this before.

I was in a medical study in 2009. We were supposed to be at the facility for more than a week. There was a man who said he has written a book, who also uploaded it to the same online company I used in 2006, Lulu. I asked to see his book.

The book looked like a book. I randomly opened a page, I read a few lines and noticed his sentences could have been better. The closing quotation marks came before periods, etc. His sentences and the way he conveyed his story did not make sense to me. The book needed heavy editing. He was still proud of his work. I was happy for him.

He was on the right track. We all have periods of learning. It has been years. I'm sure he has produced more books. I make an assumption that we all write badly. What makes our writing better is editing.

When you're feeling the high of just having finished writing your book, you can easily think that the book is done. You might decide to just see the book printed without even taking a look at it. The things that happen during this time are great experiences. Nevertheless, they are great *early* experiences.

Don't get free editing with paid book design

The goal of the book designer is to design the book. Not edit and look for mistakes.

When I take over a book, I know that my goal is to make the book as close to *industry standards* and *consumer expectations* as possible.

This means that the book should be well-edited *and* well-designed. I make myself aware of this when I'm working on a book, *because* I'm the one working on it. I really put my sense of responsibility and care *and* love to the book. I know that book projects last a lifetime and in our case, 300 to 3,000 years.

Even so, I still overlook some mistakes. As long as the number of mistakes get minimized, I'm fine with it.

Taking the book to a book designer or a desktop designer too soon, without editing, will delay the book more and more.

Book designers are not editors. They might spot mistakes, but ignorance is bliss. If a client thinks the book is fine and just needs to be finalized, they will do their jobs without telling the clients about the mistakes in the book. Caring too much can delay the payment.

Once the writer proudly shows the book to a friend, the mistakes will start emerging. Ideally, the book designer will allow for one or two revisions. Those revisions better be final. The problem at this stage is that the designer would only be expecting *design* revisions, not editing revisions.

A well-edited book will not need revisions because of writer mistakes. The revisions should be for designer mistakes, like if the designer failed to italicize a word.

Traditional publishers know about all this. Just because we're mostly beginners does not mean we should have lowered expectations and standards *unless* we deliberately release the "Unedited Artist's Writing Project." Still, the second version must be well-revised.

37: Editing & Proofreading Read Your Work 8 Times

I just simply start editing my own work

Nowadays, I would personally hesitate having a relative edit my work. The only relative I would trust to edit my work would be my youngest sister, who has been editing coffee table books for more than two decades.

In chapter 27, I described how depression can be debilitating, not just for a writer, but for an editor. In 2006, when my sister tried to help me, she was having a bad time in her life. Had she said that, I would not have let her look at my work. The draft was not just personal to me—I included stories of her and the rest of our families. Maybe she was curious about how I portrayed her in the book.

As a result, I got delayed with other plans. In retrospect, the delay was only three to four months. It has been more than a decade since this happened. We're still alive.

I decided to edit my own books from 2012 and onwards, even if I felt it would be depressing and daunting.

I now also have experience editing other people's works. I now know for a fact that it is easier to look at other people's works because the content is a new sight to the editor. The mistakes and uneasiness when ideas don't flow are clearer.

I know now that editing my own work is always a big challenge. As you read this book, you might discover mistakes that I obviously missed. That's okay. I just remind myself that I did my best and that this book is not a term paper, just like what I always tell you.

So I decided to simultaneously work on three memoirs in 2013 to 2014. It was an experiment. I would go through the depression once. I surprisingly did not feel too depressed. This time, for this book, I had not felt any depression nor anxiety.

Here is one advantage if you edit your own work: You can pressure yourself to finish the editing. You can lose sleep if you want. You can drink as much coffee and even take caffeine tablets.

You can try giving yourself eight days to look through your book eight times. If despite all this, your book gets delayed, you can forgive yourself and allow for more delays.

Getting relatives to edit

(Note: You can see Jerry Miller's &
James Miller's books on page 146)

My friend Jerry Miller, the one who got in touch with me for his first book, **Empty Space: Creating a Theatre in Your Church Step-by-Step,** approached me again this year.

Like what I have told you, as soon as you can prove that you can write a whole book, you will do it again. Our brains will start telling us it's easy.

Jerry got in touch with me for his second book, which was a collaboration with his twin brother, James, entitled, **The Day the Rain Came Down: The Stories of Gay Identical Twins.** They are now 72 years old. Their book tackles their decades of struggle with various types of addiction which they attributed to the sexual abuse they received when they were mere children.

They both separately got into 12-Step programs through the years. With 12-Step programs, you have to admit to your addiction and patch things up with people who were involved, if you can.

Their sister volunteered to help edit the book, so the four of us—the twins, their older sister and I helped find mistakes.

I don't know their sister, nor had I met Jerry's twin brother, James, but I did my best to finalize **The Day the Rain Came Down** because I appreciated the fact that the book was an honest revelation of their lives to the world. I also appreciated the fact that they have a sister who was also willing to read about their tribulations.

Jerry and I met many times for each of the two books at our favorite café. For this second book, we had to meet for the edits and images. Whenever his phone rang, or when he had to ask his sister or brother to confirm details, when he had to mention me, he always referred to me as his editor.

He would say something like, "My editor is here with me, and we need a location clarified."

It's good to hear this from someone else once in a while. You have to get skilled and help someone else with their books if you want to hear this for yourself.

I think it was our level of respect and professionalism that hinted

37: Editing & Proofreading Read Your Work 8 Times   219

to his brother and his sister to treat the project in a professional way, despite the depressing personal stories all three of them had to face as they read to edit.

By involving me, who was not their relative, they looked at their book in a professional, more detached, antiseptic way.

Try editing your work yourself. If you are not yet used to it, and you notice that you are delaying yourself, backup your work, and ask someone to edit.

I can assure you that, in time, facing your own work gets easier.

Let me end this chapter by once again reiterating what I keep telling you.

Try helping others

If you feel you had gotten better at editing, you might still not feel that you are good enough. The only way to find out is to find other people to help.

Make sure that you will be credited somewhere in the book. The acknowledgment section is a good start. This way, you can show the book to others as proof of your skill.

Seeing several names of people who helped make the book can add to the image of the book, so the benefit is not just for the individuals. It is also for the book itself.

The book is not a term paper

I once worked for a free monthly Filipino community paper in Chicago. It made money from ads and paid for features of events.

Some events were formal and sponsored by organizations, some were personal, like a matriarch's birthday celebration or a wedding.

Our deadlines were flexible to a degree to accommodate the events and the printer.

The paper can get complicated. The pages with the events get complicated because the people in the pictures needed to be identified. The articles submitted by the columnists had varying lengths. The paid ads should appear.

Towards the time when the printer's representative came to pick up the final paste up, the publisher would say, "The magazine is not a term paper."

What this means is that she herself and her employees had to let it go. We did our best. Any errors cannot be helped. If there were errors, the next issue would include an erratum.

I have seen errors in books published by big publishing houses. I wonder how strict they can get. We should be more forgiving while still being professional.

hashtag #valzubiriagenda

Part 4

Publishing Books, E-Books & Our Future

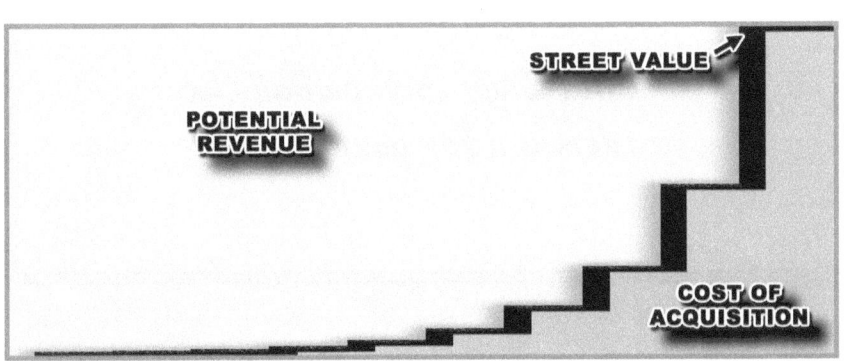

SPECIAL SECTION #4

From Chapter 3 page 27:

Our Herd Mentality is Real

Make it work for you as an investor

If you hear of a bank or a large institution invest a lot of money in an artist, they will have plans and a marketing and promotional budget that you don't have—piggyback on their efforts

Invest only in what you can afford

Get everyone else interested in the same artists

Find ways to snowball the demand for your artists

Chapter 38

A Quick Lesson in Publishing

The famous 19-year old publisher

If you go to bookstores and peruse picture books, you will notice a publisher, Taschen. Chances are you have some of the publisher's books.

Taschen is owned by Benedict Taschen. If you go online to Wikipedia, there are two entries: one about the publishing company and another about the owner. Look at his age. He started his publishing company when he was under 20 years old. He started his company in Germany. Now, his books are all over the world.

He had an ingenious idea which anyone can do.

Classic paintings are in the public domain. Basically, Rembrandt would not sue you for publishing his pictures.

Taschen basically began publishing art books that included what are unglamorously called "stock photos" of famous paintings. You still have to pay for the right to publish the photographs—you still save money, because you do not have to fly to The Louvre in France to take a picture of the Mona Lisa.

Then he published more and more books. Now, his brand is recognizable.

There are lessons to learn from well-known publishers even though there are also differences between us and them.

Taschen and other commercial publishers have the goal of making money from their books. Their books are the ultimate products. Our purpose in publishing ourselves is to sell our original art.

Our books might still end up in the bookstores. If we trend enough, we will have our own regional following. Our local bookstores might decide to carry our books and even hold events for us. All bookstores have a section about the city, province, state and country it is situated in.

The quality of our books

Look at art and picture books in the stores. Our current self-publishing companies will have limitations on the paper and sizes available for us.

We can work with whatever our companies can offer. We can be unique in how we design our covers and interiors. Remember that our memoirs also depend on how well we wrote them. We get better in time.

If the big publishers can do this, so can you

You might notice that some publishers publish different versions of the same book.

With the same exact pages, they can come up with a large hardbound version, a smaller paperback version, a pocket-sized version, a thinner version with some pages taken out, etc.

You can do this with your own art books. Nobody is stopping you.

You can have more than one title available from the same book.

Breaking notions

We have been programmed to become consumers, not producers. When someone tells you that they have a book out, our immediate response tends to be, "I'm going to have to check it out."

If you talk to someone from the publishing industry, they always have the general public in mind. They will always think, "Will your book sell to the general public?"

If only I could have taken you to the publishing conventions so you would realize that anyone can publish. That 19-year old owner of Taschen did not stop himself from becoming a publisher because he was too young. He started in Germany where he is still currently based and he has found worldwide success.

Our books, blogs and websites are exposed internationally because

38: A Quick Lesson in Publishing

they are online. That's a good start.

Our world of publishers

I have been using the term "self-publishing" for a lot of our discussions here. I know it sounds a little off. "Publishing" sounds better. Becoming a "publisher" sounds better than becoming a "self-publisher."

If you go to the publishers and booksellers conventions, you will confirm this for yourself: There are more or less 4 major groups of publishers who attend:

1. Big publishing houses
2. Small presses
3. University presses
4. Self-publishers

Maintaining "self-publishers"

Here is the definition of what a small press is: If you don't have the budget of a large publishing house, then you are a small press.

Even a university press can be a small press. Everything is relative. If you produce books, and you are at a university, and it was your university that financed the publication of the book, then you are a university press. You don't have to call yourself a small press.

Self-publishers are people who publish their own works, so they don't need to submit their books to someone else.

Here is the catch: All these are relative terms. If you decide to publish other people's works, even if you are using CreateSpace, or another online print on demand outfit, you can stop calling yourself a self-publisher. You can call yourself a publisher. You can call yourself a small press.

What I learned from Dov Simens

Dov SS Simens is someone who goes to different cities and countries to teach his famous 2-Day Film School seminar.

I learned about his seminar 6 years prior, but I was not able to match my free time and my budget to fly to the city where he was scheduled. When he finally made it to my city, I made sure to do two things: enroll immediately, and study what he will be talking about, so I can ask good questions.

As I had predicted, I asked the smartest questions. There were students who asked "unprepared" questions. Those two precious days with him were our only chances to ask relevant questions and get our money's worth. Most people did not do their homework.

Some of us flew in from out of town and some drove for 6 hours. They stayed in the hotel. One slept in his car. That's dedication.

Here is the stupid, but striking lesson I can share with you.

What's the difference between a filmmaker and a producer? According to Dov, just the semantics. When you're a straight guy and you talk to a beautiful girl, Dov said, and she asks you what you do for a living, would you say you're a filmmaker or a producer?

He gave us permission to use the word "producer," and to ditch "filmmaker" forever.

Filmmakers are people who do not have the confidence to call themselves producers. Producers are perceived as people with money, even if they don't. Producers will use other people's money anyway, he explained. As you can see, it's more about how you perceive and present yourself.

I'm now defining the term "publisher" and "self-publisher" for us, thanks to Dov SS Simens. The moment that you decide to help others see themselves in book form—this is the moment you can call yourself a publisher.

You can go as far as calling yourself a small press. I have helped others publish. I just like sticking to the term self-publisher.

Your café, restaurant, beauty salon, store or office can now become publishers, just like the university presses and small presses.

Another important lesson from Dov

He said, the moment you get an idea for a film, that becomes a film project. That's "a stage of development."

As long as you are entertaining ideas for your movie, you're already at a stage of development.

If you are entertaining more than one movie idea, you can start telling people, "I have movie projects at different stages of development."

Let's use this in referring to our books. Even if you are just planning to write or publish, then you're already at a stage of development.

If you are going to become a publisher of other people's books, then that's a stage of development. If you have two book ideas, then that makes it plural.

You can therefore easily tell everyone, "I have book projects at different stages of development," or "I'm a publisher with book projects at different stages of development."

This is legitimate. You're not lying.

What I learned from a large, famous publisher

I don't want to name names again, but I eventually figured out what a publisher that makes seven figures does.

Almost all of their books are the same size. They have the same theme, same book design, same look.

I initially thought that they stick to the same look for their books as part of their branding. I still think this way. However, I discovered something more useful to us.

They go to the same printer—a print on demand printer. The same people we use.

There is no need to keep changing the sizes of their books because their readers had gotten used to the same format anyway.

Basically, if a bookstore needs 20 copies of a book they publish, all this publisher needs to do is to order 20 books from the print on demand printer. The printer sends the books straight from the printing press to the bookstore.

This is obviously an aspect of their business that nobody needs to know. I'm telling you this so that you eventually realize that all this is doable and is getting easier and easier.

Their books look as professional as any other book. We just need to be as professional as we can, and make our books look like any other book.

What some galleries can learn from us

Some gallery owners also make art. They mix their own art with the art of the artists they represent.

Some high-end galleries frown on this. I have heard some galleries say if you're a gallery, be a gallery, and if you're an artist, be an artist. How can you promote other artists when a customer comes in, when you're also telling the customer to buy your own art?

Once again, we see the pecking order of people here.

The #valzubiriagenda once again evens out the playing field. We're doing things and even calling ourselves publishers because we can.

If some of us only recently decided to become artists, then so be it.

If a gallery owner wants to make art, so be it.

We're all in good company and our company will just keep getting bigger and bigger.

I encourage those galleries that carry their own owners' art pieces to look into #valzubiriagenda sooner than the galleries who want to stick to the traditional approaches and views.

Becoming a publisher

Here is why I like to call myself a self-publisher.

When someone approaches me to help them with their books, I coach them on how to open their own accounts with CreateSpace.com, Lulu.com or elsewhere. Because they have to maintain their own books, they become self-publishers themselves.

I become just a helper in their own publications, even when it was I who helped edit, rewrite, design the books, photograph images, photoedit all their pictures, and even make suggestions on promotion and what to do next. I want them to experience the process of publication, promotion and owning their books.

I do call myself a publisher at times—I just need to be consistent in this book. I will have a call for artists, but that will be for later. I need to establish myself as an artist and a memoirist, just like all of us.

Chapter 39

Which Print on Demand Company to Use

When you do your own research

There are many companies that offer print on demand publishing or printing. Search one for yourself. Make sure you use the terms "self-publishing" and "print on demand." Do not use "vanity press." I cannot endorse one single company, because these companies compete with each other and they can easily change prices and policies, etc. to make themselves more appealing to us.

If you go to Wikipedia's "Self-publishing" entry, you will see an updated list of print on demand publishers.

Your major considerations are the following:

1. The ISBN
2. Distribution online, physical bookstores and other venues
3. Your upfront costs
4. The confidential wholesale prices of your books
5. How you want your books to look like
6. The fact that you are new to all this
7. Can you submit and manage your works and book sales from your country

This is an intricate web of considerations. I can name two companies to consider, and there are more on the internet. As you will eventually discover for yourself, they have different advantages and disadvantages.

The two companies I can recommend are:

1. CreateSpace.com (owned by Amazon.com)
2. Lulu.com

Here are a few more companies to look into:

3. IngramSpark.com (owned by Ingram)
4. BarnesAndNoble.com (owned by Barnes & Noble)
5. SelfPublishedAuthor.com (owned by Bowker.com)
6. BKConnection.com (Go to Open Book Editions at the Berrett-Koehler website)
7. TheBookPatch.com and PrintToPress.com

Once again, check online, including Wikipedia for self-publishing or print on demand companies.

As you can see, even the traditional publishers have gotten into self-publishing or print on demand. This is because this past few years, up to 700,000 new self-published titles are introduced to the market in the United States alone *every year.*

As I have said before, most self-publishers want to make money from the sale of their books.

We are more after the sale of our art. As a rule, we will take advantage of self-publishing and print on demand.

We can publish as much as 20-30 art books per artist, maybe more.

Investors and art collectors will also be able to produce them. Cafés and other venues can also produce books.

Some of these companies have fees up front, so if you don't want to pay for anything, you can use CreateSpace or Lulu.

Online and venue distribution

Don't worry too much about this anymore. Your books will show up in just about all the bookstore databases online and in actual bookstores. When you upload your printed book version in one, they will be

39: Which Company to Use

picked up elsewhere.

Once your book is available to the public on the print on demand company's website, give it a day to a week. It should start appearing in other online stores. Research or ask your company if your book has not shown up.

If you need to supply books to your cafés, offices and other venues, you have a choice: You can order the book wholesale or let the venues order the books retail. If you're a later investor who is reselling the art, you may have to pay retail for the artist's books.

The books you own yourself have a wholesale price. Each site should have a wholesale cost calculator. You can order your books for your venues and investors, so they can also enjoy the discount you get.

ISBN

The ISBN is a unique number. You will need a new ISBN for every version of the books you release. You do not want your customers receiving a paperback version if your ISBN was originally for a hardbound.

If you use a free ISBN from your print on demand company, you cannot use the same ISBN elsewhere. Paid for ISBNs are used by the more traditional publishers. Imagine ordering 5,000 copies of books from China, warehousing them, and distributing them to the stores. This is when you pay for one ISBN from Bowker.

Lulu allows books without ISBNs. Books without ISBNs will only be seen on Lulu.

Variations in formats

CreateSpace.com has a more limited variety of finishes and sizes, especially for full-color books. They don't have hardbound.

Lulu has hardbound options.

Here is my suggestion

Stick to CreateSpace.com or Lulu.com for now. Choose one because you will need their requirements to format and finalize your book.

Once you start making art sales, you can upgrade and reformat your books as needed. Research some more and pay the necessary dues.

TheBookPatch and PrintToPress are managed by the same company.

They have different interfaces. If you want to use a smaller company, then go to them. They do tend to be more costly. However, I have used them before.

I don't want to make this chapter too complicated, so I listed the next 6 locations for you to look into for the future. You're better off learning about them online. Each website has a good number of pages of information for self-publishers.

Once again, Wikipedia. There are many bloggers who also discuss print on demand.

If your country is not served by CreateSpace or Lulu

Check if your country has its own version of CreateSpace or Lulu.

If you don't, partner with a relative whom you can trust who lives in another country, where CreateSpace or Lulu is available, to help you maintain an account. Ask for help.

Chapter 40

Publishing Your Book
What You Should Watch Out For

Why you should visit a bookstore first

When you visit a bookstore, pick out some books you would be interested in looking at and sit somewhere, like their café. Go to the store's bargain section and pick up some books from there as well. Get both fiction and nonfiction titles.

Look at the parts of the book. Look at the cover, back cover and the spine. The spine is the section where the sheets of paper are glued.

Now that you will also become a publisher, look at the copyright page, the dedication page, the table of contents. Look at the cover and how it repeats in the interior title pages.

I tend to repeat the cover three times. I like repeating the cover design with some variation.

Sometimes, there will be an introduction, a preface and acknowledgments. Usually, the nonfiction books will have an index and a glossary of terms. These are all considerations for your book.

If your book needs footnotes, bold letters, italicized letters, etc., then make sure to look at some in the already-published books that have them.

Bring a large notebook and a pen. Write notes, especially on how footnotes are formatted.

Many years ago, I took a few pictures of the interior of a few books. I was approached by a clerk who said that the books were copyrighted material. I told her why I was doing it, and she allowed me to continue.

Remember that your book is *not* a term paper. There is no need to fully study everything about formatting. You just need to have your first book published as you learn a few new pointers here and there.

Operate on a per project basis. If you only have one footnote, there is no need to study how all possible combinations of footnotes are made. Just imagine mimicry. You're supposed to "mimic" what is already expected of a book.

Assume that people do judge a book by its cover and interior. So match your book with what is expected of your book.

Parts of a book

The interior usually has three parts:

1. The frontmatter
2. The body
3. The backmatter

I'm just listing the more specific parts here.

Frontmatter
    Half title page
    Title page
    Copyright page
    Dedication
    Foreword
    Preface
    Acknowledgments
    Introduction
    Table of contents
    Prologue

Body
    Parts
    Chapters

40: Publishing Your Book What You Should Watch Out For

Backmatter
- Epilogue
- Afterword
- Postscript
- Appendix
- Notes
- Bibliography
- Index
- About the author

*You might also want to include an index of art pieces included in your book and their page numbers.

Most of these are self-explanatory.

The half title page is usually at the beginning of the interior, which repeats only a few elements from the cover design.

You might confuse Preface with Introduction. Look for the difference online. You probably do not need a preface if you decide to include all the preliminaries in the introduction. Don't bother with the index if you are not writing a biography.

Here is how I define Preface and Introduction. The Preface is the introduction to the book. The Introduction is the introduction to the topic—it can be the beginning of the narrative.

If you're writing a memoir, go to the bookstore and look at some of them. I would never include an index for memoirs because I fictionalize the names of my characters. I would never name locations nor businesses if I have nothing good to say about them.

If you're writing a biography, see if some biographies use indexes (or indices—these two plural forms are correct). Biographies usually use correct names of people and are more technical. I don't see a lot of beginners in our group writing biographies.

I'm giving you enough pointers and technical knowledge to help you work with someone who would be more knowledgeable than you are. If your desktop designer has experience designing posters and newspapers, and no experience in books, you both could use these more "generalized" tips. Because this is the first book about #valzubiriagenda, I want everyone to continue to these last few pages courageous enough to start all this.

Two words: Eyeball and Mimicry

I'm talking about "eyeball" as an idiom.

When you "eyeball your book" or "get an eyeball on your book," you look at it to spot things that seems off or wrong.

If it is obvious to you that your book is not right, don't pretend like you don't know it's there or not there.

For example, you might think that your background for the cover looks wrong, your title design is not right for your book, or your title is not centered or balanced on the cover. If you feel something is wrong, you can be sure the public will feel it.

One way to come up with a good-looking book is to mimic a book that is already published by professional publishers. Make sure to look at the latest book designs.

Maybe you want to look like a movie poster.

Maybe you like large block letters.

Eyeball your book design to see if it has the look you were aiming for.

I purposefully designed my memoir, **Dollman the Musical, A Memoir of an Artist as a Dollmaker,** to look like a poster for a musical. Then I made my next three memoirs look like indie books from the 80s and 90s, with the thought that as soon as I make another three memoirs, I will redesign all of them.

This book has the look of a business book, even though it has a lot of stories from my life. It is a memoir of sorts, but I will have it classified as a book on business and marketing.

You will notice that Silverio and I have our names elevated, because the exponential graph is below it. That's a design decision that has been done many times. Usually, the image placed below is a skyline. By doing so, the authors' names get elevated toward the center.

Your book design and the elements found in the books will be affected by your own disposition, your country and culture, your design-

40: Publishing Your Book What You Should Watch Out For

er's skills, your text and title designs and your color choice. Colors and color combinations can feel cold, neutral or warm.

I just want you to become aware of certain things. As you "practice" publishing your books, you will become familiar with these.

The interior page margins

I will mention what's important about the interior margins before tackling the cover, because this is easy to miss.

The book is no longer a manuscript. The edges are no longer left, right, top and bottom. They are inside, outside, top and bottom margins.

Here is where "eyeballing" your book becomes useful.

The inside margin is where the pages are glued, where the spine will be. Because the adhesive glue will make it hard to see the letters near it, you must have more empty area on the inside margin than the outside.

The reader's subconscious will pick this discrepancy up. If you make the inside and outside margins equal, the mind of the reader will feel uneasy, because the letters toward the inside margin will feel difficult to view.

You also need the bottom margin to have the largest empty area. The subconscious also picks this up. When you read, you usually see your thumb holding the book at the bottom.

The subconscious needs to feel that you will not keep moving your thumb to read the lowest lines on each page. Your readers' thumbs will tire if they have to keep moving it at every page. The subconscious will dislike your book if this keeps happening.

Even if there is ample empty space on the pages, the subconscious feels at ease if the inside and bottom margins have larger values than the outside and top margins.

Give the bottom margin the most empty space, followed by the inside margin, followed by the ouside margin. As for the top margin, read the next section.

Running heads

The top margin will have the least empty space, because you will also need to place what is called "running heads" or "running headers."

If you open a book that reads from left to right, the running head on the left pages will have the title of the book, while the right pages will either have the chapter title or the author's name.

The top corners also have the page numbers.

For this book, we have opted to place the title and our last names on the left pages, and the chapter names on the right pages.

Finally, all the chapters begin on the right page, with no running head. The page number goes to the bottom center of the page.

Know these "shortcuts"

"Shortcuts"

InDesign has shortcuts in place. You are supposed to use "master pages" to design the pages. There is a way to get the page and chapter numbers automatically produced and updated. There is a command called "preflight" which checks to make sure your links to images and other files are still working correctly.

Let's say you are working on a book on InDesign where each chapter is a separate file, all compiled and ordered on the Book window.

You can assign one file to be the "style source" that other files will follow. You can program "paragraph styles" and "character styles" on that one file, so you can be assured of style consistency throughout your book.

If you need to change a paragraph style, like if you need to change the font for subheadings, you just need to change the paragraph style on that document that you selected to be the source style. Then you just need to "synchronize" all the documents, so all the subheadings that were assigned that same paragraph style will change.

Go online for instructions. I'm using words and phrases from the InDesign software.

The cover

Your covers need to look good. Your decisions on design will be up to you. Obviously, you should have a title, a subtitle, the names of the authors, etc.

Go to your favorite bookstore, and compare book covers and magazine covers. They have different sensibilities. What I find funny with the magazines, you see a famous person on the cover, and right next to that celebrity's face are phrases like, "How to have the most sex in an hour."

40: Publishing Your Book What You Should Watch Out For

Did you ever notice that no celebrity really complains about that? It's part of the culture and the way magazines are marketed.

Celebrities should be thankful to be on a monthly magazine cover because these magazines only have 12 issues a year. That's 12 chances for only 12 celebrities.

The back cover

I will begin with what might escape your attention:

1. The barcode on the back cover
2. *and...* You have to include your retail price on the barcode. If you generate a barcode without a price, your book will look like it came from the bargain section of the bookstores. I can't stress this enough. It escapes many self-publishers
3. On the top left corner of the back of the book, you must make a suggestion of where a normal bookstore should file your book. For example, I'm suggesting that this book should be filed in the marketing section of bookstores, even though I have stories about my life.

    The clerks at the bookstores will follow your suggestion. Since we are writing artist, art collector or art investor memoirs or biographies, you can use "Art / Artist Memoir" or "Art / Artist Biography" or whatever you feel would be the good words to use.

    Go to the Biography and Artist Profile sections of your bookstore, and see what other publishers choose to put on their books.

    I don't want to clump us all into one way of classification. You might creatively produce a children's book about yourself. I personally plan to write fiction in the future based on my misadventures.

    Do not dismiss this just because you think you won't end up in a bookstore. Keep dismissing elements and you will look less and less like a readable book.
4. There is something called "QR codes" which look like cryptic squares with smaller squares inside. Check if

there are more and more books which have those. I haven't bothered using them, but you can. Remember that you're marketing not just your books, but your websites, and whatever else, so look into generating QR codes for your purposes

What text will be on the back of the book?

You will need to add a short blurb about yourself. I am still not comfortable putting a small picture of myself on the back cover to date.

I must warn you about big face pictures / headshots on the back cover. This was used in the past, but not as much anymore. Surely, you must have things to say on the back versus putting a large, smiling mug shot there.

If the book is not about your children, then they should not be on the book cover smiling with you. I personally would not pose with my pets, unless they are part of the story.

You can include an introduction to what people will be reading. You can also include early, advanced praise by other people. If you want to print other people's praises with their names on the back cover or elsewhere in the book, you will need their written permission to do so.

The problem with that is that some of these people will want to read your work *before* you get their go signals. This means that you should already have a well-written, well-edited, well-designed "advanced reading copy" to give to your advance readers.

Then you have to give these readers ample time to read, before you even finalize and release it, because now, other people's reputations are at stake. Some friends they are, delaying your publication.

I also suggest that you repeat the ISBN numbers and your retail price somewhere on the back of the book, besides being on the barcode.

The spine

When you stack books on your shelves, the spine will be the only visible part of your book. It will become an eyesore if your title is upside-down compared to the other professionally made books on the shelf.

You must make sure that your spine's text is rotated correctly.

At the publishers conventions, you will see books with upside-down

40: Publishing Your Book What You Should Watch Out For

spines at the booths of the biggest publishers, the small presses and the self-publishers, although they are a rare sight.

This is a costly mistake for traditional publishers, because they print books by the thousands.

We, on the other hand, only need to revise the cover design and upload the revision. CreateSpace only needs 24 hours or less to approve the new book file.

The spine calculators

You may have noticed that some books have text on their spines that are not perfectly positioned. This is because the size of the spine was off.

Each online print on demand publisher has a spine calculator on their website.

The width of the spine is calculated based on the number of pages your interior pdf file has, and the type of paper you choose.

For example, CreateSpace.com gives you a choice of three types of paper. For black and white interiors, there is a choice of white or cream. For color interiors, there is one choice, white, but it's different from the white paper for black and white interiors.

Let's say you have written your memoir. The total number of pages for your finalized, well-designed 6-inch (width) x 9-inch (height) book is 210.

If you chose the cream-colored paper, the width for your spine will be:

210 pages x .0025 = .525 inch. The dimensions of the spine will be .525 inch x 9 inches.

If you chose white paper, the width for your spine will be:

210 pages x .002252 = .47292 inch, or .473 inch. The dimensions of the spine will be .47292 inch width x 9 inches height.

If you have a full-color interior, the width for your spine will be:

210 pages x .002347 = .49287 inch. The dimensions of the spine will be .49287 inch x 9 inches.

As you can see, you have to be as exact as possible. Different paper and inks produce different thicknesses of books.

All the online printers will have their own sections instructing you about spines.

Have you heard of bleeds and slugs?

If you're going to use an image for your cover, my first suggestion is to use a continuous image that will occupy your back cover, the spine in the middle, and the front cover.

Imagine your book. The printing press will trim your book so that the image you placed continues or "bleeds" all the way to all the edges. The only way for this to happen is to use a slightly enlarged picture so that the edges of the image can get trimmed.

If the size of your book is 6 inches width x 9 inches height, and the spine size is .47292 inch x 9 inches, then the dimensions of your pdf will be 6 + .47292 + 6 = 12.47292 inches width x 9 inches height. Your background image should be larger than 12.5 inches width x 9 inches height.

Most online print on demand printers require an extra .125 inch bleed on each edge—left, right, top and bottom. The cover above at 12.47292 inches width x 9 inches height with the .125 bleed will be 12.72292 inches width x 9.25 inches height.

(IMPORTANT NOTE: CreateSpace might simply require you to use a file size of 12.72292 inches width x 9.25 inches height, with the bleed being 0! Call them to make sure.)

Your background image should be 12.72292 inches x 9.25 inches.

If you have an interior page that has an image that needs to bleed, you need to add a .125 on three edges and none on the edge where it is glued.

This means that right from the beginning, when you started using InDesign, your document settings should be set at 6.125 inches width x 9.25 inches height for a 6" x 9" book. Make sure to check "Facing Pages" as well.

InDesign and other desktop publishing software has a document setup setting which will ask you for both Page Size and Bleed.

So, for your cover, if the size you calculated from the spine calculator is .47292 inch, you will enter:

Page Size:
>Width: 12.47292 in, Height: 9 in

Bleed and Slug:

Bleed:
>Top: .125 in, Bottom: .125 in,
>
>Inside: .125 in, Outside: .125 in

Slug:
>Top: 0 in, Bottom: 0 in, Inside: 0 in, Outside: 0 in

Once again, the values might be different if you're using CreateSpace. The bleed values would be 0, and the file's height and width would include the bleed. Call the company you are using!

If your **interior** does not have any page that has a bleed, you will enter:

Page Size:
>Width: 6, Height: 9 in

Bleed and Slug:

Bleed:
>Top: 0 in, Bottom: 0 in,
>
>Inside: 0 in, Outside: 0 in

Slug:
>Top: 0 in, Bottom: 0 in, Inside: 0 in, Outside: 0 in

If your **interior** has one or more pages that has a bleed, you will enter:

Page Size:
>Width: 6, Height: 9 in

Bleed and Slug:

Bleed:
>Top: .125 in, Bottom: .125 in,
>
>Inside: 0 in, Outside: .125 in

Slug:

>Top: 0 in, Bottom: 0 in, Inside: 0 in, Outside: 0 in

I'm just defining "bleed," so you'll be aware of this. Research some more if you think this is complicated.

Slugs are not required for our purposes for the online printers, but I'll just define this for your information. The area beyond the bleed is the slug.

Together with the area of the bleed, they will be cut out of the final product. The slug can include instructions to the printer. If you're printing posters, you will see marks for cutting the poster correctly in the area of the slug.

Your face on the book cover

If you feel you should include your face on the cover, by all means, do so. If you think you're ugly and your face won't help sell the book, then don't have your face on the book.

I have my own very stupid rule for not getting any large images of my face on the book cover or anywhere on the book.

Have you seen large advertisements at bus and train stops, where the smiling faces became toothless, thanks to pens and markers? Sometimes, people use markers on eyes to make them look cross-eyed.

If you are comfortable with people defacing faces, then by all means use a large image of your face in your books, including your covers and back covers.

I should caution you not to wear anything that has a recognizable logo. You would not feel comfortable if someone comes up to you and asks a disturbing question like, "Oh did you need permission from the company for wearing that?"

Better be safe than sorry. Always think: you publish books, not to get sued. Not to release, only to recall. You publish books to release. I invented all the names in this book except for the ones I helped publish and am currently helping to promote.

Just wear something plain. You're calling attention to yourself, not to your clothes. You don't need to wear the most expensive outfit, because your book is one accomplishment that already ranks you with the elite.

Speaking of revisions, be careful if you cannot revise your books later. Some of us will acquire grants or a one-time influx of money for writing and publishing books. You must really finalize your books if this is the case. Make sure to edit 8 times. Do as I say, not as I do. Oops.

Collaborate within the #valzubiriagenda community

I hope you collaborate well and productively with your #valzubiriagenda group. Avoid compromises if your goal is greatness. If you wrote a full-length book, which took time, energy and emotions, why would you sacrifice design and final touches?

I am encouraging you to design a single pdf cover for your book. If you cannot figure that out, use one of your contacts.

Do the same thing with the interior

When you use pictures and fonts (the letterings), make sure you have permission or that you are using copyright-free pictures and fonts that also allow free use for commercial purposes.

We are producing books for commercial purposes, because we are placing prices on our books and putting them in online publishing stores and physical bookstores, like Amazon, Lulu.com and Barnes & Noble.

Just as a reminder, if you don't want to ask people for their "honorary inclusion" in your book, just fictionalize their names.

I want to tell you why I am encouraging bartering with other #valzubiriagenda participants.

Your goal is $0 cost or near it

There are vanity book publishers that have detailed pricing for their services. They can add up.

I saw a book that a vanity publisher produced. It did not look like a book. It looked like a booklet.

I was shown the book and then was offered a small amount to have it fully redone, and only after a lot more money had already been given to the vanity press. I refused.

A year later, I learned that they could not have released any book I can design anyway, because the agreement the author signed stipulated that they can only order copies of the book through the company. They pretty much abandoned the project. It is stuck with the vanity press.

I would not know who really is at fault here, but if the author kept seeing typographical errors, then he really did not proofread the book from start to finish as much as he should have.

He gave money thinking he will receive a perfect book.

I did notice that he was given a really lousy cover—just the title and his name on white glossy paper. The book was thin, because the paper used did not feel like book-quality paper.

Barter to keep costs down, and work with people who will agree to this.

The good thing about collaborating with people in your own city is that you can meet once in a while to see how the book or books are progressing. Everyone will feel in control. I would discourage collaborations online where you would only be emailing back and forth.

I have, however, worked with a friend who was in Cambodia.

Working with an author abroad
(Note: You can see Bob Couttie's book on page 152)

I have worked with someone abroad. I edited and designed a book for someone who lives in Cambodia, Bob Couttie—his books can be found on Amazon. I edited and designed the paperback edition of one of his books, **Temple of the Leper King (André Velon Mysteries) (Volume 1)**.

He still has two versions of this book on Amazon. Mine is the one with the line drawing of two people on the cover. I think he did not want to lose the book reviews from the earlier version.

He collaborated with other publishers and individuals for his other books.

He initially approached me decades ago for permission to use my original oil painting of a bell for a book cover. I originally used my painting for a theatre poster. I also designed the poster for my theatre group.

Bob and I continued to keep in touch with each other ever since the use of my painting. Look for **Hang the Dogs** by Bob Couttie on Ama-

40: Publishing Your Book What You Should Watch Out For

zon. I painted that bell in oil. I also did some of his mobi e-books.

Bob and I used Google Drive. He uploaded all the text and images to his Google Drive folder and gave my email address permission to view, change, download and upload files to our folder.

As you collaborate with people, you will give them access to sensitive information, so be careful who you trust.

Whenever I help with books, I always give all the files I had ever worked on to the authors. This way, they can bring the files to someone else anytime they want, in case something happens to me.

I don't hold the working files ransom.

What can happen with your online book publisher

CreateSpace.com is Amazon's company that is in charge of self-publishing.

If you are savvy with publishing your own book, all they easily require you to do is upload the two pdf files—one for the cover of the book and another for the interior. As such, you need to finalize the editing and design of both. It only takes a few seconds to upload your files.

They actually have two options.

I have been telling you to design your own book's cover and interior, which is their "professional option."

There is also the novice self-publisher's option, where the uploader goes through a step-by-step form. The online form will ask to upload a background image. Then it will ask for the title, author's name, subtitle, etc. Their software will automatically generate the spine, front and back covers from the information provided.

The form will also ask you for your interior text. Good luck. I have seen a book that came out double spaced with many other errors.

The problem with all this is that we are supposed to be artists. We eyeball our works to know what is right and what is off, not necessarily wrong.

The principle of triangulation is also a design consideration. A nicely designed page needs at least three elements to look good. When it comes to a page of text, the mind likes to see at least three or more seemingly disjointed fonts or typestyles.

If you look at this book, I assigned different fonts for the chapter, subheading, content text, page number and running head. I did the same for the cover text. There is a slight degree of separation between paragraphs.

You must collaborate with someone else to decide on these details if you cannot do this alone.

Remember that you are competing with the rest of us. You might have great art in a lousy book while someone would have great art in a great-looking book.

CreateSpace has their own book designers that you can work with. Once again, just like the vanity publishers, they will work on books by novices. The problem is that they charge for their services, that's fair enough, but you cannot sit with them to finalize and be fast. You will still end up going back and forth.

You are delaying yourself with all this. If you go to your nearest bookstore, you know for a fact that each book by a big publisher used a professional designer. These big publishers make sure that each book looks unique. You should require the same option for yourself.

Don't forget we're still just talking about your black and white books—your memoirs, biographies, artistic essays, manifestos, poetry. You have art books to work on. You really should work with collaborators.

You're not alone here. You can bet that others in our community will have the same challenges.

What software programs are used by the professionals

Know that photographs are different from line illustrations. Adobe Photoshop and other similar professional level photoediting software are used to retouch photographs.

Adobe Illustrator is used for line drawings. This includes the designs of the title, subtitle and the author's names.

The importance of using Illustrator for the title / subtitle design is that the the text remains crisp and the design remains intact and in place when blown up to use for banners and posters and shrunk for repetition on the back cover, postcards, press releases and letters, just like a logo. You can also reproduce the design for use online, on your websites and blogs.

I highly recommend a smaller-scale repetition of the title on the

40: Publishing Your Book What You Should Watch Out For

back cover.

Adobe InDesign is what I highly recommend to design the books. The Photoshop and Illustrator files get imported into the InDesign file. When you need to edit the Photoshop or Illustrator files, all you need to do is right-click > Edit Original, and the image will open in Photoshop or Illustrator.

If you go to a bookstore and see a book that has text on the cover that looks blurry and smudged with the background image, the book designer only used Photoshop or a similar photoediting software.

If you think there is a way to "cheat" by including the text titles with the background image using a photoediting program, there is, although it will require you to have even more knowledge of the program. Even I would not dare do it.

You can get away with current digital cameras

Books continue to be small in size. The technology of today's digital cameras—which are even "more primitive" than digital SLR (single lens reflex) cameras, have surpassed the requirements for printed books.

I already mentioned in Chapter 24 that you can use a digital camera to photograph your art. I also mentioned to use indirect lighting, no flash and to watch out for the yellows, because yellow is the most difficult color to photograph.

Remember to "embed" your fonts

I mention embedding fonts in Chapter 24.

Imagine this. You worked on your computer. You designed the pages and you finally converted, or "exported" the cover and interior files to pdf. Then you sent the file to your print on demand company and hoped for the best.

The printer's computer cannot guarantee that they have all the fonts in the world, just so they can print out all the fonts you used in your book.

CreateSpace has an online interface to show you how their computers see your pages. Check to see if they are displaying your text with the correct fonts.

You must order a proof of your book before you approve the book for the public to buy.

Only when everything is good should you release the book to the public.

If you see problems, you can call them to find out what it was you missed.

Your fonts have to come "embedded" in your pdf file.

For Adobe InDesign, the command for embedding fonts is seen in the "Advanced" selection in the Export Adobe PDF window.

As a beginner, try putting 1% in the box for "Subset fonts when percent of characters used is less than:"

If you go online and research on embedding fonts, you will come across a confusing discussion on embedding fonts. There is only one thing you should consider: The typestyles you chose should show in the book.

If your software showed you an option for embedding fonts, and you think you set it right, then upload your pdf files to your online printer, then order a proof copy of the book. Check to see if the printer printed all the typestyles correctly. If not, then research to find out what setting you may have overlooked.

Here is a faster way to check embedding

You will need two computers: The one you have been working on, which has your chosen fonts for the book, and a second one which does not have any of the fonts you are using in the book.

From the first computer, export your file to pdf. Take the pdf file from your first computer and open it in the other computer. See if there are missing letters. Print one or two sample pages—the pages which will include all the fonts you ever used in the file.

Print the same pages from the first computer.

Compare the pages. If they have similar fonts, then you had successfully embedded all the fonts.

Glyphs

Glyphs are additional characters in the fonts. If you noticed, I have been using "café" instead of "cafe" in this book. The "é" is a glyph. The designers of the fonts sometimes don't bother designing glyphs. If you don't see the glyph you need to use, you may have to change the font.

When you embed fonts correctly, the glyphs you used get included as well. This might be hit or miss.

This is why you need to look at the sample proof of your book before you approve it for the public to buy.

The design decision from Towering Inferno

Look at posters from the 1974 movie, **The Towering Inferno.**

The production company wanted to hire Steve McQueen and Paul Newman, who were at the time popular rivals. The problem was they needed to share top billing without being better than the other.

They made a smart decision by positioning the actor on the left and his name on the lower left, while positioning the actor on the right and his name higher.

A huge consideration, especially for collaborative books is fairness. Books last 300 to 3,000 years, so be fair or forever turn in your grave.

And now, learn from embarrassing experiences

As you mimic the professional look, know that you have power over your own book. You *can* abuse your power. If you do, you will look like a delusional dictator of a country that has no communication with the outside world.

Let me show you some personal incidents.

The book of acknowledgments

My friend Jaime received a book in the mail. With it was a form. The author/publisher was asking to get paid for what he sent.

The sender was a distant friend of his. Jaime figured that if the author sent him a copy, then he sent everyone else whom he knew a copy.

Jaime opened the acknowledgment section. The acknowledgment section listed everyone the author knew. It was pages upon pages of names.

He named people from his former school, work, church, relatives, etc. There were people clumped together in paragraphs, depending on their organizations and associations, formal or informal.

This writer self-published and pretty much abused the acknowledgments page. Once again, this happened 20 years ago.

I won't stop you from doing this. I don't think this is good practice, but people continue to do this.

This might be your first attempt at publishing. Maybe you feel you need to acknowledge a lot of people in your life. Most of these people do not need to see their names in a book. Only acknowledge people who helped make the book possible. Otherwise, the book will become amateurish after all your hard work.

I don't require my friends and relatives to read my books

I personally only tell people I have books out. I don't ask my relatives and friends to read my works.

The reason for this is that I used to, and still do, consider my friends and relatives as just that. I need to just go home to relatives and hang out with my friends. Our books should be for the public.

Another reason is that I come up with lessons to learn based on what people near me—my friends and relatives, provide. As a rule, the best stories are the bad, mean ones.

When I wrote about having been a victim of pedophilia, I looked at myself as someone who was "hiding in plain sight." My friends and relatives knew I had written books, but I never required anyone to read them nor had I told them what my stories were. I don't need to tell them about my traumatic childhood.

All of my memoirs include what happened to me, but the trauma gets told in different ways based on the context.

By the way, here's a lesson to learn. I used to have Zig Ziglar's books. Zig Ziglar is an expert in business sales. I also listen to his audiobooks a lot. Here is what I learned from him.

He always mentioned that he loves his wife very much. There's always a way to insert the same thing. Don't be afraid to mention the same topic, as long as it is needed.

The most memorable souvenir program

When Jaime and I were members of a theatre group, we participated in a large, week-long symposium at a university.

This honorary member of our theatre group may have been one of the organizers. Honorary members usually don't do the work. They supposedly just lend their "prestige" to the group.

40: Publishing Your Book What You Should Watch Out For

We members were asked earlier on to come up with ideas on how we can contribute to the symposium. I took charge of a one-day group art show on the last day. We showed art by the entrance of the university's auditorium, where the theatre group performed.

The members of the group obviously rehearsed their lines, there was a director, technical crew, and the playwright was Jaime.

It was only on that last day that the week's program or souvenir program got delivered—when everything and everyone's efforts finally converged.

The convergence included a panel discussion in another auditorium, which included our honorary member; the show, which had Jaime's play, a dance number and something else; the art show, which I organized; and a few other attractions.

A month before the week-long event, my group was busy looking for sponsors and soliciting ads to raise money. I took charge designing the display ads. Our honorary member was the one in charge of the entire program, so I handed my work over to the one above me, who handed it to her.

We all took a look at the souvenir program and looked for our names. The section with the events included the names of us volunteers. The speakers on the panel had bios.

Guess who included her entire curriculum vitae and whatever else she can muster to include on a page and a half? That was probably why she chose to release the souvenir program on the last day. It was crucial that we all showed up to cooperate. I'm sure she knew that what she did was insulting.

It's good to have experienced these things, because now I know what to avoid doing. This happened in the '90s, so you can see how much it got stuck in my head. We can forgive; we cannot forget.

If you're coming up with a collaborative book, make sure to be fair.

My first art show was hogged by the organizer

This happened to me months before that symposium at the university.

I was living at an "artist in residence" type of apartment. Basically, the two buildings' draw was to rent out to artists.

Somebody posted an invitation to participate in an art show. The group of us who responded started to meet once a week. I did three works in pastel—it was my medium then. Someone had a 16-inch sculpture of a dinosaur. Another one had an installation. I guess most of us had paintings.

I spent a lot of money to frame my works at the nearby frame shop. My three works had mats, glass covers and metal frames. I took pictures of my works for the "souvenir program."

We were finally given the invitations and the souvenir programs. They were just photocopies in black toner! That would have been okay, except that the organizer, who was also a participating artist, gave us photocopied postcards that served as invitations that only had her painting.

She did the same with the program. The photocopied folded program only had her work again as the cover.

We all felt cheated. I was working in an office that had a copy machine. It would have been easy to make different versions of postcards and programs that equally featured all of us.

Later on, this lady, who was also a musician, had performances at a nearby café. I saw her once, to support her. What she did to us at the art show was obviously something memorable. Once again, you can forgive, but you cannot forget.

As you prepare and finally publish your books, make sure you make professional, not selfish, decisions. If you organize artists, don't aggrandize yourself without permission. People would agree to your plans, if you tell them in advance.

Remember, now that all of us are encouraged to write book-length rhetoric. We can all end up in someone else's memorable story.

Chapter 41

Producing Your Art Books Before You Proceed

I still have my art intact

In 2008, my source of income suddenly dried up! I'm going to write about this in another memoir. I was so depressed.

I was in Madison, Wisconsin, miles away from Chicago, in the cold of winter. I was running out of funds. I was waiting for the bus to take me back to Chicago, having been rejected by that mystery source of income (which I will write about in a future memoir).

So there I was, at home trying to figure out what I needed to do next. As you can see, I finished my first draft of a book-length manuscript in 2006, just a year and a half ago. I was still depressed about it, and now, my money had slowed down to nothing. It was easy to jump in Lake Michigan.

This was in January. A week later, I opened up my portfolio of nude drawings and a few nude paintings.

I took them out, and signed each and every one of them, dating them as I remembered making them—1995 and 1996.

I started photographing them one after the other. The pictures totaled to 138. I photographed both the good ones and the bad ones, including the ones which had "x" marks. I placed x's by the spots which I eyeballed were wrong—mistakes in drawing, so that I would be aware of what I needed to improve.

I photographed them because I decided to produce a book of my nude drawings and paintings. I can remember the day I finished photoediting, finishing and uploading the book: January 31, 2008. I used my laptop and digital camera of that time.

When I finished the book, I had it in my mind that my works had become more precious than before.

Later that summer, I was asked by a gallerist friend in the expensive River North District Galleries to see my works. I told her I had nudes. She asked to see what I had.

I seriously felt disturbed. I did not want her to get anything from me, because it will disrupt the exactness of the book.

I brought her my works, but she critiqued them, telling me that they were good, but had gotten dirtied up. She decided not to get anything from me.

At least she spent time giving me an audience. We were familiar with each other as professional, not personal, gallery friends.

On my part, I was thankful. I was praying for her to decide not to get anything, so that I can keep my art.

For the week between her asking to see my art, and myself returning to her with it, I just could not get my mind and heart to let go of my works. I felt flustered. When I left her gallery that day, with my art intact, I felt relieved.

I kept remembering a documentary about artist Robert Crumb where he said he was approached by a collector who wanted an entire notebook of his drawings.

My idea for my works, was that it would be nice to have my book and the entire collection of my art go to one single art collector.

As soon as you see your works in book form, you might lose interest selling them. You might realize that your art has become more valuable. This is a valid feeling. I still feel it now. I still have all my nudes from that book, which is still available on Lulu.com.

Three books versus one book
(Note: You can see Richard Lau's books on page 70)

When I helped artist Richard Lau produce his first three art books, he never asked for me to help him sell his works. He continues to tell people to this day, as I write this, that at his age, he cannot believe that he has 3 books authored by him (because he is the artist) on Amazon.

41: Producing Your Art Books Before You Proceed

We produced his three books simultaneously in 2014 when he was turning 70 years old.

I was continuing to go to church in 2014 after my dad passed away in 2013. After morning mass, I went to Jewel, the nearby grocery. He was behind me at the register when I heard his voice.

He asked me how can anyone get to volunteer at church. I had been going into the sacristy behind the altar after daily mass to help out, I just took my volunteerism for granted.

To cut this story short, we became friends and started hanging out after daily mass. I was grieving for my dad and I felt that God probably wanted me to connect with this old man.

I learned that Richard had just moved to Chicago. He was from Michigan.

For a few times, he told me he painted, but he wasn't really pushing it. He showed me his iPhone a few times to show me less than five of his works. We just kept hanging out for about more than 5 months.

Finally, in October of 2014, when he showed me new works, it occurred to me to finally ask him how many works he really had. He said a little more than a hundred. They were mostly in Michigan. We were in Chicago.

I told him I can help him publish his works. He had seen my four books, so he believed me. We started planning what to do. I required for him to get an acceptable digital camera. We went to Microcenter, the nearby technology and computer store to get one.

I showed him what to do with the camera. He eventually drove to Michigan to take pictures of his works. As soon as he arrived, I got his camera and SD card, and downloaded the pictures to my laptop.

Lo and behold, there they were. Pictures of more than 200 works.

Guess what? All of them had the shadow of his head at the bottom part of the paintings, and most of them had glares from light sources.

I had already told him to take pictures where there would be no direct lighting. I also told him not to use the flash. I certainly told him not to get any shadows on the works. I told him about yellows. I told him that the pictures can be dark, because Photoshop can correct the darkness. They can also be skewed; Photoshop can correct that as well. (You can check out Chapter 24 again!)

So, guess what he had to do. He had to return to Michigan, six hours away, and return to Chicago with all of his paintings the next day.

In Chapter 22, I talked about seeing art at a museum, an art show opening and at the artist's studio or home. I appreciated Richard's effort to cooperate with me.

He and I finally photographed a total of 273 paintings. It was good that we collaborated. Even if the first batch of photographs he made were correct, he would have been guessing the size of his works.

With me working with him, he was also able to name each work, sign them before we photographed them, and provide the medium used. We measured the works, which he also wasn't able to do alone.

I uploaded the photographs to my laptop and for three months, I worked on the books to finality. Towards the later stage when I needed his face picture or headshot for the back of the books and the inside, we drove to the nearby park for his photograph.

Here is one hurrah.

I was finishing his one single volume of 273 works. I went to CreateSpace.com to calculate the retail price, which I needed to include in the bar code and cover design. The smart retail price for a thick art book that had one image per page was $59.95. It felt a little expensive.

This was when I decided to divide the book into two. I reshuffled the pages and split the book into Volume 1 and Volume 2. I figured I still had the files in my laptop, so either I do this now or forever shut up.

So I surprised him with three titles:

1. **Richard Lau Paintings: 273 Works by the Artist,** $59.95
2. **It Dropped Out and Other Works: 133 Paintings by Richard Lau** (Works by Richard Lau Volume 1), $37.95
3. **Happy Again and Other Works: 140 Paintings by Richard Lau** (Works by Richard Lau Volume 2), $37.95

(Note: Page 70 shows Artist Richard Lau's books)

All of them have the same release date: Dec 17, 2014

So now, each one of Richard's paintings is guaranteed to be included in two books—the big one and one of the smaller ones.

If you analyze Richard's works, you might think that they might be

41: Producing Your Art Books Before You Proceed

easy to fake. The books will discourage that.

Once again, self-publishing allows all of us to come up with multiple titles. Why have only one book?

If more and more artists, art collectors and investors begin to do self-publishing, just like us, more and more will want 10 books instead of just one. An artist with 2,000 works can have 10 art books with 200 works each. No one can stop us from producing our books.

We're not the big-time publishers who depend on book sales. We are self-publishing artists, art collectors and investors who depend on art sales, with books being the supplemental attractions.

There is a great chance that bookstores all over the world will proudly devote shelves to their local self-publishing artists, investors, art collectors and all our other collaborators under the #valzubiriagenda.

One of these days, when we gather to meet, we will have a laugh at our over-accomplishments in self-publishing. We do it because we can!

For now, we need to find each other.

Should you put #valzubiriagenda on your books? Yes and No

If you go to Amazon to look at my books, I have my "normal versions" and versions that have what I call "Special Insert for Bankers." I charge more for the books with the insert.

I released my current books in 2012 and 2014, when I thought I was alone and had no competition. Now, if you publish your books, your purpose is to be found as an individual and as part of the #valzubiriagenda group.

I suggest that you come up with two versions of your books. One will have #valzubiriagenda and your proposed scarcity and pricing schedule. You can bring both books to all your outlets.

Add a few pages at the beginning of your book's interior. There, you can include an acknowledgment that you are following all or some of the #valzubiriagenda conditions, your contact information, your online presence that has up-to-date information, where your art is currently sold, contact information of other investors, art collectors and venues reselling the works you previously owned (list them with permission), the plans you have for yourself—your planned price schedule, your planned quantity, what publishing plans you have, etc.

The other version would be the vanilla versions of your art books and memoirs.

When our potential investors and art collectors check out our book at our venues, they will see your price schedule and scarcity announcements in your books.

Make sure you have a disclaimer—that you still reserve the right to change plans.

Once our local bookstores and other locations have started to feature us, it will be up to each one of us to get on their local list. We will need to check the stores once in a while to make sure they are aware of us. We should get invited to local events related to the #valzubiriagenda so we can meet new artists, investors and collectors.

Let's all come up with new ways to see one another online.

Do whatever you can, add the hashtag #valzubiriagenda as you see fit. Add #valzubiriagenda in t-shirts and mugs. Even sell them if you want. Just understand that I'm not responsible for you decisions.

(Note: Go to page 18 for the t-shirt illustration)

Chapter 42

The Basics of Producing E-Books
Just an Overview

If you are familiar with the internet, you may have heard of html files. Websites are stored on servers, which serve the html files to browsers like Chrome, Microsoft Edge, Safari, Firefox and Opera.

Besides html, there are other file formats like php and asp, but let's stick to html for this discussion.

Html is the important format we need to tackle to understand e-readers.

When you look at an html page, those pictures you see are actually separate files, usually jpegs.

Early on, someone came up with the idea of e-readers, where a book gets packaged as a set of html pages and jpeg images.

That one epub or one mobi file for e-readers that you see is actually a cloaked collection of html text and images.

Each chapter is normally assigned its own html file. You anticipate this early on, as you assign a chapter per file right from the start when you begin working with the initial print version in InDesign.

I'm still giving you general knowledge here. There are tutorials online as usual about all this.

The InDesign Book file

InDesign has a Book option, wherein a Book window manages the list of chapters in sequence, as arranged by you in that window. That window has an option not only to manage your books for physical printing, but also for exporting the files to become an epub format. Epub is the format used by Android devices, iPads and iPhones.

Use Sigil to tweak epub files

There is a free software, Sigil, which can make your epub books from scratch. Sigil is free, and is owned by Google.

You will discover that the epub file you generated from InDesign needs tweaking. Sometimes, the font size and indentations are wrong. Sometimes, you might want a link to a website or email added. You might want your phone number to link correctly so the reader can immediately call you. You might want to add your address with Google Map directions to your location.

The way to discover what needs tweaking is by viewing the epub file on an Android device, like a tablet or a smartphone. If you see something that needs to be changed, you will need to return to Sigil to make the change.

Use Calibre to make mobi files

Once you have the epub version, I recommend that you use Calibre, another free software, to produce mobi, which is the format for Kindle readers.

There might be newer ways of making mobi files.

You must use Sigil and Calibre together

Go back and forth between Sigil and Calibre to produce corrected epub and mobi formats and use Sigil and Kindle devices and apps to check your work. There are "emulators" online that you can download for your PC or Mac.

These are apps that you can use on your PC or Mac so you can view your epub and mobi files as if you are looking at them from real e-readers, smartphones and iPhones.

As you can see, you need to be patient. You would not want a paying customer to discover that your letters overlap, or that your pictures are not positioned correctly.

Smartphones, iPhones and e-readers have variations that can affect how your book looks like as an e-book.

42: The Basics of Producing E-Books Just an Overview

Your problem if you only try to produce e-books

If you think that you only want e-books of your book, use Sigil first, produce your epub, then use Calibre to convert the epub to mobi.

Here is your real world problem. #valzubiriagenda is a group effort with group meetings and get-togethers. You cannot just pass around your e-reader to proudly show what book you have on your device. Someone might drop your smartphone. If you really get lucky, someone will steal it.

A café with your art will want to have all of your relevant books—those published by you, the café and their other artists on a shelf to show off. People who chase and purchase the available art will want to purchase copies of the books.

As you can see, producing epub and mobi files will require you to go from one software to another. You will need to know html basics.

Preferably, it would be good to have an Android phone, Android tablet, iPhone and iPad devices around to make sure that your files work on these devices. After all is said and done, you really still need to have a book physically printed.

If you want a workaround, you can sell as an e-book the pdf file that combines the cover with the interior. If that's the case, then you're back to producing the pdf for the printed edition anyway.

Permanence & Repetition

PERMANENCE

Our books at any location, like cafés, offices and stores, and online, give real, long-term permanence to art, for artists, investors, art collectors and resellers.

A location, like a café, without #valzubiriagenda, will only show work for a month or more, then it's over for the artist. This is a self-imposed limitation for the same time and energy invested in putting on any acceptable art exhibit.

Having the #valzubiriagenda memoirs and art books, the locations become permanent representatives of all their artists, and even their investors, as art ownerships and everyone continues to resell the art, as and prices continue to increase.

REPETITION

More buzz happens as the art gets permanently represented by more and more locations and resellers.

The artists won't be able to control this anyway, as more and more investors resell.

End of special section. First special section is on page 4

Chapter 43

Beginning #valzubiriagenda Let's Organize & Make Progress!

Our status quo

There is a status quo with people who have been in the banks and galleries. I have talked to people whom I can trust with this idea.

In Chapter 3, I mentioned a vice president of a bank who said that he has been quite comfortable with his status in life, that he was just waiting a few years to retire. He did not want to stir the pot himself, because although the banks do need a good influx of money, he might lose his job and retirement if he became instrumental in something that might lose money.

I just recently shared this idea with another bank president, a few months ago. He feels that the ideas that comprise the #valzubiriagenda has to happen with the public. Then the banks can come in. What he said was the same thing that was in my mind.

My gallery friends have also heard about my idea. They said it would be safe for them to respond later. These people know that I have already written four memoirs, and now this book. They know I'm serious and building my case. They said it's a matter of time.

This book will be our status quo. The previous memoirs I wrote did not give any artist, investor nor art collector any "permission" to work on the #valzubiriagenda.

Us and them

People tend to think grass is greener elsewhere. Some artists make an attempt at art, except that they focus on the other side of the art business fence. Those artists find ways to interpret who would be "us" and who would be "them." They find ways of "internal, mental" discouragements and "real world" disqualifications. They think there is an impenetrable fence. Those demarcation lines vary from person to person.

Some would-be investors and art collectors do the same thing. Those people look at current prices and wish they had bought art in the past. They had been focused on higher-priced art and because of that, they shut themselves out of artists they can afford.

They also feel that the artists they can't afford shut them out. Once again, these demarcation lines vary.

Now, here we are, wherever we are. We can look at current prices and look forward to higher potential returns. As we all move forward, we connect with each other.

We might also get into the practice of sharing returns through commissions.

We can see what's good. What we can do for ourselves right now, we can make our normal. We can be both rare and prolific.

Remember the gallery who told me that publishing the art in her gallery sounded like too much work and just might give her artists big heads that they would go elsewhere?

I never really analyzed her situation. In retrospect, I think she was already struggling to keep her gallery open. Had someone like myself volunteered to make her an art book, maybe things would have changed for the better for her. Had I also presented this idea to all the artists she represented, they probably would have been the ones to start the books for her.

This was also in 2008, when people were losing money and the economy was on the downturn.

I was also doing my version of creative procrastination in 2008. I did not have the books I have now to show, because I decided to rest. I did not work on and release my first draft.

My future books probably could have convinced her. She did listen to what I had to say.

43: Beginning #valzubiriagenda Let's Organize & Make Progress!

I have had more people asking me for advice now, than way back—it might be my "older" age right now. I tell them something new.

"Act right now...

"I can advice you—if you tell me that you will wait for my own success before you act on your own success, good luck. I'm following my own instincts and path. I take my time. I procrastinate. I have all my knowledge, skills and insights through years of encounters, reading and improvement of my own skills...

"Any advice you ask me for yourself means that you would appreciate some help in speeding up your own development. I fully support that. Let me tell you a set of ideas that I now call #valzubiriagenda. Pick and choose what you like from it. Remember that we should not have to go to hell because of something as stupid as art...

"Okay, so listen to me now and I hope that right now is exactly when you are definitely going to act on my advice. Let me now tell you everything I know so you can do with all of this as you will, because...

"...where you are, there you are. It's the best place to be."

- Artist, Memoirist, Co-Author Valentino Zubiri
- Artist, Co-Author Silverio Perez

About the Authors

Valentino Zubiri

Artist & memoirist Valentino Zubiri believes that everyone should publish their memoirs and art books, especially now that publishing is accessible. He has authored four memoirs to date and has helped others with their books.

Silverio Perez

This is Silverio Perez' first book. He and Val are also collaborating on a series of art pieces, several art books and a screenplay.

We're too sexy for pix

Index

Symbols

1-Hour Mentors, A Memoir of an Artist as a Masseur xxviii, 36, 44, 46, 99, 101, 129, 149, 201
1% writing 194, 213
1% writing and 99% editing 194, 213
2-Day Film School 225
3D computer file 24
3-D hologram trading cards 51
4/0, 1/1 and 4/4 140
8 Times 213
12-Step 192, 218
19-year old publisher, The famous 223
21 Irrefutable Laws of Leadership 61, 63
55,000 words 39, 145, 158, 186, 193
99% editing xviii, 194, 213
101st 119
300 dpi, 300 dots per inch 38, 136, 137
300 to 3,000 years xxvi, 35, 41, 42, 43, 94, 147, 171, 184, 204, 216, 251
$0 cost 245
$50 million dollar artists 58
$51,200,000 7, 9, 22, 24, 25, 26, 31, 50, 55
#valzubiriagenda xviii, xx, xxix, xxx, xxxi, xxxii, 4, 5, 6, 7, 15, 20, 21, 23, 25, 28, 32, 35, 36, 38, 39, 43, 50, 52, 56, 63, 65, 66, 67, 69, 71, 72, 73, 74, 81, 83, 85, 87, 90, 92, 93, 98, 101, 117, 123, 127, 128, 130, 147, 172, 189, 193, 212, 213, 228, 236, 244, 245, 259, 260, 263, 265, 267
#valzubiriagenda The Basics 5
#valzubiriagenda, valzubiriagenda, Valzubiriagenda xviii, xx, xxviii, xxix, xxx, xxxi, xxxii, 4, 5, 6, 7, 15, 20, 21, 23, 25, 28, 32, 35, 36, 38, 39, 43, 46, 50, 52, 56, 63, 65, 66, 67, 69, 71, 72, 73, 74,

A

A bank near me closed 71
About the author 235
About the Authors 269
A bubble that would not burst 60
acceleration region 31
Acknowledge your crankiness 161
acknowledgments, Acknowledgments 89, 143, 206, 233, 234, 251
acrylic 4
activist 4
Actual Writing Bigger & Better Tips! (Chapter 35) 201
Additional reasons why you need high-resolution images 139
add or not add hyphens 213
Adobe Illustrator, see also Illustrator 143, 248
Adobe InDesign, see also InDesign 141, 142, 143, 206, 215, 238, 242, 248, 249, 261, 262
Adobe Photoshop, see also Photoshop 143, 152, 248
advanced praise 240
advanced reading copy 182, 240
After Notepad I use InDesign 206
Afterword 235
age range 4
A great lesson from the comic book industry 48
alien abductee art, see also UFO abductee 62
Amazon 36, 37, 39, 66, 110, 111, 112, 133, 141, 152, 182, 230, 245, 246, 247, 256, 259
Amazon trends 110
American veteran artists 62
AmeriTrade 63
An accepted publishing practice 38
Andersen, Hans Christian 200
And now, learn from embarrassing experiences 251
Android 262, 263

Angels We Have Heard On High 208
Another important lesson from Dov 226
anyone can publish 224
apology, apologies, apologize 103, 104, 136, 139, 161, 181
Appendix 235
A Quick Lesson in Publishing (Chapter 38) 223
Are you too busy to read this book? 71
army, army veteran 4, 85, 86
Art / Artist Biography 239
Art / Artist Memoir 239
Art / Artists 195
Art / Biography 195, 196
art book, art books xiii, xxvi, xxvii, xxix, 6, 15, 16, 21, 23, 24, 29, 32, 35, 39, 41, 42, 43, 44, 49, 50, 51, 60, 62, 63, 64, 67, 70, 74, 76, 80, 82, 86, 88, 101, 117, 119, 121, 141, 165, 172, 193, 195, 223, 224, 230, 248, 256, 258, 259, 260, 266, 269
Art book copyrights 32
art bubble 59
Art / Collection 195
art collection, art collections xxiv, 212
art collector, art collectors xiii, xx, xxiv, xxvii, xxix, xxxii, 4, 5, 6, 7, 15, 16, 17, 19, 21, 23, 25, 28, 30, 31, 32, 35, 41, 42, 43, 52, 55, 56, 57, 60, 62, 64, 75, 77, 78, 80, 81, 82, 90, 91, 94, 101, 118, 120, 127, 139, 147, 164, 180, 182, 212, 230, 259, 260, 266
art collectors, definition xxiv
art commission, art commissions 17, 24, 32, 80, 123
Art / Crafts 195
Arthur 199
art investor, art investors 57, 63, 77, 215, 239
art investors and collectors 63, 215
artist, artists xvii, xix, xx, xxii, xxiii, xxiv, xxvii, xxix, xxx, xxxi, 5, 6, 7, 8, 15, 16, 18, 19, 22, 23, 24, 25, 26, 28, 30, 31, 32, 35, 41, 48, 49, 51, 52, 53, 54, 55, 56, 58, 60, 62, 63, 65, 72, 73, 74, 75, 76, 77,

271

78, 80, 81, 82, 83, 85, 86, 87, 90, 94, 95, 101, 106, 108, 115, 118, 119, 121, 123, 124, 126, 127, 139, 147, 160, 171, 189, 195, 222, 227, 228, 247, 253, 254, 259, 260, 263, 266
artist from Manhattan publishes his books xxviii
artistic essays 6, 43, 44, 248
artist in residence 253
Artist Richard Lau's 3 art books 70
"Artist's Final Edited Version" 182
"Artists - Fine Art" 123
artist's home or studio 118
"Artist's Manifesto, Original Raw Version" 181
"Artist's Original Unedited Manuscript" 181
"Artist's Original Unedited Masterpiece" 181
"Artist's Unretouched Writing" 181
artist who died in the '90s, The xxx
art is unregulated 6, 27
Art is unregulated 6, 27
Art / Memoir 195, 196
art museums 118
Art / Reference 195
art sale, art sales 75, 231, 259
Art sales can help your café 75
art show, art shows xxi, xxviii, 30, 42, 92, 252, 253, 254, 258
Art versus brain surgery xxx
A Selection of Mixed Media Porcelain Dolls 84
assistant, assistants xxi, xxiv, 24, 121, 127
A suggestion if you cannot decide on pricing and scarcity 49
Augusten Burroughs 129
authenticity 87
Authors, About the 269
A vision a café owner told me 74
"A Visual Artist's Attempt To Write Without Editing" 181
Avoid validation 204
Ayers, Nathaniel 89

B

back cover 38, 134, 136, 143, 152, 181, 195, 233, 239, 240, 242, 248, 249
back cover, The 239
Backmatter 235
backmatter, parts of a book 234
back of the book 143, 239, 240, 258
Back to the gallery with the investors 50
backup, backups 214, 219
Backup your files 214
bait and switch 154, 155
bandwagon, "bandwagon effect", bandwagon mentality (see also "herd") 28, 52, 231
bank xxiv, 19, 20, 37, 59, 71, 222, 265
"bar" 190
barcode 143, 144, 239, 240
barcode generator 144
bargain bin 144
bargain section 144, 233, 239
bar graph 30
BarnesAndNoble.com 230
Barnes & Noble 37, 39, 230, 245
barter xxxii, 39, 62, 78, 86, 91, 132, 179, 180, 184, 192, 245, 246
Barter! 132
Basics 5
Basics on Producing E-Books Just an Overview, The 261
Because you can! 181
Beckstrom, Rod A. 61
Become an Artist Now & Join #valzubiriagenda It's Never Too Late! (Chapter 22) 117
Become aware of this term: "embedding fonts" 142
Becoming a publisher 225, 228
Becoming Artists & Writers (Chapter 21) 115
becoming a self-publisher 225
Beginning to Write Some Nice Simple Pointers (Chapter 33) 189
Beginning #valzubiriagenda Let's Organize & Make Progress! (Chapter 43) 265
Benedict Taschen 223

Be online as you edit 213
Bernie Madoff 20, 25, 26, 28, 49, 95
Berrett-Koehler 230
Beware of fake success 167
Bibliography 235
big new idea 58
Big publishing houses 225
Billy Elliott 192
biography, biographies xiii, xxvi, xxvii, 6, 39, 43, 44, 60, 79, 129, 153, 154, 172, 235, 239, 248
bird, birds 4, 31, 191, 210, 211
BKConnection.com 230
black and white 39, 137, 138, 141, 197, 214, 241, 248
black and white books 39, 141, 248
black and white images 137, 138
black and white interiors 241
black and white pictures 39
Blake Snyder 169
bleeds and slugs 242
blurb 240
Bob Couttie 152, 246
Bob Couttie's book 152, 246
body, Body 119, 120, 140, 234
body, parts of a book 234
book cover, Your face on the 244
book design 135, 145, 159, 206, 215, 216, 227, 236
book designer, book designers xiii, xx, xxxii, 5, 7, 38, 40, 56, 65, 75, 77, 78, 90, 115, 118, 127, 128, 129, 132, 135, 153, 154, 155, 157, 171, 179, 180, 189, 198, 204, 206, 215, 216, 248
BookExpo America 33, 34, 158
book ideas 77, 78, 172, 227
Book ideas you can come up with 63
book, parts of a 234
Book Production Preliminary Basic Knowledge (Chapter 25) 147
book project, book projects 7, 22, 24, 29, 63, 75, 77, 78, 192, 216, 227
booksellers conventions 33, 225
bookstore, bookstores xiii, 33, 44, 48, 55, 57, 58, 59, 76, 87, 101, 105, 107, 112, 113, 114, 131, 143, 144, 149, 169, 195, 196, 223, 224, 227, 229, 230, 233, 235, 238, 239,

Index

245, 248, 259, 260
bookstore databases 55, 230
Books vs. postcards 42
book writers xiii, xx, xxxii, 7, 38, 40, 56, 65, 75, 77, 78, 89, 90, 93, 115, 118, 127, 128, 129, 132, 135, 153, 154, 155, 157, 171, 179, 189, 198, 204
Bowker.com 230, 231
Brafman, Ori 61
brain surgeon, brain surgery xxx, 92
brand, branding, brands 38, 62, 122, 133, 137, 141, 144, 196, 223, 227
brand yourselves 62
Breaking notions 224
bronze 24
bubble 20, 21, 59, 60, 94, 123, 125, 166
Burroughs, Augusten 129
Business Authors, Business Writers & Economists (Chapter 17) 93
business cards 42, 44, 54, 91
"but" 198
But and define famous 198

C

café, cafés xxxii, 6, 15, 29, 35, 43, 55, 56, 58, 73, 74, 75, 76, 80, 82, 121, 122, 127, 178, 201, 202, 214, 218, 226, 230, 231, 233, 250, 254, 263
café owner 74
Cafés, Restaurants, Offices & Other Locations (Chapter 12) 73
Calibre 136, 142, 262, 263
call for artists, calling for artists xiii, xx, xxxii, 38, 40, 56, 63, 65, 72, 75, 77, 78, 90, 115, 118, 127, 128, 129, 132, 135, 153, 154, 155, 157, 171, 179, 189, 198, 204, 228
cancer, cancer victim 4, 62, 85, 87, 159, 201
Cancer victim paintings 62
cards 4, 42, 44, 51, 52, 54, 91, 119, 129, 199
Casablanca 192
celebrities, celebrity 4, 44, 46, 101, 130, 173, 238, 239
cellphone 136, 140
Ceramicists 62
Chapters 234
check embedding 250
check the spelling of words 213
Chicago xv, xviii, xix, xx, xxii, xxiii, xxv, xxviii, xxxii, 34, 47, 81, 82, 83, 85, 121, 124, 125, 129, 149, 150, 168, 173, 174, 201, 219, 255, 257, 258
Chicagoan xv, xviii, xix, xx, xxii, xxiii, xxv, xxviii, xxxii, 34, 47, 81, 82, 83, 85, 121, 124, 125, 129, 149, 150, 168, 173, 174, 201, 219, 255, 257, 258
Chicago gallery 34
"chick magnets" 80
Child, Julia 111
children 23, 87, 115, 154, 207, 208, 210, 211, 218, 239, 240
children's audiobook 207
children's book 239
china paint 164
choice of words 208, 209
Choose your book's size at the editing stage 215
Christmas carol 208
Christmas Eve, December 24, 2017 xv
Christmas Eve party xvi
chromium trading cards 51
classy rich lady xxvi
"click bait" 190
closure 48, 49, 199, 200
cloud storage 86
CMYK 140
Co-authors, definition 38
coffee, coffee mugs xxxi, xxxii, 74, 118, 122, 148, 170, 183, 201, 202, 217
collaborate 4, 7, 22, 28, 29, 30, 39, 55, 64, 74, 77, 89, 90, 91, 92, 122, 128, 132, 133, 139, 146, 152, 172, 179, 192, 198, 206, 218, 244, 246, 247, 258
Collaborate within the #valzubiriagenda community 244
collaborative books 251
collaborator 61, 89, 127
collectible xxiv, xxxi, 29, 56, 68, 82, 87, 94, 125, 193
collectible art xxiv, 87, 94
Collectible art from UFO abductees and other famous paranormal authors 87
Colored images only need to be 300 dots per inch 38
color interior, full-color interior 241
commercial or noncommercial galleries 118
commission xix, xxxii, 4, 5, 7, 8, 16, 17, 23, 24, 26, 27, 31, 32, 52, 53, 60, 64, 75, 80, 123, 266
community building 58
Comparing this with the Tulip Mania in 1636-1637 94
competing with the rest of us 247
computer file 24, 172
concrete 24
confuse Preface with Introduction 235
"Connect ten" 28
consumer expectations 216
contract 8, 16, 17, 23, 24, 31, 32, 44, 80, 180
convention 33, 34, 44, 45, 88, 100, 104, 105, 110, 112, 113, 130, 131, 134, 158, 183, 224, 225, 240
Cook County 19
copyright 142, 143, 144, 145, 152, 206, 233, 245
copyright-free 152, 245
copyright page 143, 144, 145, 206, 233
Copyright page 234
copyright page template 145
core group 22, 75, 78
cost of acquisition, Cost of Acquisition 9, 10, 11, 12, 13, 26
Could there be others like Madoff out there? 95
countries, country xix, 4, 17, 19, 20, 37, 62, 69, 83, 144, 185, 186, 211, 224, 225, 229, 232, 236, 251
Couttie, Bob 152, 246
cover 30, 33, 34, 36, 38, 49, 57, 69, 106, 109, 112, 121, 128, 129, 134, 136, 140, 141, 143, 145, 146, 152, 181, 186, 189, 195, 206, 224, 233,

234, 235, 236, 237, 238, 239, 240, 241, 242, 244, 245, 246, 247, 248, 249, 253, 254, 258, 263
cover size, calculating 242
cover, The 238
coworking, coworking space 77
crazy 123, 124, 125, 126, 204, 253
crazy pair 125, 204, 253
CreateSpace.com 37, 112, 225, 228, 230, 231, 232, 241, 247, 248, 249, 258
"creative procrastination", procrastination 45, 266, 267
current asking price, Current Asking Price 16, 17, 23, 26, 27
current market value, Current Market Value 26, 27
current street value, Current Street Value 26, 31
Cyprus 20

D

Dale, Jim 207
December 24, 2017 xv
December 2017 xv, 191, 192
dedicate, dedication, Dedication page xxvi, xxx, 44, 49, 143, 166, 226, 233, 234
dedicated to me, autographed 106
"Define 'famous'" 199
depressed, depressing, depression 40, 122, 123, 153, 154, 156, 157, 158, 159, 160, 171, 217, 219, 255
depression can be debilitating 217
designer xvii, xviii, xix, xx, xxii, xxxi, xxxii, 5, 7, 56, 65, 75, 77, 78, 82, 83, 90, 127, 143, 180, 206, 215, 216, 235, 236, 248, 249, 250
designer mistakes 216
design revisions 216
desktop designer 5, 216, 235
desperate calls for help 123
Did you notice this method that I used for this book? 190
Different price ranges for everyone's various budgets 53
digital camera 38, 136, 137, 249, 256, 257
direct reservation 4
disbelief 199

Display #valzubiriagenda on café windows and websites 74
doll art, doll, dolls xvi, xxi, xxvii, xxviii, 4, 34, 45, 68, 69, 80, 84, 120, 121, 162, 164
doll-making xxi
Dollman the Musical, A Memoir of an Artist as a Dollmaker xxvii, 36, 45, 99, 159, 169, 201, 210, 236
dominatrix 124
Don't get free editing with paid book design 216
Don't say it's an "Advanced Reading Copy" or "Proof" 182
Don't take yourself for granted 89
dopamine 167
Do the same thing with the interior 245
Dov SS Simens 225, 226
Do Warm Ups Pretend You're Already Writing (Chapter 32) 185
Do you know about negative space? 117
drag queen artists 4, 62
drawing xxi, 49, 87, 88, 115, 118, 120, 125, 143, 152, 246, 248, 255, 256
Dukakis, Olympia xvi
Duncan, Isadora 200

E

"é" 213, 250
early bird region 31
earn commission xix, 4, 5, 7, 32, 60
Easy Technical Knowledge To Help Make You Stop Flinching (Chapter 24) 133
e-book xiii, 36, 38, 133, 134, 135, 136, 137, 139, 141, 142, 214, 246, 262, 263
  Your problem if you only try to produce e-books 263
economic bubble 59, 94, 123
economic trend 59
economy 74, 189, 266
edit, Edit, editing xviii, 34, 75, 78, 91, 112, 127, 135, 137, 142, 147, 148, 150, 152, 158, 159, 163, 175, 177, 179, 181, 184, 191, 192, 194, 197, 202, 203, 206, 213, 214,

215, 216, 217, 218, 219, 228, 244, 247, 248
Editing & Proofreading Read Your Work 8 Times (Chapter 37) 213
editing revision 216
edit my own work 217
edit my work 217
editor xx, 7, 65, 75, 77, 90, 91, 127, 131, 157, 158, 206, 215, 216
eight times 213
Email: A way to entertain a cue for reservations 28
Email your contacts regularly 16
embarrassing experiences 251
embedding fonts 142, 249, 250
Empty Space: Creating a Theatre in Your Church Step-by-Step 146, 191, 218
emulators 262
encounter with a very classy rich lady xxvi
Encouraging a friend to write her memoir 190
endorphins 167
enlisted army 4
Entertain agents and commissions 53
Enticing investors and collectors with books 56
envious, envy 100, 165, 172, 193
Epilogue 235
epub files 133, 136, 141, 142, 261, 262, 263
e-reader, e-readers xiii, 38, 133, 134, 135, 136, 137, 139, 141, 142, 214, 246, 261, 262, 263
erratum 220
E-Trade 63, 65
event 44, 58, 76, 78, 90, 113, 121, 122, 128, 160, 208, 219, 224, 253, 260
Everybody's Coffee 202
exclusive, exclusivity xxi, 15, 34, 35, 76
expert xxiv, xxv, 26, 110, 138, 252
exponential graph, exponential pricing 6, 7, 236
exponentially increasing bar graph 30
Export Adobe PDF 249
External Conflict How Others can

Index

Affect You (Chapter 29) 165
eyeball, eyeballing 90, 236, 237, 247

F

Fables, fairy tales and your memoir 154
face on the book cover, Your 244
face picture / headshot 240, 258
fair, fairness 56, 58, 132, 198, 248, 251, 253
fair (street fair) 85
fake, fakery, fakes xxvi, 6, 43, 167, 188, 259
fake success 167
fame, famous xvi, xvii, xxii, xxx, xxxi, 28, 30, 32, 34, 40, 43, 45, 82, 87, 88, 101, 104, 105, 106, 107, 108, 111, 112, 118, 119, 120, 121, 122, 124, 129, 130, 149, 150, 151, 153, 157, 173, 179, 190, 198, 199, 223, 225, 227, 238
famous 19-year old publisher, The 223
famous paintings 223
famous paranormal authors 87
fantasy and science fiction trading cards 119
fiction 34, 42, 43, 119, 128, 233, 239
fictionalize 235, 245
file storage 214
Files you should become aware of 135
Filipino 194, 204, 219
"Filipinoness" 204
Finally, guess what? 58
finance books 4
financial company 8, 71
financial success 8
fine art 4
Fine Art (Artists - Fine Art) 123
First and foremost: Do this! 138
first two conditions, The 6
Fixation 202
flash drive xxiii, 86, 140, 214
flower 4, 117
Follow the leader 53
font size 39, 145, 186, 215, 262
font, typestyle 39, 142, 143, 145, 186, 206, 215, 238, 245, 247, 249,

250, 262
Foreword 234
form groups now 4, 30
foundries 24, 127
Friend of the Galleries xix
friends and family 105, 167, 169, 170
friends and relatives 252
From janitor's closets to cafés to galleries 55
frontmatter 234
Fry, Stephen 207
full-color xiii, 18, 51, 119, 138, 141, 231, 241
full-color interior 241
funny writing ideas 198

G

galleries have seen this before xxviii
galleries reject a lot of artists xxii
Galleries Some Considerations (Chapter 14) 81
gallery assistant xxiv
gallery friends 74, 81, 256, 265
gallery, galleries xvii, xviii, xix, xx, xxi, xxii, xxiii, xxiv, xxv, xxvi, xxviii, xxix, xxx, xxxi, xxxii, 15, 24, 29, 30, 34, 35, 41, 42, 43, 47, 48, 50, 52, 53, 54, 55, 56, 58, 68, 73, 74, 75, 76, 81, 82, 83, 118, 121, 227, 228, 256, 265, 266
commercial galleries 118
noncommercial galleries 118
gallery owner xvii, xxii, xxiv, xxv, 34, 35, 43, 47, 48, 82, 227, 228
gallery status quo 48
gallery tour xxv, 43
gatekeeper 31, 34
Generating local demand 82
Germany 19, 223, 224
Germany-based bank 19
Get a blog 67
Get a blog and join the popular blog links 69
Get comfortable! 201
Get included in group books 62
Get someone to produce your books 127
Getting relatives to edit 218
Getting the next investors and art

collectors to produce books 56
Get to know the icons on other people's blogs 67
ghostwriter xxvii, 5, 7, 38, 89, 90, 127, 128, 179
Ghostwriters, definition 38
Giving your book a title 194
glass is half empty, glass is half full 208
glyphs 143, 250
Glyphs 250
Google can find us fast 66
Google Drive 86, 152, 214, 247
government agencies 19, 22
government pension funds 19, 94
graphic design, graphic designers 77, 90
Greece 20

H

half title page, Half title page 234, 235
Halsted Street 201
Hang the Dogs 246
Hans Christian Andersen 200
Happy Again and Other Works: 140 Paintings by Richard Lau (Works by Richard Lau Volume 2) 70, 258
Happy Hooker, The 101
hardbound, hardcover 89, 183, 224, 231
hard drive 139, 214
Harry Potter 183, 207, 208
hashtag 4, 7, 65, 66, 69, 74, 90, 260
Have a crowd of talents around you 132
Have you ever read articles like this one? 59
Have you heard of bleeds and slugs? 242
headers 237
Hear this audiobook 160
hell xx, xxxii, 66, 124, 193, 267
Hello Dolly! 192
help xiii, xvi, xvii, xx, xxxii, 4, 5, 8, 17, 19, 24, 25, 29, 30, 32, 37, 56, 60, 61, 62, 64, 65, 73, 74, 75, 81, 85, 86, 87, 91, 92, 94, 95, 107, 108, 118, 123, 131, 133, 140, 167, 175,

179, 189, 193, 202, 203, 211, 213, 217, 218, 219, 226, 228, 232, 235, 244, 246, 256, 257, 267
Help others get ahead 64
"herd behavior," herd mentality 28, 52, 222, 231
Here are some collaboration pointers 90
Here are some funny writing ideas 198
Here is a faster way to check embedding 250
Here is also something beginners don't know much about 145
Here is an example of size 209
Here is an example of time 210
Here is an idea that came from the galleries 30
Here is another insight I got from him 150
Here is a principle of hypnosis 209
Here is a visualization exercise prior to writing 196
Here is a way to move forward xxxi
Here is my suggestion 231
Here is one way to get prices to the next level fast 52
Here is something relatively easy which the internet-savvy do 67
Here is the new #valzubiriagenda approach 15
Here is the traditional situation with cafés 15
Here is the traditional situation with galleries 15
Here is where we begin to differ from traditional publishers 57
Here is why you should keep believing that you can produce your books 110
Here's a Simple Business (Chapter 2) 15
Here's the minimum number of words for a book 39
Herman 183
183
high-end galleries xix, xxx, xxxi, 42, 118, 227
Hilton, Paris 130
Hocus Pocus Lately 36, 45, 87, 99, 129, 159, 201

Hollander, Xaviera 101
homebound 4, 87
homeless, homeless street artists 4, 56, 62, 84, 85, 86, 94, 183, 184
Homeless Street Artists, UFO Abductees & Others (Chapter 15) 85
"honorary inclusion" 245
honorary member 252, 253
Hotdog-eating contests 173
How All This Started Years of Evolution So You can Use This Now! (Chapter 4) 33
How bookstores arrange books 195
How galleries define these two groups of people xxiv
How the high prices might be reached soon 27
How to Come Up with 2 Books from 1 Draft (Chapter 31) 181
How to edit your work 213
How to get your money back fast 24
How to ruin the writing process for a book 203
How to save yourself from going to jail 25
How to think if someone tells you that 109
How to use the 5 stages to get you motivated 148
hyphens 213
hypnotic writing 207

I

idea, ideas xxxi, 4, 5, 6, 18, 20, 21, 22, 25, 26, 29, 30, 32, 34, 36, 41, 44, 45, 48, 49, 53, 54, 58, 59, 61, 63, 64, 65, 66, 73, 74, 75, 77, 78, 79, 81, 82, 86, 87, 94, 95, 100, 101, 107, 113, 120, 122, 124, 132, 133, 141, 161, 172, 186, 187, 194, 197, 198, 203, 205, 217, 223, 226, 227, 252, 256, 261, 265, 266, 267
idea people 77
Ideas for Banks & All the Other Financial Companies (Chapter 11) 71
I don't require my friends and relatives to read my books 252

I follow a lot of YouTube channels 79
If the big publishers can do this, so can you 224
If you can't join them, beat them! 132
If your country is not served by CreateSpace or Lulu 232
If you're underage, bring a guardian 92
Ignorance is bliss 215
I had a crazy dominatrix for a neighbor 124
"I have book projects at different stages of development" 227
I have book projects at different stages of development 227
I hope galleries profit! 81
I just simply start editing my own work 217
I know some people freeze when they begin to write 207
Illinois 19
Illustrator, Adobe Illustrator 143, 152, 248
image for your cover 242
"I'm a publisher with book projects at different stages of development" 227
I'm a publisher with book projects at different stages of development 227
InDesign, Adobe InDesign 141, 142, 143, 206, 215, 238, 242, 249, 261, 262
InDesign Book file, The 261
index, Index, indexes, indices 129, 233, 235
industry standards 216
I never heard this-some of us might 174
Ingram, IngramSpark.com 230
"in" New York City 214
interior, calculating size 243
interior, interiors xvii, xviii, xix, xx, xxii, xxxi, xxxii, 34, 38, 82, 83, 134, 136, 141, 224, 233, 234, 235, 237, 241, 242, 243, 245, 247, 249, 259, 263
interiors, black and white 241
interiors, color 241

Index

277

interior title pages 233
Internal Conflict Preparing Your Mind to Write (Chapter 27) 153
"in the plane" 214
Introduction, definition 235
introduction, Introduction xv, xvi, xxx, xxxi, 19, 39, 47, 57, 75, 76, 80, 89, 110, 143, 179, 181, 193, 233, 234, 235, 240
investor xiii, xx, xxiv, xxvii, xxix, xxxii, 4, 5, 6, 7, 15, 16, 17, 19, 21, 23, 24, 25, 26, 27, 28, 30, 31, 32, 35, 41, 42, 43, 50, 52, 53, 54, 55, 56, 57, 58, 59, 60, 63, 64, 67, 72, 75, 76, 77, 78, 80, 81, 82, 86, 90, 91, 94, 101, 118, 120, 127, 139, 147, 164, 180, 182, 212, 215, 222, 231, 239, 259, 260, 265, 266
Investors might chase art 76
invitation 253, 254
iPad xiii, 38, 133, 134, 135, 136, 137, 139, 142, 214, 246, 262, 263
iPhone xiii, 38, 133, 134, 135, 136, 137, 139, 142, 214, 246, 262, 263
Is $100,000 to $51,200,000 realistic? 24
Isadora Duncan 200
ISBN 143, 144, 145, 229, 231, 240
ISBNs and LCCNs 144
I still have my art intact 255
It Dropped Out and Other Works: 133 Paintings by Richard Lau (Works by Richard Lau Volume 1) 70, 258
It is okay to display #valzubiriagenda on the sidewalk 85
It's a bait and switch only better 154
It was in 2009 when I started getting into porcelain doll-making xxi
I use a laptop and the Notepad software 205
I've seen some cafés close in my area 73

J

Jaime 251, 252, 254
James Miller 146, 191, 192, 218
jealous, jealousy xxvii, 165, 172, 193

Jerry and Jim's book 191
Jerry Miller 146, 191, 218
Jerry Miller's & James Miller's books 146
jewelry xxvi, 4, 120
Jim Dale 207
J.K. Rowling 207
John C. Maxwell 61, 63
John Ventimiglia 131
Julia Child 111

K

kiln 120, 164
Kindle 36, 133, 136, 141, 262
Know the "why" or the "salvation" 155
Know when to move along 132
Know your "bar" so you can set it higher and higher 190

L

laptop 73, 86, 91, 149, 150, 151, 173, 191, 201, 205, 214, 256, 257, 258
Lau, Richard xxix, 258
  Happy Again and Other Works: 140 Paintings by Richard Lau (Works by Richard Lau Volume 2) 258
  It Dropped Out and Other Works: 133 Paintings by Richard Lau (Works by Richard Lau Volume 1) 258
  Richard Lau Paintings: 273 Works by the Artist 258
Law of the Lid 63
lawyer, lawyers 8, 75, 89, 91, 127
LCCN 144, 145
leaderless organization 63
Learn so you don't get fooled! 135
Learn to take comments in stride 172
Leave the World's Greatest Novel for another writer 155
Leave those people be 165
Let's begin with a non-technical tip 37
Let's Crunch Big Numbers First The Yet Unusual Big Challenge (Chapter 3) 19

LGBTQ artists 4, 62
Library of Congress 144, 145
line illustrations 248
List me as first in my city for ... 4
local artists xxxi, 73, 74
locations xiii, 5, 7, 15, 16, 17, 18, 35, 55, 58, 76, 78, 80, 82, 88, 90, 118, 121, 136, 232, 235, 260
Looking at ourselves as kids again 51
Looking at ourselves as traders 55
Lopez, Steve 89
Louvre 223
Lulu.com 33, 34, 37, 39, 109, 112, 182, 215, 228, 230, 231, 232, 245, 256

M

Mac 262
Madoff, Bernie 20, 25, 26, 28, 49, 95
magical letters, The 204
Magic the Gathering for adults 54
Maintaining "self-publishers" 225
Making the art books 82
Making your books look more professional 143
Manhattan, see New York xxviii, xxix
manifesto, manifestos xiii, 6, 43, 44, 60, 153, 172, 181, 248
margin, margins 215, 237
margin (profit margin) 56
marketers 77
marketing 26, 58, 122, 128, 195, 196, 222, 236, 239, 240
Mastering the Art of French Cooking 111
Maxwell, John C. 61, 63
McQueen, Steve 250
media (mass media) 104, 121, 122, 161
medical study 215
medium, media (art) 4, 24, 25, 80, 253, 258
meeting, meetings xiii, 7, 8, 21, 22, 44, 47, 54, 72, 76, 77, 78, 83, 87, 89, 90, 91, 92, 132, 136, 173, 189, 263
memoirist, memoirists 45, 92, 228,

267, 269
memoir, memoirs xiii, xx, xxi, xxvi, xxvii, xxviii, xxix, xxx, 6, 21, 23, 29, 33, 34, 35, 36, 38, 39, 42, 43, 44, 45, 49, 60, 66, 67, 68, 74, 79, 80, 86, 87, 99, 100, 101, 103, 110, 118, 121, 128, 129, 138, 143, 145, 149, 153, 154, 155, 156, 159, 160, 165, 166, 169, 172, 182, 186, 189, 190, 191, 193, 195, 196, 197, 199, 201, 205, 210, 217, 224, 235, 236, 239, 241, 248, 252, 255, 260, 265, 269
Memoirs are just stories 129
Meryl Streep 111
metallic trading cards 51
metal, metals xxvii, 4, 27, 32, 80, 84, 120, 121, 188, 253
middlemen 8
mild stroke theory xxv, xxxi
Miller, James 146, 191, 192, 218
Miller, Jerry 146, 191, 192, 218
mimic, mimicry 128, 234, 236, 251
misadventures 101, 107, 239
mixed media 4, 80
mobi files 133, 136, 141, 142, 246, 261, 262, 263
Mona Lisa 223
most important factor for your financial success, The 8
multiple artists 75
museum, museums xvii, xviii, xxii, xxxii, 118, 182, 258
music 93, 105, 119, 180, 210
musical xxvii, 45, 68, 119, 160, 169, 192, 209, 236
musician 89, 254
My doll art 120
My early version of permissions and apologies 104
My Encounters with a Very Famous Author (Chapter 26) 149
My encounter with a very classy rich lady xxvi
My experience in theatre 90
My first art show was hogged by the organizer 253
My life-changing author 106
My mild stroke theory xxv
My secret, subconscious way to becoming artistic 117
My triangulation 45
My two "desperate calls for help" from a yellow page ad 123
My "unofficial designation" xix
My Writing Secrets Get Started with These Techniques (Chapter 36) 207

N

Nathaniel Ayers 89
negative space 117, 118
new age 4, 195, 196
Newman, Paul 250
newsletter 4, 28, 63
New York, see Manhattan xvii, xviii, xx, xxiii, xxviii, 34, 83, 214
noncommercial galleries 118
Not all 3,000 will circulate 23
Notepad 205, 206
notes, Notes 140, 233, 235
Not every artist will care about selling 59
Nothing can really cheapen art 29
nudes xxi, 4, 60, 256
nurse 4

O

office, offices xxvi, xxxi, 6, 21, 26, 43, 53, 55, 56, 58, 73, 86, 90, 113, 127, 226, 231, 254
official release date 183
"Oh Val, we're all doing the same thing!" xxiii
Oh Val, we're all doing the same thing! xxiii
oil xxiv, 4, 67, 161, 246
Olympia Dukakis xvi
"on" Earth 214
One gallery-related reason why I came up with this idea 82
One Porcelain Doll in Fur Coat & Boots 80
Online and venue distribution 230
online book publisher 247
online distribution 230
online file storage 214
"on the plane" 213
Open Book Editions 230
Oprah's trends 111
Oprah Winfrey 111
Ori Brafman 61
original drawings 87, 88
original files, originals 136, 138, 139, 164, 214
"Originals Do Not Touch" 214
Our Herd Mentality is Real 222, 264
Our minds always look for resolution and closure 199
Our new practice for #valzubiriagenda 38
Our status quo 265
Our world of publishers 225
outsider art 4
overprice 27, 74
oxytocin 167

P

paper xxi, xxv, xxviii, 4, 22, 26, 40, 42, 72, 83, 87, 88, 90, 99, 104, 105, 107, 115, 125, 126, 140, 155, 160, 168, 183, 187, 193, 197, 205, 217, 219, 220, 224, 233, 234, 241, 246
paperback version 89, 224, 231
paper, white or cream 241
paperwork 8, 24
paranormal memoir 87
Paris Hilton 130
parties 167, 170
Parties and friends 167
Parts 234
Parts of a book 234
pass along, pass-along, Pass-Along 58, 59, 262, 263
pastel 4, 253
Paul Newman 250
PC 191, 262
pdf file, pdf files xiii, 34, 38, 133, 134, 135, 136, 137, 139, 141, 142, 214, 246, 247, 250, 263
pedophilia 252
pension fund, pension funds 19, 94
Perez, Silverio xiii, xv, xvi, xvii, xix, xx, xxiii, xxvii, 4, 116, 120, 162, 179, 236, 267, 269
permission, permissions 24, 94, 103, 104, 105, 107, 139, 142, 150,

Index

152, 162, 226, 240, 244, 245, 246, 254, 259, 265
Permissions & Apologies (Chapter 19) 103
photocopies 107, 254
photoedit, photoediting, "photoediting" 138, 140, 214, 228, 248, 249, 255
photographer, photographers 5, 8, 65, 75, 89, 90, 127, 135, 137
photograph, photographs 82, 86, 135, 136, 137, 138, 143, 223, 228, 248, 249, 258
photographs of art pieces 136
photographs of your works 86, 137
photography 135
Photoshop 64, 140, 141, 143, 152, 248, 249, 257
Picasso, Pablo 25, 118
pilot 4, 115
plateau region 31
pocket-sized version 224
POD 41, 112, 135
poetry xxviii, 183, 192, 248
porcelain doll xxi
porcelain doll art xvi, xxi, 80
Porcelain Doll Heads 164
porcelain doll-making xxi
Porcelain Doll Shoes 188
porcelain slip, "slip" 164
portfolio 91, 255
postcard 107, 254
Postscript 235
potential revenue, Potential Revenue 9, 10, 11, 12, 13, 26
praise 240
praise, advance 240
Preface xiii, 89, 234, 235
Preface, definition 235
Preparing to Become a Writer (Chapter 18) 99
presenter 21
Pressfield, Steven 160, 161
prestige 252
price point, price points 4, 7, 16, 22, 23, 25, 28, 31, 53, 56, 72, 75, 78, 121
price, retail 239
principle of hypnosis 209
print on demand 6, 37, 39, 41, 112, 135, 142, 144, 182, 198, 225, 227, 229, 230, 231, 232, 241, 242, 249
Print on Demand Company 229
PrintToPress, PrintToPress.com 230, 231
prismatic trading cards 51
private investment companies 19, 95
Producing Your Art Books Before You Proceed (Chapter 41) 255
professional designer 248
professional family 167, 172
professional friends 167, 172
professionalism 218
professional parties 167
professional software programs 248
programmed to become consumers, not producers 224
Programming e-books 135
Prologue 234
Proof 182
proof of your book 249
proofread 75, 78, 91, 127, 213, 245
proofreaders, Proofreaders 5, 8, 75, 77, 89, 90, 91, 127
proofreading, Proofreading 213
prototype 24
proud artist I know xxix
public domain 223
public meetings 21, 22
publisher, publishers, Publishers xiii, xxi, 33, 37, 40, 42, 43, 44, 49, 57, 59, 65, 75, 89, 100, 104, 105, 107, 110, 111, 112, 113, 115, 130, 131, 132, 134, 138, 143, 155, 157, 158, 172, 175, 182, 183, 195, 198, 216, 219, 223, 224, 225, 226, 227, 228, 229, 230, 231, 232, 233, 236, 239, 240, 241, 245, 246, 247, 248, 251, 259
publishers and booksellers conventions 33, 225
Publishing Books, E-Books & Our Future 221
publishing conventions 112, 224
publishing, Publishing xxix, xxxii, 3, 6, 33, 35, 37, 38, 39, 41, 43, 45, 49, 55, 56, 57, 58, 59, 60, 74, 76, 77, 92, 94, 101, 102, 107, 108, 110, 111, 112, 113, 114, 120, 127, 130, 131, 132, 134, 138, 147, 153, 155, 157, 163, 165, 171, 172, 175, 179, 182, 183, 184, 194, 215, 220, 221, 223, 224, 225, 229, 230, 233, 237, 242, 244, 245, 247, 251, 259, 266, 269
Publishing Your Book What You Should Watch Out For (Chapter 40) 233
publish others now 4

Q

QR codes 239
quality of our books, The 224

R

"read bait" 190
Reading between the lines 175
Really Stupid, Really Easy Technical Knowledge Just So You Know (Chapter 5) 37
Redgrave, Vanessa 200
Regression 202
reject a lot of artists xxii
relatives xix, 165, 170, 171, 218, 251, 252
release date, release dates 183, 258
Rembrandt 223
Remember to "embed" your fonts 249
resellers 7, 8, 16, 17, 29, 32, 52, 56, 147, 231
reselling art, reselling the art 52, 78, 82, 231
reselling, Reselling 32, 51, 52, 55, 72, 78, 82, 231, 259
Reselling to Friends & Colleagues (Chapter 8) 51
resolution and closure 199, 200
respect 218
Respect agents who will work for commissions 64
respect and professionalism 218
Respect collaboration 139
retail price xxi, 55, 135, 144, 231, 239, 240, 258
"Revised 001" 214
revision, revisions 181, 204, 216, 241, 245
RGB 140

Richard Lau xxix, 4, 70, 256, 258
Richard Lau Paintings: 273 Works by the Artist 70, 258
rich lady xxvi
Rod A. Beckstrom 61
Rowling, J.K. 207
running head, running headers, running heads 144, 237, 238, 248
Running heads 237
Running with Scissors 129

S

samples xvi, 91
sans serif and serif fonts 145
Save the Cat! The Last Book on Screenwriting You'll Ever Need 169
Scarcity & Pricing The Next Pair (Chapter 7) 47
scarcity, Scarcity 3, 6, 22, 47, 75, 78
science fiction 34, 43, 119
science fiction author 34
science fiction trading cards 119
Secrets Before You Begin Writing (Chapter 34) 195
SelfPublishedAuthor.com 230
self-publisher, self-publishers xxix, xxxii, 6, 33, 37, 39, 40, 41, 43, 57, 58, 59, 94, 112, 113, 147, 153, 157, 171, 172, 215, 224, 225, 226, 228, 229, 230, 232, 239, 241, 247, 259
Self-publishing and POD or print on demand 41
Self-publishing is now cheap 39
self-publishing trend 58, 112
Self-publishing vs. vanity presses 39
Selling lower 23
Selling price varies for color and black and white books 39
September 183
serif and sans serif fonts 145
serotonin 167
"Shortcuts" 238
Should you put #valzubiriagenda on your books? Yes and No 259
Sigil 136, 142, 262, 263
Silverio Perez xiii, xv, xvi, xvii, xix, xx, xxiii, xxviii, 4, 116, 120, 162, 179, 236, 267, 269
Silverio Perez' art commentary 162
Silverio Perez, Untitled, porcelain & permanent marker, 2018 116
Simens, Dov SS 225, 226
sister 157, 158, 159, 217, 218, 219
size, hypnotic writing 209
"slip", porcelain slip 164
SLR (single lens reflex) camera 136, 249
slug, slugs and bleeds 242, 244
small press 225, 226, 241
smartphone 67, 93, 136, 142, 262, 263
snobbery xxiv
snowball 8, 52, 231
Snowball the demand and trade contracts 8
Snyder, Blake 169
social category 4
soda tax 19
Soloist, The 89
Some additional pointers 77
Somebody invented the word "photoediting" 140
Some illusions we have are misleading 197
Some pension funds are in the spotlight right now 94
Some popular mentions of large-scale finance 19
Something my friend encountered 174
souvenir program 252, 253
spelling 131, 150, 213
spider 61
spine calculator 241, 242
spine, The 240
spite, spiteful 166, 172, 193
"stage of development" 226
starfish 61, 63
Starfish and the Spider, The 61
Start with a pen and paper 205
status quo xxxi, 20, 48, 265
Stephen Fry 207
Steve Lopez 89
Steve McQueen 250
Steven Pressfield 160, 161
stock photos 223
storage 214
Streep, Meryl 111
street artist, street artists xxv, 62, 85
stroke xxv
student 4
studio 118
  artist's home 118
  artist's studio 118
subconscious 104, 117, 121, 145, 155, 166, 173, 174, 210, 237
Subset fonts when percent of characters used is less than 250
Subvocalization 202
sugary drinks 20
suspension of disbelief 199

T

Table of contents 233, 234
Take charge of your #valzubiriagenda community 72
Taking over the work of the galleries 55
Tales of the City xvi
"taming the porcelain" 164
Taschen 223, 224
Taschen, Benedict 223
teacher 4, 40, 156, 173, 212
Temple of the Leper King (André Velon Mysteries) (Volume 1) 246
term paper 40, 155, 156, 217, 219, 234
text file 133, 205, 206, 214
The 21 Irrefutable Laws of Leadership 61, 63
The 101st is always better than the first 119
The army veteran who was missing a hand 86
The artist can decide on the top price 31
The artist decides for himself 48
The artist is the gatekeeper 31
The artist who died in the '90s xxx
theater 199
theatre, theatre group xxi, 45, 69, 90, 138, 146, 174, 191, 212, 218, 246, 252
The author/public speaker/television interviewer 44

Index

The back cover 239
The Basics on Producing E-Books Just an Overview (Chapter 42) 261
The bestselling sci-fi author and visual artist 43
The biggest misconception most people have 133
The biggest misconception people have 38
The blogger trend 111
The book is not a term paper 40, 219
The book of acknowledgments 251
TheBookPatch.com 230, 231
The Christmas Eve party xvi
The cover 238
The crazy pair 125
The Day the Rain Came Down 218
The Day the Rain Came Down: The Stories of Gay Identical Twins 218
The depression might take a long time to get over 157
The design decision from Towering Inferno 250
The difference between my friend then and you now 21
The e-readers are glorified web-page viewers 141
The famous 19-year old publisher 223
The first two conditions 6
The galleries have seen this before xxviii
The galleries reject a lot of artists xxii
The gallery status quo 48
The Happy Hooker 101
The importance of The quick brown fox 187
The InDesign Book file 261
The initial 55,000 words in this book 193
The interior page margins 237
The interior page margins, The 237
The lady with the stack of manuscripts 172
The Little Match Girl 200
The magical letters 204
The mathematics of art and publishing 163
The most important factor for your financial success 8
The most memorable souvenir program 252
Theoretical activities 185
The picture of a family whose dad had cancer 87
The proud artist I know xxix
The quality of our books 224
The second two conditions 6
The self-publishing trend 112
The separation between artists and collectors 54
The similarity between cafés and art galleries 73
The simplest way to form a cue: Email 63
The smaller investors will piggyback on your budget 72
The snowball effect might happen 27
The Soloist 89
The Sopranos 131
The Sopranos Family Cookbook: As Compiled by Artie Bucco 131
The spine 240
The spine calculators 241
The stages of book production 147
The Starfish and the Spider 61
The Starfish and the Spider: The Unstoppable Power of Leaderless Organizations 61
The suspension of disbelief 199
The three regions of sales 30
The Towering Inferno 250
The traditional publishing industry is declining 113
The two files required for printed books 134
The two ladies and I talked about art xvii
The two most important lessons from a publisher 40
The two words I mistakenly interchanged 165
The #valzubiriagenda The Basics (Chapter 1) 5
The War of Art: Break Through the Blocks and Win Your Inner Creative Battles 160
The World's Easiest Way to Produce Books! (Chapter 23) 127
The young man Herman 183
thinner version 224
This artist from Manhattan publishes his books xxviii
This chapter only has general information 133
This is a career 92
This man said he wanted to become a famous artist 121
This might become an economic bubble 94
Three books versus one book 256
Three different but similar movies 192
Three negative emotions 153
"Throw your books out!" 173
time, hypnotic writing 210
Tips for Publishers, Writers, Ghostwriters, Editors, Book Designers, Proofreaders, Lawyers, Photographers, etc. (Chapter 16) 89
Title page 234
Towering Inferno, The 250
trade contracts, trade paperwork 8, 24
trading cards 119
traditional publishers, traditional publishing 42, 43, 57, 59, 132, 183, 216, 230, 231, 241
transfer funds 8
trauma 252
trend, trended, trends xviii, xxix, 33, 41, 58, 59, 76, 110, 111, 112, 172
triangulation, Triangulation 36, 42, 44, 45, 46, 247
Try helping others 219
Try this: Publish First What Your First Book Will Do for You (Chapter 28) 163
t-shirts xv, 18, 260
Tulip Mania 94
two groups of people xxiv
two ladies and I talked about art xvii
Two words: Eyeball and Mimicry 236
typestyle, font 39, 142, 143, 145,

186, 206, 215, 238, 245, 247, 249, 250, 262

U

UFO abductee, alien abductee 62, 85, 87
Understanding a little of the software needed 141
Unedited Masterpiece 181
university 101, 252, 253
university press 225, 226
"unofficial designation" xix
"Unretouched Writing" 181
upfront costs 229
upgrade and reformat 231
Us and the future 60
Us and them 266
Use Calibre to make mobi files 262
Use hashtag #valzubiriagenda 66
Use Hashtag #valzubiriagenda to Find Each Other (Chapter 10) 65
Use Sigil to tweak epub files 262

V

Valentino Zubiri xiii, 60, 110, 267, 269
Valentino Zubiri: Nude Drawings and Paintings from 1995 to 1996 60, 110
Valentino Zubiri's 4 memoirs 36, 49, 159, 265, 269
valzubiriagenda@gmail.com 4
valzubiriagenda, Valzubiriagenda, #valzubiriagenda xviii, xx, xxviii, xxix, xxx, xxxi, xxxii, 4, 5, 6, 7, 15, 20, 21, 23, 25, 28, 32, 35, 36, 38, 39, 43, 46, 50, 52, 56, 63, 65, 66, 67, 68, 69, 71, 72, 73, 74, 81, 83, 85, 87, 90, 92, 93, 98, 101, 117, 123, 127, 128, 130, 147, 160, 172, 189, 193, 202, 212, 213, 228, 236, 244, 245, 259, 260, 263, 265, 267
Vanessa Redgrave 200
vanity book publishers 39, 112, 113, 192, 229, 245, 248
Variations in formats 231
Ventimiglia, John 131

Venues will matter less 28
venue, venues xxxii, 7, 15, 28, 29, 55, 56, 58, 82, 90, 110, 139, 147, 229, 230, 231, 259, 260
version, versions 18, 36, 43, 44, 65, 89, 104, 135, 139, 141, 142, 146, 155, 160, 161, 163, 181, 182, 183, 207, 208, 216, 224, 230, 231, 232, 246, 254, 259, 260, 261, 262, 266
veteran 4, 62, 67, 85, 86, 153, 154
vision, visions xxii, 34, 74, 103, 104, 121, 163
Visual Artist's Attempt To Write Without Editing 181
volunteer, volunteers xxix, 77, 78, 90, 91, 174, 253, 257

W

"Wait and See Program" 28
Warhol, Andy 24
watercolor 4, 125, 126
way to move forward xxxi
We all make rules to include and reject xxii
We are already doing the CEO's suggestions 58
We are not traditional publishers 57
We are self-publishers 157
We'll Be Like Children 210
we're all doing the same thing! xxiii
We're not the traditional publishing industry 113
We should not have to go to hell for art xx
We will All Become Marketers & Collaborators (Chapter 9) 61
What a Christmas carol can teach you 208
What are serif and sans serif fonts? 145
What artists can learn from writers 189
What can happen with your online book publisher 247
What fantasy and science fiction trading cards taught me 119
What I expect from a professional book 143
What if the artist died? 24
What I learned from a comic book artist 119
What I learned from a large, famous publisher 227
What I learned from a speed reading workshop 202
What I learned from a widow of a famous sports player 129
What I learned from Dov Simens 225
What I learned from music lessons 119
What I learned from Paris Hilton 130
What I learned from the high-end galleries 118
What I learned from the Soprano Cookbook 131
What inspires me to keep believing that this would succeed 85
What is happening to the world 93
What is your status quo? 20
What software programs are used by the professionals 248
What some galleries can learn from us 227
What's the minimum word count for a memoir? 145
What text will be on the back of the book? 240
What will motivate you and your company to do this? 22
What you can learn from Harry Potter 207
What you can learn from politicians 131
When you do your own research 229
When you write, you write for the public 166
Which Print on Demand Company to Use (Chapter 39) 229
wholesale price, wholesale price of your books 57, 76, 135, 229, 231
Who the F#%k Told You to Get Yourself Published? (Chapter 20) 109
Who would be the leader? 63
Why Books (Chapter 6) 41

Index

Why I don't advise friends 168
"Why Not?" 129
Why you're still cranky and irritable 155
Why you should visit a bookstore first 233
width of the spine 38, 241, 242
Wikipedia's "Self-publishing" entry 229
Winfrey, Oprah 111
Wonder xxx, 36, 45, 99, 129, 201
Wondering about expertise xxv
word count 145, 185, 193
Working with an author abroad 246
Working with an editor and a book designer 215
Working with a small group 61
Working with editors and book designers 206
World Wars 1 & 2 19
Write as if you're talking 204
Write in the language you are comfortable in 194
writer, writers xiii, xvi, xx, xxvii, xxxii, 5, 38, 40, 41, 56, 65, 75, 77, 78, 90, 101, 110, 115, 118, 127, 128, 129, 131, 132, 135, 150, 151, 153, 154, 155, 157, 159, 170, 171, 175, 179, 187, 189, 197, 198, 200, 202, 203, 204, 210, 216, 217, 251
Writing is 1% writing and 99% editing 213
Writing sexy books 106

X

Xaviera Hollander 101
"xxxxx" markers 203

Y

You can form groups and focus on the same artists 30
You can get away with current digital cameras 249
You can reshuffle your life 197
You can Use Other Writers or Write Your Own Book! (Chapter 30) 179
You do not need a fancy camera 136
You don't need to print 1,000 books 135
You might realize that the art is almost inconsequential 32
You must use Sigil and Calibre together 262
You only need a few tips to get started 212
Your area of business 56
Your art vs. someone else's 41
Your brain as a whole pie (chart) 156
Your choice of words 208
Your circle of friends and colleagues 22
You're not competing with the cafés 82
You're supposed to spend only what you can afford 22
You're writing about your life 157
Your face on the book cover 244
Your first move 21
Your goal is $0 cost or near it 245
Your good intentions are not theirs 161
Your problem if you only try to produce e-books 263
Your quarterly and annual financial statements 26
You should know these three fractions: 4/0, 1/1 and 4/4 140
YouTube 62, 79
YouTubers 62, 79
YouTubers, Other Videographers & Their Followers (Chapter 13) 79
YouTube videos 215

Z

Ziglar, Zig 252
Zig Ziglar 252
Zubiri, Valentino xiii, 60, 110, 267, 269

www.ingramcontent.com/pod-product-compliance
Lightning Source LLC
Chambersburg PA
CBHW020629220526
45464CB00001B/72